Poetry, Politics, and the Law in Modern Ireland

Irish Studies
Kathleen Costello-Sullivan, *Series Editor*

Select Titles in Irish Studies

Avant-Garde Nationalism at the Dublin Gate Theatre, 1928–1940
Ruud van den Beuken

Fine Meshwork: Philip Roth, Edna O'Brien, and Jewish-Irish Literature
Dan O'Brien

Guilt Rules All: Irish Mystery, Detective, and Crime Fiction
Elizabeth Mannion and Brian Cliff, eds.

Literary Drowning: Postcolonial Memory in Irish and Caribbean Writing
Stephanie Pocock Boeninger

Modernity, Community, and Place in Brian Friel's Drama, Second Edition
Richard Rankin Russell

Politics, Culture, and the Irish American Press: 1784–1963
Debra Reddin van Tuyll, Mark O'Brien, and Marcel Broersma, eds.

The Rogue Narrative and Irish Fiction, 1660–1790
Joe Lines

Science, Technology, and Irish Modernism
Kathryn Conrad, Cóilín Parsons, and Julie McCormick Weng, eds.

For a full list of titles in this series,
visit https://press.syr.edu/supressbook-series/irish-studies/.

Poetry, Politics, and the Law in Modern Ireland

Adam Hanna

Syracuse University Press

First Edition 2022

22 23 24 25 26 27 6 5 4 3 2 1

∞ The paper used in this publication meets the minimum requirements of the American National Standard for Information Sciences—Permanence of Paper for Printed Library Materials, ANSI Z39.48-1992.

For a listing of books published and distributed by Syracuse University Press, visit https://press.syr.edu.

ISBN: 978-0-8156-3766-0 (hardcover)
978-0-8156-3761-5 (paperback)
978-0-8156-5558-9 (e-book)

LCCN: 2022011111

Manufactured in the United States of America

To my parents, Rosalind and David Hanna

Contents

Acknowledgments

All acknowledgments are partial acknowledgments. This book owes its existence to the sustained kindness, generosity, and enthusiasm of more people than can be listed here. At the inception of this project, an Irish Research Council postdoctoral fellowship enabled two crucial years of full-time research under the inspired mentorship of Heather Laird. During this time and after, my work has been buoyed along by the friendship of the staff and students of the English Department at University College Cork (UCC). Great thanks to all my colleagues, and especially to the most recent heads of department: Alex Davis (who also provided generous feedback on several draft chapters of this book), Lee Jenkins, and Claire Connolly.

Beyond the UCC English Department, I am indebted to the following people for their help, friendship, good examples, or combination of these three things: Charles Armstrong, Lauren Arrington, Matthew Campbell, Lucy Collins, Peter Crooks, Ailbhe Darcy, Kathy D'Arcy, Peter Davidson, Gerald Dawe, Sophie Doherty, Eric Falci, Elaine Feeney, Tadhg Foley, Kit Fryatt, Colin Graham, Jane Griffiths, Hugh Haughton, Veronica C. Hendrick, Fiona Kearney, Ken Keating, David Kenny, John McAuliffe, Fiona McCann, Eugene McNulty, Ellen McWilliams, Julie Morrissy, Ailbhe Ní Ghearbhuigh, Doireann Ní Ghríofa, Julia Obert, Patrick O'Callaghan, Bernard O'Donoghue, Billy Ramsell, Paige Reynolds, Christabel Scaife, Ronald Schuchard, Rajinder Singh, Jane Stevenson, Anna Teekell, Molly Twomey, Tom Walker, and Kathleen Williams. Additional thanks to Lucy Collins and Kathy D'Arcy, who generously shared their books and papers when all the libraries closed. I know this list could be three times as long; if you should be on it and are not, my thanks to you as well.

I gratefully acknowledge the support of the Research Publication Fund of the College of Arts, Celtic Studies, and Social Sciences at University College Cork. The School of English at UCC and the Information Services Strategic Fund, UCC, were very generous in supporting the costs of my quotations. I am grateful for the permission of Faber and Faber as well as Farrar, Straus & Giroux to quote from the works of Seamus Heaney; to the National Library of Ireland, who gave me their permission to quote from a draft version of Heaney's "The Unacknowledged Legislator's Dream"; to Carcanet Press, Manchester, United Kingdom, for their kind permission to reprint "Penal Law" by Austin Clarke; to Dedalus Press for permission to quote from the poetry of Doireann Ní Ghríofa; to Dan Sproul for permission to reproduce his painting *Scales of Justice*; and to Elaine Feeney and Julie Morrissy for their permissions to quote from their poems in chapter 7. A version of chapter 1 was published as "The Senate and the Stage" in the *Oxford Handbook of W. B. Yeats*, edited by Matthew Campbell and Lauren Arrington. Part of chapter 4 was published as "Thomas Kinsella: The Civil Servant–Poet at Mid-Century" in *Poetry Ireland 124* (2018). Some of the research that went into chapter 5 was initially published as "Seamus Heaney's 'Settings, xiii' and the Troubles," *Notes and Queries* 263 (September 2018). Some of chapter 7 was published as "Irish Poetry and the Law," *Honest Ulsterman* (October 2020). I gratefully acknowledge the permission granted to reproduce the copyrighted material in this book. Every effort has been made to trace copyright holders and to obtain their permission for the use of copyrighted material. I apologize for any errors or omissions and would be grateful to be notified of them.

Thanks, too, to Annette Wenda for her scrupulous copyediting, the team from Syracuse University Press, especially Kathleen Costello-Sullivan and Deborah Manion, and to the two anonymous readers who, if they read this book again, will find their suggestions incorporated everywhere.

My greatest thanks, as ever, go to my family: my mother and father; my sisters, Rebekah and Erika, and their families; and, of course, Isabella and Ralph.

Poetry, Politics, and the Law in Modern Ireland

Introduction

Unacknowledged Legislators' Dreams

> I sink my crowbar under the masonry of state and statute, I swing on a creeper of ~~cadences~~ secrets into ~~the~~ our Bastille.
>
> —Seamus Heaney, "The Unacknowledged Legislator," draft poem[1]

"The Bastille" or "our Bastille"? In the early 1970s, near the outset of the long conflict that came to be known as "the Troubles," Seamus Heaney wrote a prose poem, "The Unacknowledged Legislator," whose poet-hero protagonist breaks into a prison. A note on the manuscript states that Heaney wrote it on May 30. It does not specify a year, but it was most likely in the violent years 1972, 1973, or 1974. In the same note he also records that when he wrote it, he was waiting for his Volkswagen to be fixed in Bray, County Wicklow, the nearest large town to the mountain cottage that he had recently moved into after leaving Northern Ireland in 1972. The poem that he drafted that day would eventually be published under the title "The Unacknowledged Legislator's Dream" in his landmark 1975 collection, *North.* In its manuscript form, quoted above, it shows evidence of how, as he drafted it, Heaney hesitated over how close to home to situate that symbol of discredited laws and unjust authority, the Bastille.

This book is an exploration of the relationship between a number of modern Irish poems and the legal contexts in which they were written. It explores how poets, like Heaney, have weighed their words in the balance and measured the claims of existing jurisdictions and laws against more broadly conceived ideas of law and justice. This book is therefore about the intersection between poetry, laws, and the lawmaking authorities—both official and unofficial—that have operated in Ireland in the past century. Further, this book seeks to explore the relationship between the individual imagination and the society and culture in which that imagination operates. It is, among other things, an attempt to revisit and gauge the pressures that Heaney felt as he stopped and, momentarily, thought twice about what involvements the words "our Bastille" might get his "unacknowledged legislator" into.

When Heaney shifted from the monosyllable "the" to "our," the poem's center of gravity changed as well. The first word he chose, "the," had avoided dangerous territory by ostensibly situating the poem in the Paris of the French Revolution. This choice spoke of analogy rather than allegiance, creating a more distanced and playful perspective on contemporary issues than his second choice of word. "Our Bastille," however, edged the poem onto more controversial ground, placing its speaker on the side of those individuals who looked on Northern Ireland's prisons and internment camps as being the tools of an illegitimate power. The idea that there is a "Bastille" in Ireland is, as Heaney would have known, one of the country's oldest republican tropes.[2] The shift from "the" to "our" Bastille made the poem something close to an indictment of the recently reintroduced internment policy and courted controversy by seemingly aligning the poet with the republican forces that, like their predecessors in France, were engaged in violent revolt against the extant regime.[3]

By the time the poem came to be published, however, it was once again set in that far-off location, "the" Bastille. In composing this poem, Heaney had faced a decision about where to direct its energies, and, ultimately, he made the decision to aim them a fraction closer to the ironical than in his first draft. This minuscule recalibration, preserved among the manuscripts that Heaney deposited in the

National Library of Ireland, is suggestive, showing how this unacknowledged legislator's dreams were subject to careful adjustments.

This book considers how a range of poets who have lived and worked in Ireland—among others, Austin Clarke, Rhoda Coghill, Paul Durcan, Elaine Feeney, Miriam Gamble, Seamus Heaney, Thomas Kinsella, Paula Meehan, Julie Morrissy, Doireann Ní Ghríofa, and W. B. Yeats—have deployed the finest linguistic and formal subtleties in response to public questions. Rather than looking at how we might better understand legal doctrines through reading literature, this book explores how the works of modern Irish poets respond to, and are shaped by, legislative and constitutional changes, court judgments, and legal scandals.

A significant thread that runs through this book is the persistent, legally sanctioned, marginalization of women and their exclusion from the public sphere that has been such a marked element of modern Irish life. Recently and notably, it has involved poets writing work that engages with and challenges the abortion laws of Northern Ireland and the Republic. These laws include the Eighth Amendment of the Constitution of Ireland, a provision that, between 1983 and 2018, effectively copper-fastened an existing ban on abortion by asserting the equal right to life of a fetus and the woman who carried it. Analyses of poems that respond to these laws form part of the sixth and seventh chapters of this book. These poems respond to a body of legislation from the outset of the state that denied agency and opportunities to women through the twentieth century and beyond.

Legislative attempts to drive women from the public sphere began early in the history of the Irish state. The exemption on women from jury service (Juries Bill, 1927), the banning of the sale or importation of contraceptives (Criminal Law Amendment Bill, 1934), and the ban on married women being employed in pensionable posts within the civil service (Civil Service Regulation Act, 1956) were just some of the ways by which the Irish state asserted its values in law.[4] This book will acknowledge the often indirect role that laws played in keeping women from the kinds of opportunities to write, publish, and be recognized for their work that were available to their male peers. It will therefore be alive to the conditions that meant that, while W. B. Yeats and Seamus Heaney might fairly be called Ireland's "unacknowledged legislators," Rhoda Coghill, to give just one example, remained for many decades largely unacknowledged.[5]

For any poet, man or woman, to even muse on that grand role, that of "unacknowledged legislator," as Heaney did as he drafted a poem in the early 1970s, seems out of kilter with modern sensibilities. However, Heaney's use of the term becomes more understandable in the light of the particular ideas and values of the society in which he was writing. The Irish nationalist tradition from which Heaney derived has historically had an acute sense of the poet as a keeper of national, and then nationalist, sentiment: one who acts as an alternative legislator. The anomalous high status traditionally enjoyed by poets and poetry in Irish culture was confirmed as an inheritance of the first internationally recognized Irish state in 1922, when the country's most prominent poet, W. B. Yeats, was appointed to its first Senate. Declan Kiberd points out that at this time a fellow senator could claim, without drawing ridicule, that without Yeats, "there would be no Irish Free State."[6] The *Freeman's Journal*, too, remarked at the time that Yeats's appointment restored an "ancient relationship" between the Irish bard and councils of state.[7] Yeats himself embraced this status, writing to Augusta Gregory in 1922 that "we have to be 'that old man eloquent' to the new governing generation."[8]

Decades after the death of Yeats, Seamus Heaney, too, was imagined by his contemporaries in similarly exalted terms: in 2010, Danny Morrison, the former publicity director of Sinn Féin, teasingly introduced Heaney at a festival with the words, "You know what Shelley said about poets being the real legislators of the world, so would you not consider running for President?"[9] In the same year, Heaney was indeed invited by one of Ireland's main political parties to be their candidate for this office.[10] At a state banquet held during the British queen's visit to Ireland the next year, Heaney was seated at the top table as Ireland's most prominent poet. Though he ultimately declined the invitation to run for president, a published poet, Michael D. Higgins, was eventually elected to this post. (Higgins's supporters adopted #keepthepoet as the unofficial Twitter slogan for his reelection campaign in 2018.) At Heaney's funeral in 2013, the taoiseach, Enda Kenny, cast Heaney's national role in august language, saying that "for us, [he] was the keeper of language, our codes, our essence as a people."[11] If Heaney was, however ironically he did it, willing to countenance the role of "unacknowledged legislator" in one of his poems, it was because, for deep-seated reasons, many in his country were willing, even eager, for him to occupy this position.

The idea that the poet might play a significant and challenging role in public life has existed in Ireland for centuries. Its origins go too far back to see them clearly, but it glimmers in some of the oldest documents. The twelfth-century *Book of Invasions* (whose core appears to be in seventh-century sources) sets out the mythological origins of the Irish people and contains the story of the first Irish poet, Amergin.[12] According to the legend recorded in this book, he set foot on Ireland's soil and introduced lyric poetry to the country at the same moment, announcing himself to be one with the wooded and wild country in which he found himself:

> I am a stag: *of seven tines*,
> I am a flood: *across a plain*,
> I am a wind: *on a deep lake*.[13]

The nature of the authority Amergin demonstrates is significant: his words suggest that the early role of the poet was to act as a shaman, an otherworldly oracle through whom a people were linked to a place. He also, according to an early text, made Ireland's first judgment, setting a precedent that "the judicature belonged only to the poets."[14] As Paul Muldoon has pointed out, Amergin's words bespeak a profound authority: "[He] has a mandate, it seems, from the *Míl Espáin* [mythical progenitor of the Irish people] to speak on national issues, to 'speak for Erin.'"[15] This is a case of an Irish poet acting as an unacknowledged legislator avant la lettre.

There are a number of tantalizing clues as to the ways in which law and poetry were entwined in the Celtic society that traced its mythical origins to Amergin and the Milesian invasion.[16] Though the role of people with skill in verse in making and administering law in Gaelic Ireland is, according to Fergus Kelly, "difficult to assess" and subject to "considerable variation," there is clear evidence in various copies of documents in Old Irish that there were links between these areas.[17] The *Senchas Már*, a series of documents compiled in the eighth century, contains laws that are both in verse and rhymed and traces the origins of some of its contents to "the true laws of the poets." Another Old Irish document on law, the *Uraicecht Becc*, thought to have been composed in Munster at some point between the seventh and tenth centuries, states that the two highest grades of judge needed to have knowledge of both law and poetry. A further document from the same period, known as the *Airecht*-text, indicates that the chief poet, or *ollamh*, had a role in judging legal cases. These individual pieces of evidence all point to the supposition that, at least from the sixth century, there were recognized overlaps in Gaelic Ireland between people who had ability with poetry and people who had competence in law.[18] The links between law, verse, and authority, whether they influence the phenomenon or not, provide an intriguing backdrop to the high status that more recent Irish poets have enjoyed.[19]

Of course, the elision of the roles of poet and lawmaker is not unique to Ireland, but has varied roots and parallels in other ancient and modern societies. Indeed, in Roman poetry from the Augustan era, the word "carmen" signified both song and law.[20] On the other side of Europe, in medieval Iceland, the heroes of the sagas were praised for their skills in law and poetry.[21] A recent study has anatomized the quasi-lawmaking status that was ascribed to poets, including Alphonse de Lamartine and Victor Hugo, in postrevolutionary France.[22] Such a diverse range of societies have posited links between poets and lawmakers that it suggests there is something that links poems and law, and not just in Ireland.

The links between laws and poetry have been explored by many modern scholars of law and literature. In one foundational work from 1924, the American jurist and lawyer Benjamin N. Cardozo, whose name has come to be synonymous with the study of law and literature, sought to anatomize the links between the two fields. At the heart of a series of lectures he gave was a meliorative vision of law as an engine of growth and change, and therefore as linked to the arts in its restless orientation toward the promise of the next horizon. The exploratory journey that literature took into the future of humanity, Cardozo argued, was powered by the generative confinements of literary form. They were equivalent to the confinements that were imposed on social life by the law. He provides this argument in his lecture "The Function and Ends of the Law":

> As new problems arise, equity and justice will direct the mind to solutions which will be found, when they are scrutinized, to be consistent with symmetry and order, or even to be the starting points of a symmetry and order theretofore unknown. [. . .] We find a kindred phenomenon in literature, alike in poetry and in prose. The search is for the just word, the happy phrase, that will give expression to the thought, but somehow the thought itself is transfigured by the phrase when found. There is emancipation in our very bonds. The restraints of period or balance, liberate at times the thought which they confine, and in imprisoning release.[23]

In his assertion that the restraints provided by a desire for form, pattern, and balance that acted on both writers and lawyers would create necessary and hitherto-unimagined ideas, there is a hopefulness that has come to characterize much of the writing on law and literature. This field of study has, since its inception, taken much of its impetus from the idea—notably propounded in works by James Boyd White, Richard Posner, and Martha Nussbaum, among others—that if practitioners of law were attentive to the linguistic specificity and imaginative engagement with the world that are features of literature, then it would enable legal systems, and, by extension, societies, to operate in a more empathetic, and in a more just, manner.[24]

One of the early and influential proponents of the idea that the just practice of law needed the kinds of qualities that were inculcated by the study of literature was critic Northrop Frye. The theme of the address he gave to the Law Society of Ontario in 1970 was the necessity of the imagination, and, by extension, literature, to the humane operation of a legal system: "Law still depends upon the imagination, and the fostering and cherishing of the imagination by the arts is mainly what makes your profession honourable, perhaps even what makes it possible," he told them.[25] The ideas Frye raises here inform writing on law and literature studies to this day. At the heart of much law-and-literature scholarship is a desire to combine legal studies with the imaginative insights into human and social life that are stimulated by literature and to stress the necessity of this activity.[26] For this reason, law-and-literature studies tend to focus on parts of texts that have immediate relevance to the operations of laws: the punishment of Raskolnikov in Dostoyevsky's *Crime and Punishment*, for example, or the interminable legal machinations of Dickens's *Bleak House*, or the absurd trials suffered by the protagonists invented by Franz Kafka.

Critic Jahan Ramazani, in an essay in which he considers the links between law and poetry, suggests, as Benjamin Cardozo did before him, that poems and laws have significant parallels.[27] Both are linguistic constructions to which word choice and form are central, and both have traditionally been associated with painstaking scrupulousness about language.[28] In a post-Wittgenstein, post-linguistic-turn environment, the perplexities caused by a poem, a law, a constitution can all be considered as emanations of and problems of language. In this mode of understanding, words are flawed entities that simultaneously make communication possible and impossible, while laws are an equally flawed attempt to regulate and order the inchoate vagaries of human relationships.[29] However, when words, those insubstantial things, take the forms of laws or of poems, they are placed in frames that are intended to give them something extra, a status as objects that both have resulted from and demand deliberation and concentration. The status of a text as a law or a poem gives it the aura of something that will be read and attended to in the future. Both laws and poems partake of forms that give them access to a kind of afterlife, and a power to linger and haunt.

The laws that pass through legislatures or are created by the judgments of courts are usually framed in forms of words whose accordance with established precedents underscores their significance and authority. In poetry, this authority and sense of continuity has, at times, been achieved through the employment and adaptation of extant forms. Furthermore, the rhythmic patterns of poems can help them to stay in the mind. Perhaps their deep connections with memory are what give both poems and laws what status they have as valued shared possessions and repositories of wisdom.

The link between laws and poetry in Ireland, however, has been seriously complicated by the long reverberations of the establishment of an Anglo-Norman polity on the island in the late twelfth century and successive invasions and attempts at legal and administrative integration that created distinct but overlapping legal entities on the island. These dynamics created a conflict of jurisdictions in Ireland whose effects were to be felt for centuries and are to this day. Long wrangles for territory, and the disabilities that were imposed from the early seventeenth century by the anti-Catholic Penal Laws, ruptured the bonds of reciprocity that linked governor and governed. Legal theorist Lon L. Fuller, in *The Morality of Law* (1969), a meditation about the relationship of trust between the individual and the state, writes of how the breaking of these bonds compromises the operability of any legal system.[30] The failure of this reciprocity in Ireland, especially in the period after 1690, resulted in what Michael Brown and Seán Dolan have called a "low-grade legitimacy crisis that warped social and political relations on the island."[31] One of the consequences of this state of affairs was the emergence of an Irish-language tradition of poets who upheld a conception of justice that was separate from and often in opposition to official sources of law.[32]

Protest at "lawful" but unjust authority is a consistent theme in the landmark collection of Irish-language poetry from the three centuries that followed the Elizabethan conquest, Seán Ó Tuama and Thomas Kinsella's *An Duanaire, 1600–1900: Poems of the Dispossessed* (1981).[33] One of the most notable of the poems in this tradition is an eighteenth-century Munster poem, the "Caoineadh Airt Uí Laoghaire," translated as "The Lament for Art Ó Laoghaire." Attributed to the widow of its subject, Eibhlín Dhubh Ní Chonaill, it was written in response to the killing of her husband following his feud with a local magistrate. It shows both an acknowledgment of existing legal structures and a willingness to have recourse to other alternatives.[34]

In this poem, the widow vows to spend everything she has on lawyers to prosecute her case. However, if these official channels do not yield the desired result:

> [. . .] I'll come back again
> to the black-blooded savage
> that took my treasure.[35]

There is other evidence of a similar knowledge of, and selective disregard for, official sources of justice in Irish-speaking Ireland. Declan Kiberd writes of how the eighteenth-century "courts of poetry" that convened in taverns subverted and mocked the official legal system. Presided over by a chief poet in the role of "High Sheriff," the attendees were summoned with a "warrant" beginning with that talismanic legalism "Whereas."[36] This co-option and inversion of the authority of the courts hints at the existence of a similarly sidelong and ambivalent view of the official legal system in the country more generally.

In a colonial society where the link between law and justice was contested, and where the official record and official law were not trusted to be impartial, the capacity of the poet to be both a truthful recorder of events for posterity and a dissenting voice in the present was all the more highly valued.[37] From the clash of jurisdictions that arose on the island resulted a suspicion of law as the codification of the interests of the powerful. This idea, for all that it has found strong expression in Irish literature, is present in many other places in the world. Irish poet Theo Dorgan, in an essay on poetry and law, quoted philosopher Bertrand Russell, who saw in law something whose purpose might be the obliteration of justice: "Law in origin was merely a codification of the power of dominant groups, and did not aim at anything that to a modern man would appear to be justice."[38] Ireland, because of its colonial history, has been a place that has been especially receptive to the idea that official laws are designed to regulate and subordinate rather than serve the populace.

In the late twentieth century, Irish poet Anthony Cronin, looking deep into the history of Europe, saw the first imposition of laws on the agrarian societies of the Continent as legitimated theft:

> A new exclusion, worse than frosts of winter:
> Tongued in the trees, writ in the running brooks,
> The law of contract and of property.[39]

The use of law to deprive the original inhabitants of a land of traditional rights was also vividly imagined in Ulster poet John Hewitt's poem "The Colony." In this poem, he peopled his allegorized origin myth of Protestant Ulster with "young law clerks skilled with chart and stylus / their boxes crammed with lease-scrolls duly marked."[40] Memories of laws as language that might deprive those individuals who depend on land from full ownership of it are not far beneath the surface in Ireland.

Irish critic Denis Donoghue identified literature as being, by its nature, inherently oppositional to officially formulated laws: "Society makes statements and sends forth instructions, edicts, laws, definitions of reality. Literature makes counterstatements, Greek when the official designations are Roman," he wrote.[41] In the way that Donoghue imagined, many modern Irish poets have written in opposition to both prevalent legal tendencies and specific developments. W. B. Yeats, the subject of the first substantive chapter of this book, inherited a long tradition of speaking justice to law through mid-nineteenth-century rebel-poets like Thomas Davis.[42] Yeats announced early in his career that he, like the Young Ireland poets before him, had a restorative role to play. According to himself, he "sang, to sweeten Ireland's wrong, / Ballad and story, rann and song."[43] Because of the intensity with which ideas of law have been contested in Ireland, special expectations of fairness, justice, and defending the dispossessed and marginalized against the unjust exercise of authority have accompanied the role of the poet.

A central concern of this book is with how the traditional high status of the poet in Irish culture has been complicated by developments in English-language poetry since around the time of the First World War. This period is, in Ireland, almost coterminous with the period since the foundation of the two official states on the island, the Irish Free State and Northern Ireland. Since this time, both in Ireland and beyond, a self-conscious and ironic approach to art has commonly found expression in polysemous poetry to which no definitive meaning, let alone purpose, can be assigned.[44] Twentieth-century relativism, and a concomitant suspicion of totalizing narratives and identifications in art, meant that, at almost the same moment as legislative powers were first being exercised in modern Ireland, poets were asking new questions about the relationship between their work and the societies that they inhabited.[45]

Irish nationalism, like those other grand narratives Marxism, Christianity, and the Enlightenment, had provided poets and their publics with a shared belief in an end state in which progress toward justice would arrive at its conclusion.[46] Rather than a workers' revolution, the last judgment, or the scientific conquest of nature, however, Irish nationalist hopes were vested in the promise of a self-governing island. The reality of Irish self-government for most of the island from the early 1920s onward at the very least complicated this kind of millenarian thinking. However, this very disillusionment was in keeping with rather than at odds with the dislocating direction of broader international philosophical currents. For reasons connected to the widespread questioning of all teleological narratives, Irish poets in the twentieth century have frequently balanced on the scales the weight of strong traditional, public, expectations with changes in ideas that would have them question these same expectations.

One of the consequences of this double modern tradition is the deployment of, in Paul Muldoon's useful term, "Eriny." The author who engages in this supremely ambiguous and ironic Irish literary mode, according to Muldoon, simultaneously speaks for and against the nation. "Eriny," according to Muldoon, allows James Joyce to "[undercut] the rhetoric of cultural nationalism, revelling in the very thing he repudiates, delighting in what he disdains."[47] Muldoon also discusses this mode in relation to Patrick Kavanagh's short poem "Epic."[48] Though space does not permit a detailed engagement with the work of either Kavanagh or Muldoon in this book, the approaches of both poets have helped to shape it.

The framing of Kavanagh's fourteen-line "epic" poem, with its depiction of a small-scale territorial feud among farmers in County Monaghan, is for Muldoon a classic deployment of "Eriny." On the one hand, there is self-deflation in aligning a short and super-local poem under a title that connotes the exemplary deeds and adventures of a hero who embodies the virtues of his nation.[49] On the other hand, there is something more than irony at work: Kavanagh's poem does something in between ironizing its own claim to epic status and concentrating it. "Here is the march along these iron stones," cries one of the poem's protagonists; in this depiction of the law being flung down like one of the poem's pitchforks, there is indeed the performance of the values of the nation. Its depiction of furious possessiveness over territorial rights parallels wider Irish and, indeed, international dissensions.

Kavanagh's "local row" has wider concomitants: it is written about a place just a few miles from the Northern Ireland border; it refers to "the Munich bother," a 1938 international crisis that centered on a central European border. In the case of both of these larger-scale disputes, as in "Epic," the balances between law and force, kinship group and territory, are central. However, in Kavanagh's poem, neither of these larger parallels are pressed, and recruitment of an imagined Homer in the poem's final lines is simultaneously both ironic and sincere: "I made the *Iliad* from such / A local row. Gods make their own importance," he whispers. This finely poised ending both acknowledges and dismisses the epic salvific claims in relation to territory and nationality that might have attended the works of earlier generations of Irish poets. Kavanagh's ventriloquized lines also suggest that, in the face of the legal and political claims of the shared social world, poets can insist on identifying and defining their own epic ground and on imagining and asserting their own codes.

Two tides can be seen flowing counter to each other in modern Irish poetry. One is the specific Irish inheritance of the idea of the poet as a popular guardian and protester against injustice; the second is a twentieth-century countertradition of poets who bridled at this status as an imposition. Again, Patrick Kavanagh is exemplary here. In the middle of the twentieth century, he wrote a fantasy-poem, "The Hero," that depicts a poet who disappoints the crowd who proclaim him their "poet-king" by informing them that "he had no intention of dying / For virtue or truth."[50] The speaker of Derek Mahon's "The Last of the Fire Kings" initially expresses his desire to be a heroic rebel, escaping the authorities like "the man / Who drops at night / From a moving train" before admitting that fate has not fitted him for this role. Paul Muldoon imagines a protagonist who was "desperately wishing" to be the coauthor of the revolutionary pamphlets by a suspiciously Irish-sounding fantasy version of the Mexican revolutionary Pancho Villa, before too rejecting this grandiose idea at the end of the poem.[51] Speakers who shrug off heroic, societally imposed expectations crop up so frequently in modern Irish poetry, it is as if they are the fitful dreams of reluctant legislators as they work out their place amid clashing value systems. Heaney's "The Unacknowledged Legislator's Dream" is in the same tradition. By expending so much effort in deflating heroic expectations, poets evidence the persistence and the pressure of the same expectations.[52] This book is, in part, a testament to the ways that the incommensurable claims of history and literature can get under the skins, and into the poems, of the people who are subject to their contradictions.

There is much in Heaney's "The Unacknowledged Legislator's Dream" that lends itself to being read in accordance with precepts developed by scholars of law and literature, as well as in the modern Irish poetic tradition of resistance that is mingled with troubled self-questioning. In particular, much in the poem seems to act as a response to and critique of the consequences of the Civil Authorities (Special Powers) Act (Northern Ireland) of 1922–43: that is to say, of the reintroduction of internment.[53] This piece of legislation from early in Northern Ireland's history was revived in the face of increasing violence in early 1971. In August of that year, shortly before Heaney drafted "The Unacknowledged Legislator's Dream," the first of the internment sweeps that this legislation authorized yielded 337 men, almost all from nationalist areas.[54] It is notable that the protagonist of "The Unacknowledged Legislator's Dream," like the internees, is not granted any trial before he is imprisoned:

> I sink my crowbar in a chink I know under the masonry
> of state and statute, I swing on a creeper of secrets
> into the Bastille.
>
> My wronged people cheer from their cages. The guard-
> dogs are unmuzzled, a soldier pivots a muzzle at
> the butt of my ear, I am stood blindfolded with my hands
> above my head until I seem to be swinging from a strappado.
>
> The commandant motions me to be seated.
> "I am honoured to add a poet to our list." He is
> amused and genuine. "You'll be safer here, anyhow."

> In the cell, I wedge myself with outstretched arms
> in the corner and heave, I jump on the concrete flags to
> test them. Were those your eyes just now at the hatch?[55]

The word "cages," which Heaney uses, is not a neutral term, but a name that nationalist prisoners and their families used for Long Kesh internment camp (differing from "the Compounds," used in official prison terminology and adopted by loyalist prisoners).[56] The poem's reference to "wronged people" in "cages," therefore, responds both to the discrimination suffered by Northern Ireland's Catholic population and to the legislation that permitted internment. Shortly before writing this poem, Heaney wrote of the atmosphere in Belfast that "it hasn't been named martial law, but that's what it feels like"; his awareness of the legal context in which he was writing is also present in the imagery and language of this prose poem.[57] For example, a contemporary legal controversy is echoed in the way the protagonist is blindfolded and forced to stand with his hands above his head until he feels he is "swinging from a strappado"—an implement of torture that places all the weight of its victim on their arms. In 1971 and 1972 the government of the Republic of Ireland lodged applications with the European Court of Human Rights against the United Kingdom, accusing the Northern Irish security forces of using brutal interrogation techniques on republican prisoners. Among the accusations were ones that prisoners had been hooded and forced to stand for long periods with the weight of their bodies mainly supported by their fingers against a wall.[58] The conditions in which prisoners were held shape the constraints that the poet imagines his shadow-self protagonist suffering.

However, it would be an absurd misreading to characterize this poem as a protest against internment or the cruel conditions suffered by prisoners in Northern Ireland (though both these things clearly haunt it). Indeed, images of the doubts that caused Heaney to think twice about his position in relation to the loaded word "Bastille" are everywhere present in the poem. From its opening judgments about where to sink a crowbar to its end, dilemmas of positioning, weight, and balance that Heaney grappled with in writing the poem find expression in its imagery. The opening of the poem, anxiously flipping between metaphors (from "Billy Hunter," presumably a childhood friend, to Archimedes, to the Bastille), demonstrates the difficulties of finding a stable position from which to speak. Childish dreams of shaking the world by weight and force are balanced by ideas of seeking the leverage with which to shift the weight of "state and statute." The poem ends as it begins, with the speaker trying to work out how to use his weight to shift stones. "The Unacknowledged Legislator's Dream" ends with a dark sense that too much engagement with the exterior social world of laws and politics might bring an end to Heaney's speaker's necessary freedom. The poem's preoccupation with physical positioning and leverage is reflected in the finely balanced verbal positioning that the manuscript shows was part of its composition.

Broadly speaking, the revisions that Heaney made to "The Unacknowledged Legislator's Dream" when he was drafting it exchanged anger and involvement for irony and commentary. In this way, Heaney's eventual choice of "the" over "our" Bastille works in a similar direction to many of his other revisions to the draft poem. A reference to imprisoned "acquaintances" in the original draft was replaced by one to "My wronged people," an adjustment that overwrites a claim of personal acquaintanceship with prisoners with words that, for all their biblical weight and relevance to Northern Ireland's Catholic population, come close to the inert language of cliché.

Heaney similarly lightened the poem's load by changing "I am stood naked" to "I am stood blindfolded," a change that loosens the ties between this prose work and his more severe poem "Punishment," which appears earlier in *North*. The commandant vaguely threatens the poet in the first draft, but this passage is excluded from the published version, meaning he expresses only glib concern for the poet's safety. With each granular adjustment, Heaney enhances the comic or self-satirizing elements of the poem.[59] These changes suited the poem to its eventual position at the head of part 2 of *North*. This section sees a pronounced change of key from the volume's subterranean first part, as its grave bass notes are exchanged for a lighter, perhaps Mozartian, register in which qualities of self-referentiality and contemporaneity come to the fore. The intense fine-tuning that Heaney put the language of the poem through, in particular where it touched on contemporary issues of law enforcement, demonstrates his determination not to exacerbate an inflamed political situation, and not to inflate his own role.

In its uneasy weighing up of potentially redemptive action and self-mockery, this poem is as alive to the revolutionary force of Shelley's idea of the unacknowledged legislator as it is to Auden's needle-sharp observation that "the unacknowledged legislators of the world describes the secret police, not the poets."[60] In the evidence it offers of relentless self-questioning, Heaney's "The Unacknowledged Legislator's Dream" is more expressive of self-reflexive dubiety about the poet's status than the authoritative, vatic sway at which its title hints.

What about the other side of Irish poetry, the tradition that uncomplicatedly asserts its own authority and status and embraces its subversive, unacknowledged legislative function? Heaney's poetry, with its finely balanced involvements and ironies, can be contrasted with the poetry written by his contemporaries, men and women imprisoned for paramilitary activity.[61] Provisional Irish Republican Army (IRA) member, poet, and (briefly and nominally, after he was elected as a member of Parliament [MP] shortly before his death while on hunger strike in 1981) lawmaker Bobby Sands is a prominent representative of a strong strain of belief in Ireland that would challenge the legitimacy of the official legal authorities on the island.[62] Since the implementation of the Anglo-Irish Treaty in 1922, believers in an all-Ireland state, like Sands, have threatened, and at various times taken up arms against, the established governments of the polities centered on both Dublin and Belfast. In contrast to Heaney's twice-thought ambiguities, Sands writes in his *Prison Poems* (1981) in praise of a revolutionary movement that "burst forth through pitiful

Paris streets, / And stormed the old Bastille."[63] When the guard in Heaney's poem tells him he is honored to add "a poet to our list," it is an acid reminder that the only list he had been added to was that of Faber and Faber. As Eugene McNulty points out, though poetry like Heaney's may "prove a disappointment to the 'political activist' [. . .], the poetic imagination's architecture of self-reflexive language can reveal the discursive forcefields that shape our lives *as* discursive forcefields—cultural artefacts that we can examine, unpick, change. In this respect we may see the literary as a site of resistance, acting to force the law into open ground, to reveal its historicity."[64] Though Heaney was a contemporary of Sands and, like the prisoner, had a highly developed sense of injustice, his poetry was one whose very self-reflexiveness is a significant factor in its questioning of the status quo.

In place of the uneasy mix of self-directed humor and constant self-questioning that characterizes Heaney's prison-based poem, Sands's expresses ideological certainty more suited to a very different conception of an Irish poet. This difference is reflected in the respective forms employed by both poets: the rhymes and rhythms of Sands's work march along with predictable certainty; Heaney's wavering prose piece is more tuned to the limitations of poets and poetry. Heaney's "The Unacknowledged Legislator's Dream" depicts an Irish poet speaking back not only against the legal system that enabled internment and torture, but also against the ghosts of historic heroic expectations that came with his own role as a poet. In short, Heaney's portrayal of imagined jail-breaking reads as a corrective to a mismatch between expectation and ability, just as Canute demonstrated not the extent but the limits of his power when he commanded the sea to turn back.

Shelley's aphorism that poets are the unacknowledged legislators of the world, which Heaney borrowed for the title of his own poem, contains the idea that skill with words is connected with an ability to serve a wider ideal of justice that is unlimited by considerations of territory and time. It also suggests that poets are lonely, outcast, figures who, perhaps because of their peripherality, are capable of taking more profound and disinterested stances than the conventional kinds of legislators.[65] Unacknowledged legislators, for all that they do not have the apparatus of a state to enforce their words, might contribute to the shaping of a culture by conditioning the thoughts and feelings of people both in the present and in the future. They therefore might wield a power that is at once both more diffuse and more enduring than the power of acknowledged legislators.

Shelley wrote his famous words as the final line to his *A Defence of Poetry* (1821), where they capped an argument that the poet was a sensitive, unknowing channel through which the primacy of the imagination over reason was made manifest: "Poets are the hierophants of an unapprehended inspiration; the mirrors of the gigantic shadows which futurity casts upon the present; the words which express what they understand not; the trumpets which sing to battle, and feel not what they inspire; the influence which is moved not, but moves. Poets are the unacknowledged legislators of the World."[66] In writing this piece, Shelley was propounding an opposing conception of poetry to the one put forward by Thomas Love Peacock, whose *The Four Ages of Poetry* (1820) provocatively (if only half seriously) sought to prove that poetry had become debased in the modern era. Peacock's means of proving this point was by demonstrating how poets were subject to certain laws of economics and historic progression. His central argument was that, in an age dominated by exchange and commerce, the desire "to make a serious business of the playthings of [. . .] childhood," like verse, was "as absurd as for a full-grown man to [. . .] cry to be charmed to sleep by the jingle of silver bells."[67] Shelley, in his riposte to Peacock, argued that the creative imagination operated outside the limits identified by the other poet: poets were "the influence which is moved not, but moves." To Shelley, poets not only were free from but also shaped the restraints that Peacock had argued conditioned them.

To clinch his case, Shelley recast a phrase that his father-in-law, William Godwin, had written about Geoffrey Chaucer seventeen years earlier. Godwin had written that the author of *The Canterbury Tales*, by choosing poetry over law, had made the right choice: "The legislator of generations and the moral instructor of the world," he wrote, "ought never to have been a practising lawyer."[68] Shelley's pithier assertion was borrowed from Godwin's but contained crucial differences from it. By dropping the claim that poets were "moral instructors," and adding the word "unacknowledged," Shelley emphasized the separateness of the poet. By making this change, Shelley placed the poet in a similarly isolated and elevated position to the figure in Caspar David Friedrich's painting *Wanderer above a Sea of Fog* (1818), painted three years before *A Defence of Poetry* was written. His words were in keeping with the romantic zeitgeist that praised the outcast and wild, the free, rude, and untamed, at the expense of the urbane, polite, and politic. The ideal of the poet that Shelley's essay projected was, like the figure depicted in *Wanderer above a Sea of Fog*, lonely with his imagination, free and unconcerned with didacticism or received notions of rectitude. Heaney's use of Shelley's conception of the unacknowledged legislator kept some of these elements: in particular, his concern with imprisonment and breakouts echoes Shelley's insistence that poetry's essence lies in an exalted state of artistic freedom.

Along with its knowledge of romantic and nationalist imperatives, Heaney's poem carries, however ironically, the message that the poet should be above all things at liberty. In his poem, a gung-ho, crowbar-wielding intrusion into the world of prisons and guards merely results in whatever power the poet has being nullified. A significant part of this poem, and of Irish poetry in the twentieth century more broadly, has been a consciously imposed distance from the circumstances and contexts, both legal and otherwise, that have shaped it.

Since the 1920s, poetic involvements in legal controversies have been balanced by an almost equal desire to speak from and for a world that is not conditioned and constrained by the limits of the extant political sphere from which temporal laws issue. This antithetical quality is perhaps most famously exhibited by W. B. Yeats. The first chapter of this book, "The New Laws of the 1920s," centers on a poet whose career as a senator gives him a particular centrality to the study of law and literature in Ireland. This chapter reads his work in relation to the legal upheavals that accompanied the foundation of the Irish Free State in 1922. It demonstrates the deep impression that his appointment to the upper house of the Irish legislature made on his writing, examining how legal developments during the years around the establishment of the Free State reverberated in his poetry, plays, and prose works. The chapter argues that Yeats's writings from these years—in particular his gyre-based philosophical work *A Vision* (1925) and his monumental collection *The Tower* (1928)—were profoundly influenced by the failure and subsequent reestablishment of civil jurisdiction in Ireland in the years around partition and independence. However, this chapter pays equal attention to Yeats's characteristic self-portrayal in *The Tower* of turning away or escaping into reverie. This attitude is perhaps most famously on display at the moment when the sixty-year-old smiling public man vanishes from his senatorial duties into a world of speculation and memory in "Among School Children." Finally, this chapter shows how the gyre-based system Yeats invented—based as it is on cyclical patterns of decline, fall, and rebirth—offers a hopeful, if characteristically esoteric, model to an artist in a society that was emerging into its first modern, troubled, period of lawmaking.

The second chapter, "Jurisdictions of the Past," reads the work of one of Ireland's most prominent poets of the late 1920s and 1930s, Austin Clarke, in light of the laws of Ireland's southern jurisdiction. At this time, the excitements of the Revival and revolutionary years were giving way to the unglamorous realities of the new Free State, which included a highly conservative legislative agenda. This chapter explores the relationship between Austin Clarke's poetry and his frequent excoriations of the Irish Free State's proclivities to censorship, bureaucracy, uncaring commercialism, and Jansenist piety. It argues that Clarke's challenges to the country's laws are implicit in his frequent depictions of former times in his poetry: the Ireland of pagan times, the early modern Ireland of the Penal Laws, and, more than any other, the early medieval Ireland of small kingdoms and great monasteries. Through close readings of poems from several of Clarke's volumes, particularly *The Cattledrive in Connaught* (1925), *Pilgrimage, and Other Poems* (1929), and *Night and Morning* (1938), this chapter shows how, in many ways, Clarke carried on the protests against the laws of the Irish Free State that Yeats had spearheaded, while developing a style, idiom, and set of images that were distinct from those of his famous predecessor.

The poetry of Rhoda Coghill, who is the subject of the third chapter of this book, "Sounding Justice," even in its depictions of nature and landscapes, manifests an uneasy sense of guilt, culpability, and retribution. However, the birds that flit through her work carry a sense of liberation, their songs a countersound to the hegemonic pressures of midcentury Ireland. For example, her collection *The Bright Hillside* (1948) depicts a robin who interrupts the solemn voices of a Mass: "Through the grave, holy rite the happy bird / Drove a light counterpoint."[69] Throughout, this chapter highlights the pressures that are visible in her poetry and suggests that they are linked to her statuses as a member of the small Quaker minority in a strongly Catholic state and as a woman in a male-dominated public sphere. It focuses on several of her poems that seem to simultaneously register and soar over these pressures.

The next chapter, "The Civil Servant as Poet," examines the work of Coghill's younger contemporary Thomas Kinsella. He published his early poems while he worked in the Department of Finance, where he was mentored by T. K. Whitaker, one of the Republic's most famed civil servants. Whitaker's *Programme for Economic Expansion* (1958) is credited with laying the basis for the modern Irish economy by envisaging the country's move from a predominantly agricultural basis to an industrial one.[70] Kinsella's poetry was sensitive to these new imperatives. This chapter shows how the energies of midcentury Irish modernity, both the conservative and the transformational, were expressed both legislatively and in his poetry and other writings.

The next chapter turns to Northern Ireland, a linked but separate jurisdiction. Seamus Heaney's rise to prominence at the beginning of the Troubles at the end of the 1960s and beginning of the 1970s meant that he had to perform a more precarious balancing act with regard to law than any of his predecessors since Yeats. The chapter "Unwritten Laws" uses his 2004 version of *Antigone*, which he titled *The Burial at Thebes*, as a frame through which to view his evolving interest in matters of law. Drawing on newly released materials from the archive of his correspondence held at Emory University, Atlanta (opened in 2016), this chapter brings to light a connection between one of the greatest legal controversies of the years of the Troubles, the inquest that followed the 1988 "Death on the Rock" shootings in Gibraltar, and a poem in Heaney's volume *Seeing Things* (1991). This chapter also analyzes Heaney's responses to prisoners, from the internees of the 1970s and the hunger strikers of the early 1980s to the far-flung prisoners that he campaigned for as part of his work with Amnesty International from the mid-1980s onward. Throughout, this chapter demonstrates how Heaney's use of oblique references, small-scale publications, and alternative versions of poems are all testaments to his lifelong preoccupation with the idea of justice.

The next chapter, "Legislators of the Unacknowledged," examines how poets Paula Meehan and Paul Durcan responded to legal, constitutional, and law-enforcement controversies during the 1980s. During this decade the position of women, and of working-class people, before the state's laws, courts, and law-enforcement agencies became the subject of fierce contention. Scandals like the Kerry Babies case and the death of teenager Ann Lovett after she gave birth in secret absorbed public attention during these years. The Constitution, too, became the focus of controversy, as successive referendums pursuing liberalizing and conservative agendas had a polarizing influence, making divisions among the population apparent. During these unsettled years poets from the Republic of Ireland, in particular Meehan and Durcan, frequently gave vivid and memorable voice to the human consequences of the laws of the state. This chapter argues that, in writing in detail about the human realities that were often hidden behind legal abstractions and political rhetoric, these poets both expressed and created empathy for those individuals whose lives had put them outside the norms that were promoted by Ireland's laws and Constitution. In this way, Ireland's poets acted as, in George Oppen's phrase, "legislators / of the unacknowledged."

The final chapter of this book, "The Body of the Law in New Poetry," centers on recent work by Elaine Feeney, Miriam Gamble, Julie Morrissy, and Doireann Ní Ghríofa. In this chapter I look at the influence of an earlier generation of poets who broke with tradition, insisting on the lived experience of the female body as a subject for Irish poetry, in particular Eavan Boland's work of the 1980s and 1990s. Though Boland is not the subject of a chapter in this book, it is clear that her influence is present everywhere in the work of younger poets. This chapter particularly focuses on the shadow of the recent abortion laws of Northern Ireland and the Republic that were, to quote a poem by Gamble, "light but present, like the watchful eye of the law / when one is a fundamentally law-abiding citizen."[71] My readings of these poets' works draw attention to their imagery of exclusion, objecthood, and animality, arguing that these features protest a situation in law whereby a woman's creaturely corporeality was valued above her status as a reasoning being. I conclude with the idea that, by questioning what counts as human, the work of these poets shows the continuation of a long tradition in modern Ireland of poetry as a means of the assertion of the rights and dignity of the individual in the face of the law.

Though this final chapter is testament to the continued liveliness of the tradition of Irish poetry as counterspeech to official laws, a theme I also pursue in the book's short conclusion, it also argues that no poem can be explained by its legal context. Though critical readings of poems might be inflected by imaginings of the real or perceived attitudes of their authors, or notions of the times and places in which they lived, there will always be elements of poems that are fugitive and not amenable to being read in their legal or any other contexts. It could be that poems are inherently wayward entities, impelled by forces too deeply laid for scrutiny or exegesis to illuminate fully. Perhaps it is, ironically, this very fugitive quality that might give poetry its value in the public sphere. Poems can represent an alternative, often disaffected, source of power, precisely because, as Shelley argued, they operate outside the terms set by and relied upon by ordinary laws. They can be the "light counterpoint" that Rhoda Coghill wrote that the robin's song provided against the voice of the priest in the 1940s. They can be the escape from confinement that Heaney dreamed of in the 1970s when he substituted the responsibilities of "our" Bastille for the imaginative distance of "the."

1

The New Laws of the 1920s

W. B. Yeats

On the afternoon of July 22, 1926, the Senate of the Irish Free State was in session at Leinster House in Dublin, debating the laws that would govern the new High and Supreme Courts of Ireland. Senator William Butler Yeats, who had been appointed by William Cosgrave, the leader of the new Irish Free State, put forward a proposal whose purpose, at least at an aesthetic level, was intended to draw a line under Ireland's legal past. Yeats recommended that Irish High and Supreme Court judges should give up the gray wig and black gown that they shared with their contemporaries in the English legal system and wear instead a new Irish-designed costume of black velvet cap and red gown. This motion, which called for highly visible changes to the machinery of the law, found favor among several of Yeats's fellow senators, who accused their opponents of attachment to "English tradition."[1] Yeats was opposed, however, by several other senators, who rejected the idea that the legal reality of the new state required new symbols. These senators argued that the Irish people had a residual respect for existing institutions and that this respect should be drawn on to bolster the authority of the new state. Senator Sir John Keane, a barrister who, like Yeats, had been one of Cosgrave's appointees to the Senate, illustrated his conservative argument with a pointed quotation from poetry:

> How but in custom and in ceremony
> Are innocence and beauty born?

> Ceremony's a name for the rich horn,
> And custom for the spreading laurel tree.[2]

These were, of course, lines from W. B. Yeats's own "A Prayer for My Daughter," first published in 1919; their quotation by Keane put Yeats in the presumably uncomfortable position of hearing his own poetry quoted against him. As is often the case in disputes over style, behind the argument between the two senators was a matter of substance. Had the official Irish legal system so lost its legitimacy during the revolutionary period 1912–23 that even its symbols needed to be done away with and replaced? Or, rather, were there elements of the past that offered desirable grounds for future developments? Did the postrevolutionary moment call for the allaying power of tradition in order to speed the reestablishment of a functioning civil society, or did it, rather, represent a brief opportunity in which the outmoded might be superseded by something newer and finer? Yeats himself wrestled with just such questions of transience and supersession—of "what is past, or passing, or to come," as he wrote in "Sailing to Byzantium" (*The Tower*, 1928), a poem that he drafted in the months after this debate.[3] The Senate debates of these years over what changes Irish self-government would bring parallel the thematic preoccupation with epochal change in *The Tower* and in the philosophical book whose first version he completed during these years, *A Vision* (1925).

The years in which Yeats composed *The Tower* and *A Vision* saw Ireland's final tumultuous days as a constituent part of a unitary United Kingdom, the emergence amid revolution and Civil War of the Irish Free State, and the establishment of a separate jurisdiction on the island, Northern Ireland. They also saw the beginnings of parliamentary home rule in these states, albeit rule that was shadowed by, and shadowed, the unrealized republic whose claimed jurisdiction they shared. Yeats wrote nineteen of the twenty-one poems that make up *The Tower* between the years 1920 and 1927; his time in the Senate was from 1922 to 1928.[4] The significant overlap between Yeats's composition of most of the volume and his tenure as a legislator gave rise to intriguing consonances between *The Tower* and the existential questions, and the legislative changes, of the early Irish Free State.

Yeats's *The Tower* responds to the acts of both the British and the new Irish legislatures at several points. It evinces a highly critical stance toward the British Parliament's adoption of legislation that muzzled the institutions of civil justice while it prosecuted the Anglo-Irish War; it also reflects elements of Yeats's speeches on subsequent moves by the Irish Free State government to legislate on issues that include censorship, primary education, and, most famously, divorce.[5] However, Yeats's involvement in the work of the Senate is reflected in his imaginative work on a less straightforward level. In particular, the system building and structure making that were a part of the work of the Senate—Yeats described it as "the slow exciting work of creating the institutions of a new nation"—are reflected in both *A Vision* and *The Tower.*[6]

The single long speech that Yeats gave on divorce has become his best-known, perhaps most notorious, act as a senator. His statement during this speech that the minority from which he claimed descent were "no petty people" has to a large extent come to define his time in the Senate.[7] However, a closer look at the text of this speech shows that savage indignation was just one of the techniques he deployed. His opening argument was an antipartitionist one, warning of the damage that a ban on divorce would do to hopes of a united Ireland; his second was an appeal to the secular intentions of the drafters of the original Free State constitution of 1922; his third concerned the dangers of enacting theologically inspired legislation in a nominally pluralist state. A fourth argument, one less likely to find favor with his audience, perhaps, impugned the validity of the gospels; a fifth pointed out that a ban on divorce would have the unintended consequence of encouraging adultery. Only at the end of the speech did Yeats issue his famous racialized vindication of the Church of Ireland sect with which he identified. Yeats's use of his Senate platform to make appeals to a variety of points of view is less well remembered than his tub-thumping reference to "no petty people."

Similarly, an analysis of his entire record in the upper house of the Irish legislature shows the surprising diversity of Yeats's concerns. In particular, it shows his devotion to the preservation of buildings and monuments from all periods of Ireland's history. On two occasions he spoke about the preservation of ancient monuments and on three about the necessity of maintaining the structures and proportions of historic buildings, especially those in which the Irish government was considering locating its parliament.[8] The preservation of buildings and ancient monuments is therefore the subject he spoke on most frequently in the Senate, with his speeches on this matter representing 12 percent of his total speaking time (the highest figure for any single subject).[9] He spoke at almost equal length on measures to preserve and promote the Irish language, sidestepping debates over whether the state should support classical or spoken Irish by advocating the funding of both research into historic manuscripts and projects that would advance "the living tongue."[10] Like the buildings and monuments that he so often spoke of in his Senate speeches, this language was another threatened element of modern Ireland's inheritance. The frequency with which Yeats spoke on issues relating to linguistic and material preservation and the length at which he did so (devoting around twice the time to them that he did to divorce) indicate the strength of his interest in the maintenance of the monuments of Ireland's past during the tumultuous years when he was a senator.

Threatened monuments are a significant theme in the poetry that Yeats wrote during his time in the Senate.[11] A concern with the fate of monuments in the modern world is evident from the opening poem of *The Tower*, "Sailing to Byzantium." In its opening stanza, old men and monuments stand at either side of the teeming, abundant country that is described at its center:

> That is no country for old men. The young
> In one another's arms, birds in the trees

—Those dying generations—at their song,
The salmon-falls, the mackerel-crowded seas,
Fish, flesh, or fowl, commend all summer long
Whatever is begotten, born, and dies.
Caught in that sensual music all neglect
Monuments of unageing intellect.[12]

The meaning of the poem is shaped by the placement of its images: old men and monuments hover at both extremes of the stanza, peripheral to its real action yet crucial to its framework. In between these embodiments of venerability are the young, the shining shoals of fish, and the flocks of birds, which fill the stanza's heaving, swirling, center. This central tension between immortal monumentality and transient vitality is evident not just in the placement of images but also in the tension between the poem's form and its rhythms. A certain grandiosity inheres in the ottava rima form in which the poem is written, but the rhythmic fluidity of these lines works against any tendencies toward stateliness. Monuments of the past and pell-mell vitality are pitched against each other both in the form and in the imagery of "Sailing to Byzantium," and each exerts its own gravitational pull. The poem's combination of a time-honored form and wandering, wavering, rhythms creates a whole in which qualities of grandeur and haphazard fleetness are mingled.

On June 10, 1925, just over a year before the composition of this poem, Yeats had proleptically commented at a reading of the Shannon Electricity Bill in the Senate that "there are many monuments which we should respect and which will become of great importance to this country," but which were being put at risk in the Free State's drive toward economic development.[13] His practical concern with the fate of the country's monuments is paralleled in the preoccupations of *The Tower*, a volume in which he makes continual distinctions between the monuments of ancient wisdom and the onward pull of life. The twenty-one poems that make up *The Tower* consistently evince admiration for the human achievement represented by monuments. To give two examples, the poet's own tower and what he calls "learned Italian things / And the proud stones of Greece" are cited in the volume's title poem.[14] Elsewhere in *The Tower*, Yeats depicts Phidias's famous ivories, ingenious golden grasshoppers and bees, stately houses, and the works of the great, the good, and the wise. These things, however, are repeatedly contrasted with what might erode and eclipse them: the depredations of historic chaos, the so-called mockers that deride their majesty, inheritors who are unworthy of their great inheritances, and, more than anything, the ever-encroaching demands of self-delighting, self-generating life. A cyclical vision underlies *The Tower*, where each completed development, whether creative or destructive, is shown to be the originating point of the counter-energy that will, eventually, lead to the fulfillment of its own opposite. This central tension means that *The Tower* both mourns and celebrates the fact that, as Yeats later wrote, "All things fall and are built again."[15]

This cyclical narrative is also central to *A Vision* (1925), a systematizing philosophical work that Yeats claimed to have written with the guidance of spirit instructors (whose ideas were mediated by the "automatic writing" of his wife, George Yeats). *A Vision* has strong thematic links to *The Tower*, in that its central image, a diagram of two rotating, intersecting cones that respectively represent solar and lunar principles, is expressive of the idea that collapse and rebuilding are inevitable and inextricable processes.[16] In this genre-defying work, Yeats uses these cones to attempt no less than a schematization of epochal change. Though the obliquity of the first two chapters of *A Vision* (in which the "geometry" of these cones is adumbrated) repels attempts at logical analysis, the volume deepens in interest in the third section, titled "Dove or Swan." In this section, Yeats superimposes the cycles that the first two chapters identify over the histories of particular historic societies and sets out an understanding of both people and eras as compounds of varying proportions of opposing solar and lunar influences. Certain people and societies, the book claims, through a harmonization of these influences, achieve a state that he termed "Unity of Being." This represented a tantalizing possibility for Yeats at the outset of the Free State; his legislative work can be seen in part as an attempt to bring about this condition in the new polity.

Yeats's speech on judges' costumes shows that he had arrived at a deep appreciation of law as both force and symbol by 1926: even allowing for the overstatement fostered by argument, it is significant that he told his fellow senators during this debate that "I cannot imagine any place where innovation is more necessary than in the outward image of the law."[17] Other speeches he delivered as a senator demonstrate a great interest in the mechanisms of the Irish legal system. He spoke on the necessity of an independent judiciary, on the dangers of increasing the rights of state security forces to enter private homes, and (on two occasions) on the importance of keeping politics out of prison inspections.[18] However, viewed from the perspective of the beginning of his career, the fact that he eventually came to understand the power of the law as being transformative, as opposed to merely regulatory, is a surprising development.

References to law in Yeats's early works are few and slighting. They indicate an understanding of laws as a set of dead rules and a belief that they were promulgated by the unimaginative and maintained by those individuals with selfish motivations. Law was, in essence, a version of the "Grey Truth" to which Yeats had complained in one of his earliest poems that the modern world was in thrall.[19] This much is indicated in his play *The King's Threshold* (first produced in 1903), in which the poet Seanchan goes on a hunger strike as a response to not being seated in the same dignity as others at the court of the high king. In this case, the "makers of the law" are one of the self-interested groups that are opposed to the high status of poets. In the play, the king describes the

> Bishops, soldiers, and Makers of the Law—
> Who long had thought it against their dignity
> For a mere man of words to sit amongst them
> At the great council of the State [. . .][20]

Yeats takes aim at the legal profession again in his play *On Baile's Strand* (1904) when King Conchubar chides the hero, Cuchulain: "You play with arguments as lawyers do, / And put no heart in them."[21]

The low opinion of law and lawyers that Yeats's plays from the early years of the twentieth century reveal has a parallel in his essays for the theatrical periodical *Samhain*. In a 1904 essay he suggests that lawbreaking is a kind of proof of life and vivacity: "Had Coriolanus not been a law-breaker, neither he nor we had ever discovered, it may be, that noble pride of his. [. . .] If we were not certain of law we would not feel the struggle, the drama, but the subject of art is not law, which is a kind of death, but the praise of life, and it has commandments that are not positive."[22] It is perhaps no coincidence that Yeats's theatrical writings from the early years of the twentieth century are the most disparaging of law and lawyers. During these years, battles over theater licensing and censorship that accompanied the foundation of the Irish National Theatre forced him and his collaborators to encounter solicitors more often than they would have liked.[23]

The practice of law in Ireland had a deeper history, which Yeats would have read in the introduction to the Ossianic Society's translation of the Middle Irish tale *Immtheacht na Tromdaimhe* (Proceedings of the Great Bardic Institution), a text he drew on as a source for his play *The King's Threshold*. In the introduction to this volume, the editors set out how lawyers in pre-Norman Ireland received training in subjects that included poetry before specializing in law.[24] Yeats's slighting references to lawyers in *The King's Threshold* are even more remarkable considering the fact that law and lawmakers are not even mentioned in the other sources that he drew on for this play, including Lady Wilde's story "Seanchan the Bard and the King of the Cats" (1887) and Edwin J. Ellis's play *Sancan the Bard* (1895).[25] Despite evidence of overlaps between lawyers and poets in ancient Ireland, Yeats's *The King's Threshold* goes beyond all his sources to depict the two professions as separate.

Though the separation of lawmakers and poets in *The King's Threshold* does not accord with the scholarship on ancient Ireland that was available when Yeats was writing, it is in keeping with Yeats's other formative cultural influences. As David Ross has noted, Yeats's attitudes reflect those of Shelley in his *A Defence of Poetry* (1821), an essay from which the famous phrase "poets are the unacknowledged legislators" of the world comes. In this work, which Yeats marked up in his edition of Shelley's essays, the Romantic poet writes that "poets have been challenged to resign the civic crown to reasoners and mechanists."[26] The "makers of the law" in Yeats's play represent just such an unimaginative cadre, and his attitude to law in this play signals his indignation at the bureaucratic, bourgeois usurpation of leading roles in society that became such a theme of his poetry. The attitude to law and lawyers in *The King's Threshold* seems to be a late echo of the strain of Romanticism that condemned the alienation of the artist and the tyranny of the worldly and unworthy. In Yeats's case, this attitude was mediated through the antimaterialistic late-Victorian counterculture that is one of his most significant contexts.[27]

Yeats went from understanding law as a tool in the deadening "hands of reasoners and mechanists" to seeing it as a more significant body of knowledge during the decades that followed the turn of the twentieth century. Conflicts both in Ireland and in Europe, and the legal changes that came with these conflicts, had a highly noticeable effect on the representation of law in his work. In 1918 the British government, alarmed by a shortage of manpower on the western front, yoked the passage of a new Home Rule Bill for Ireland to the introduction of conscription under the Military Service (Ireland) Bill of 1918.[28] Yeats was even called upon by figures in the British establishment to promote this plan, though he rejected these requests.[29] In the same year he composed "An Irish Airman Foresees His Death," published in his volume *The Wild Swans at Coole* (1919). In it the poem's protagonist states that

Nor law, nor duty bade me fight,
Nor public men, nor cheering crowds,
A lonely impulse of delight
Drove to this tumult in the clouds[.][30]

The poem's hero-protagonist is one of many people whom Yeats celebrates in poetry for their disdain for public approval.[31] The speaker's rejection of the compulsion of "law" is a part of this disdain and throws into further relief his lonely, self-willed qualities. However, ironically (considering how the poem foregrounds its protagonist's lack of regard for law), the poem carries a strong echo of developments in the legal sphere. By highlighting the airman's nationality as Irish in the title of the poem, and by making references to law and public men, Yeats weaves the fateful 1918 attempts to pass conscription laws in Ireland into the fabric of the poem. In the face of calls that he support proposed legislative changes on the participation of Irish men in the First World War, Yeats himself was compelled to balance all and bring all to mind, no less than the Irish airman he wrote about.

Increasingly, the poems Yeats wrote between 1918 and 1921 show that his faith in the embattled civil legal system that governed Ireland was coming under strain.[32] The guerrilla fighting of the Irish War of Independence that had started sporadically in early 1919 continued with varying degrees of intensity over the following two and a half years. The weakening of existing structures of civil law that this fighting precipitated caused an intensification of Yeats's interest in matters of legal process. During these years, Yeats looked on in horror as the British government adopted a semiofficial policy of reprisals against civilians in Ireland. Yeats considered it not only an abjuration of the government's duty to uphold justice, but one of many signs from around the world of the end of a tolerant, peaceable epoch. For all that the policy of reprisals was unofficial, it was enabled by the Restoration of Order in Ireland Act of 1920, a piece of legislation that was, in essence, an attempt to weaken civil law by means of civil law. It provided for the replacement of trial by jury with courts-martial in those areas where the IRA was most active and for the replacement of coroners' inquests with military courts of inquiry that were more sympathetic to police and British military actions.[33]

Yeats's poetry bears the marks of these legal changes. Two of his poems, "Reprisals" and "Nineteen Hundred and Nineteen," angrily express his growing sense that law and justice were being divided from each other. "Reprisals" was written in response to the murder of a woman from Kiltartan, not far from his own tower, who was shot from a passing police lorry. In this poem, Yeats writes of civilians like the victim that:

> [. . .] Armed men
> May murder them in passing by
> Nor law nor parliament take heed.[34]

The deaf ear that Yeats accused "law and parliament" of turning to this atrocity is attested to by *Hansard*, the Westminster parliamentary record, which shows how the chief secretary for Ireland repeatedly evaded answering questions about the incident.[35] One of the central poems of *The Tower*, "Nineteen Hundred and Nineteen," was written, despite its title (and the year attributed to it in the volume), over the two years that preceded its first publication in 1921.[36] Its fourth stanza describes the same incident in Kiltartan that "Reprisals" does. However, the historic significance of the event is broadened.

In "Nineteen Hundred and Nineteen," it is not just an individual victim whose killing is decried. Rather, "a law indifferent to blame or praise" is counted as one of the victims of the modern era:

> We too had many pretty toys when young:
> A law indifferent to blame or praise,
> To bribe or threat [. . .][37]

Caustic irony burns through Yeats's description of a body of law as being among a former era's "pretty toys," one that could be broken or cast aside by a willful executive. This reflects his public statements on law in Ireland: he had publicly come out in favor of the establishment of an Irish government headed by the revolutionary cadre that had been prosecuting the Anglo-Irish War at an Oxford Union debate in February 1921. The violent end of an operative legal system in Ireland was part of his justification of his stance. At the end of his speech he harangued his audience: "Gladstone! Salisbury! Asquith! They were Victorians. I am a Victorian. They knew the meaning of the words 'Truth' and 'Honour,' and 'Justice.' But you do not know the meaning of them."[38] The failure of the executive to provide "justice" is just one of the ways in which the poem "Nineteen Hundred and Nineteen" depicts the destruction of the achievements of a former era by the unprincipled public figures of more recent times.

The poems in *The Tower* present a cyclical vision of falling and rebuilding; so, too, do Yeats's public speeches from the period during which they were written. In keeping with the antithetical vision that characterizes his poetry from this time, during the Oxford Union debate Yeats did not just excoriate the lack of official justice in Ireland; he also looked ahead to what might supplant the fallen legal system. The *Oxford Chronicle* reported: "Mr. W. B. Yeats said the law had never broken down in Ireland. English law had broken down, but though he was not a Sinn Feiner, he would say that Sinn Fein justice was real justice, and in many places in Ireland real justice had come for the first time."[39] In making this observation, Yeats endorsed the Dáil court system, a set of civil and criminal courts that Irish republicans had established from mid-1920 that both mirrored and sought to supplant the existing system.[40] Yeats's endorsement of this republican system of justice might seem surprising, but it is in keeping with a tendency in his poetry not merely to elegize what had passed, but to envisage what would supplant what had vanished. His desire to see new shoots growing among the fragments of the old is reflected in the symbolism of the second section of "Nineteen Hundred and Nineteen," in which the dancers that spin among a ribbon of cloth reflect the constant destruction and creation brought about by the winding and whirling of the historical gyres.

Yeats's tendency at this time to combine ideas of destruction with ones of rebuilding is also reflected in his early, rejected, titles for "Nineteen Hundred and Nineteen": "The Things Return" and "The Things That Come Again." Michael Wood interprets these titles as referring to the cyclical return of violence after periods of stability, and indeed this is one of their meanings.[41] However, the poem's opening line, "Many ingenious lovely things are gone," points to another possible interpretation. In repeating the word "things" from the original title, "The Things Come Again," Yeats raises the possibility that it is the vanished "ingenious lovely things" of the first line that will come again. Seen in the light of the original title, the demise of "a law indifferent to blame or praise" could just be read as a temporary absence rather than a tragic loss. The title of the original draft of the poem, like Yeats's speech in Oxford, does not just recognize destruction; it also looks ahead to a new dispensation.

The transition from the anarchy of the War of Independence to the reestablishment of civil government following the Anglo-Irish Treaty of December 1921 was, however, not to be straightforward. The Free State's Dominion status and its lack of jurisdiction over six of Ireland's northeastern counties disappointed the hopes of many who had fought for independence. A Civil War between the protreaty Free State forces and their irredentist former comrades in the IRA, fought in 1922 and 1923, shaped Irish politics for decades after. *The Tower* was written in part during the embattled early years of the Free State and reflects the violent conditions engendered by what Yeats's friend the minister for justice Kevin O'Higgins termed Ireland's "clash of jurisdictions."[42] The house burnings that had begun during the War of Independence increased in frequency in the Civil War that followed the treaty.[43] During the Civil War the windows of Yeats's Dublin house were shot out, the bridge beside his tower was blown up, and thirty-seven of his fellow senators had their houses destroyed by explosions and fires.[44] Yeats's poetry and Senate speeches show how fires were rippling and flashing through his imagination in the immediate wake of two of Ireland's rival jurisdictions going to war with each other.

Images of the destructive capacities of fire recur in the volume *The Tower*, both in ancient and in contemporary contexts. "Nineteen Hundred and Nineteen" opines that "Incendiary or bigot could be found" to light a fire on the Acropolis.[45] Later in the volume, "Meditations in Time of Civil War" bears witness to a time in which "A man is killed, or a house burned, / Yet no clear fact to be discerned." "Two Songs from a Play" concludes with a hauntingly vivid image of fiery destruction: "Whatever flames upon the night / Man's own resinous heart has fed."[46] The preoccupation that this volume evinces with the destructive capacities of fire is matched by Yeats's Senate speeches. The records show that the safety of national treasures from fire became an obsession for Yeats by the middle of 1924, and his Senate record contains a series of speeches on the necessity of fire precautions at the National Museum, which houses irreplaceable artifacts from Ireland's distant past. The museum was in danger of being burned down as it adjoins Leinster House, the meeting place of the Senate. These circumstances added urgency to Yeats's many Senate speeches on the necessity of protecting the Irish Free State's material and intellectual inheritances.[47]

The fiery destruction of the revolutionary period appeared to Yeats as a judgment on what had come before, and quasi-legal judgments abound in both his plays and his poems from the revolutionary years and the period that immediately followed them. His play *The Dreaming of the Bones* (1919) centers on an escaped veteran of the Rising who unwittingly plays the role of judge and jury to the disguised ghosts of Diarmuid and Devorgilla, semilegendary lovers who are traditionally held to be responsible for the first incursions of the Normans into Ireland in the twelfth century. The ghosts are, in the nationalist mythos, the Adam and Eve that brought the original sin of English rule and law to Ireland. The two ghosts beg the veteran to forgive them and release them from purgatory, but, at the end of the play, realizing the ghosts' true identities, he pronounces that "never,

never / Shall Diarmuid and Devorgilla be forgiven."[48] The vanishing of the ghosts as they are swept away with a lifting cloud at the play's close is analogous to the sending down of prisoners after conviction. The sense that this play conveys of a present that stands in fierce, uncompromising, judgment on the past is also a feature of Yeats's late play *Purgatory* (1938). In this play a character stands in front of a burned house and declares that "to kill a house / Where great men grew up, married, died, / I here declare a capital offence."[49] Writers with an interest in law and literature have long pointed out the many parallels between courtrooms and theaters.[50] Yeats's plays from the postrevolutionary years, in which harsh, quasi-legal judgments are often central to the action, turn theaters into courtrooms: ones in which the past itself is on trial.

Yeats did not confine the theme of uncompromising judgment to his drama: it is also a strong feature of his poetry in the postrevolutionary years. "Meditations in Time of Civil War" ends with a vision of vengeance as the speaker climbs to the top of the tower while thinking of a centuries-old injustice: "I, my wits astray / Because of all that senseless tumult, all but cried / For vengeance on the murderers of Jacques Molay."[51] This is a reference to the unjust execution of the last grand master of the Knights Templar in 1314, a killing orchestrated by the pope and the king of France.[52] The killing of Molay, which Yeats declares in a note to be a "fit symbol for those who labour from hatred," raises more contemporary ideas of trials, guilt, inoperative laws, and unjust sentencing.

The same themes appear in other poems with modern Ireland as their focus. "In Memory of Eva Gore-Booth and Con Markiewicz" (*The Winding Stair, and Other Poems*, 1933), dated October 1927 by Yeats, carries intimations of unjust judgment. The speaker of the poem includes himself in a shadowy "us" who have been "convicted" of that most obscure of crimes, "guilt."[53] These issues were on Yeats's mind until the end of his life: one of the last poems he completed, "Cuchulain Comforted" (*Last Poems*, 1938–39), features a shadowy host of "Convicted cowards" who urge the stricken hero to quiescently adopt their own behavior.[54] During the years that followed Ireland's revolutionary period, Yeats's thoughts repeatedly turned to matters of judgment.

Franz Kafka's short years (1883–1924) were encompassed within those of Yeats, and there are parallel circumstances and common factors that shaped their lives and their writing. The retreat of the frontiers of empire left Yeats, a member of his country's Protestant minority, inclined to consider issues of ancestral guilt and to observe afresh the vulnerability of the individual in relation to the armed and powerful in situations where the law was inoperative. Kafka, a German-speaking Jew in Prague (the principal city of the Czech territories of the Austro-Hungarian Empire), was justly uneasy about the future during the same years. His best-known work, *The Trial* (written in 1914–15, but not published until 1925), was written in the years immediately before the collapse of the Austro-Hungarian Empire, as the shocks and privations of war stoked divisions among its constituent peoples.[55] *The Trial* follows the shadowy indictment and prosecution of its protagonist, Josef K., and ends with his execution. It is a work that, in part, explores the shadows that a legal system can cast on an individual psyche. Yeats's poetry and plays in the revolutionary and postrevolutionary years, like Kafka's, are full of ideas of the operations of justice and authority. In Yeats's work of the 1920s and 1930s, in a way that parallels Kafka's stories, the laws that are in operation often seem opaque and impenetrable. For Yeats's "Jacques Molay," as for Kafka's Josef K., the nature of the crimes that the "guilty" have committed, the identities of the authorities who punish, and the uncompromising codes by which punishments are meted out are all shrouded in mystery.

Yeats was keen to present 1912, at the outset of what was to become the revolutionary period in Ireland, as the foundational year of his volume *The Tower*. The year 1912 is the earliest of the dates that is ascribed to any of the individual works in *The Tower*, giving the reader a (slightly erroneous) idea that the volume was under continuous construction from that date until the time of its publication in 1928.[56] Historian Niall Whelehan dates the revolutionary period to this year, writing that "after 1912 actions increasingly spoke louder than words."[57] One of the features of a functioning legal system is that, in it, words speak louder than actions, as societally agreed standards of conduct replace the unchecked power of physical might. Yeats also directs the reader to think of the year 1912 by writing about conditions "seven years ago" in "Nineteen Hundred and Nineteen":

> We, who seven years ago
> Talked of honour and of truth,
> Shriek with pleasure if we show
> The weasel's twist, the weasel's tooth.[58]

Yeats's indication that 1912 was the last time "honour" and "truth" held sway situates the failure of these ideals in the year of the introduction of the Third Home Rule Bill to the Westminster Parliament. This measure did not lead, as was anticipated, to self-government for Ireland, but led to the division of the country into two armed camps, as the British Army in Ireland mutinied and unionist and nationalist paramilitary groups formed in response to these plans. Yeats's directing of the reader's attention to 1912, the year when law became subject to armed power in Ireland, is directing them to the time of the failure of a specific piece of legislation and to the beginnings of the collapse of the extant Irish civil legal system.

Yeats's appointment to the sixty-member Senate was recognized by contemporaries as an endorsement of the place of poets in Irish national life. This position had its origins in both the distant past and modern politics. At the time that Ireland was moving toward independence, the idea that verbal power and temporal power were linked was in the air, and Yeats became a member of his country's legislature in part because of Irish ideas of the revered status of poets.[59] At the time Yeats's appointment to the Senate was announced, the *Freeman's Journal* remarked that it restored the "ancient relationship" between the Irish bard and "councils of State," citing Yeats's own play *The King's Threshold* as evidence for the existence of this relationship.[60] It was perhaps ironic that, in referring to the "ancient" rights of poets to sit at "councils of State," the newspaper echoed a revision that Yeats had made to his 1903 play only shortly before.[61] As late as 1915, printings of the play merely referred to the poet's right to sit at the king's table during meals. The 1921 printing stated that the troubles that the play records began when the bard was refused a seat at "the great council of State." Yeats, as well as absorbing resurgent late-nineteenth-century Irish ideas on the ancient dignity of the poet, perhaps more than anyone else, helped to promulgate them.

Despite the ancient links between lawmakers and poets in Ireland, the tensions and contradictions that arose from his own dual role of poet and legislator came to preoccupy Yeats. A significant theme in *The Tower* is the disjunction between work that is widely recognized as useful and the more mysterious functioning of his own irresponsible craft of poetry: "something that all others understand or share," measured against his love of "daemonic images."[62] Although the use that wider society has for the arts is a pertinent question for any artist, Yeats's position as a legislator brought ideas of the social role of the artist home to him with special intensity. In a digression in an imagined dialogue between "Peter," a senator, and "Paul," a deputy, that Yeats published in 1924, he speaks through his protagonists: one says that "creation moves in a continual uncertainty," while his interlocutor replies, "I cannot see any means whereby a Parliament can pass uncertainty into law."[63] The divisions between creative and legislative activity that these protagonists touch on form a significant strand in Yeats's thinking during his tenure as a senator.

Yeats's sense of the disjunction between his work as a poet and his role as a lawmaker is signaled by an unusual speech he gave in June 1925, in which he quoted poetry in the Senate. It was during a debate on that less-than-poetical subject the Shannon Electricity Bill of 1925. This legislation paved the way for the setting up of the Ardnacrusha hydroelectric station on the River Shannon, a project that Yeats, reviewing the first decade of Irish self-government six years later, recalled as being among the great successes of the new state. When he thought of "the legislation of those ten years," he wrote, he thought of "the electrical works at Ardna-crusha. These works are successful. [. . .] They were the Government's first great practical success, a first object-lesson in politics. [. . .] My six years in the Irish Senate taught me that no London Parliament could have found the time or the knowledge for that transformation."[64] Yeats's contributions to the debates on the bill that brought this project about, however, are more ambiguous in tone.

Characteristically, he worried about the ancient ruins and monuments near the River Shannon that might be affected by these developments. Speaking of the ruins of Clonmacnoise, an ancient monastery on the banks of the river, he recited lines from T. W. Rolleston's late-nineteenth-century translation of bardic verses that had been composed in praise of it:[65]

> In a quiet, watered land, a land of roses
> Stands Saint Kieran's city fair,
> And the warriors of Erin, in their famous generations
> Slumber there.[66]

Yeats stated that his reason for quoting these lines was that, if the ruins were protected from being damaged by the works that were under consideration, visitors would be drawn to Clonmacnoise. He also stated that Rolleston's poem could be influential in attracting visitors to the ruins, which would be beneficial for the local economy. By quoting the poem, Yeats may have wished to remind his fellow legislators of the great literary and historic inheritances of modern Ireland. However, the oddities that surround his delivery of this quotation raise questions about how he viewed himself as a poet in a legislative body and about the place of the creative imagination in a modern polity.

Yeats followed his quotation with a double-edged reflection: "I think I am the first person who has quoted a poem in the Senate. I only do so because I am sure the poem will be, to use the appropriate words, 'a definite asset.'"[67] This comment makes it possible to see Yeats's quotation from poetry in another light: he might have wished to highlight the absurdity of his task, compelled as he was to argue for the value of Ireland's ancient monuments in the economically minded terms in which business in the Senate was typically conducted. The Senate records show that Yeats would have heard Ireland's seas and rivers described as "a national asset," or similar, on three occasions on that day alone.[68] Whatever his motivations in quoting the poem, the critics who have commented on this event agree that his description of the poem as "a definite asset" carries a tang of acidity.[69] In saying it, Yeats raises a question about the role of literature in a world governed by laws of rational political economy and gives a hint that he suspects that poetry and legislatures may not mix.

This concern was a serious one for a poet for whom the foundation of the Free State held out the possibility of a new concord between practical and aesthetic life. The excitement in Yeats's letters from the time around his appointment to the Senate is focused on this idea. He had high hopes that the arrival of an Irish state heralded the collapse of these distinctions, at least at a local level: "Dublin is reviving after the Civil War," he wrote hopefully in early 1924. "People are trying to found a new society" in which "politicians want to be artistic, and artistic people to meet politicians."[70] Yeats did what he could to help along a marriage between artistic and practical life in the Free State, telling the Senate that it was "very important for the future industrial prosperity of this country that art teaching should be brought into relationship with industry."[71] He formed a Senate committee that attempted to set up a "Federation of the Arts," a body through which Irish industry could be influenced by aesthetic ideals.

Yeats's attempts to bring practical work and art into alignment in the Free State had roots and parallels in his developing philosophy. Initially, his appointment to the Irish legislature may have appeared to him as an indication that Irish society was moving toward the fulfillment of his ideal of "Unity of Being." Yeats's first reference to this concept was in an essay of 1919, in which he expresses a wish to "begin another Epoch by recommending to the Nation a new doctrine."[72] Though his ideas on what constituted "Unity of Being" are vague, they seem a continuation of the drives toward harmonization and synthesis that animated his work since early in his career.[73] His descriptions of the state of Unity of Being (though ironically heterogenous in nature) have certain overlapping features: it is a condition that could at times be embodied by people and by societies and involves a grand idea that subordinates other ideas to it. This central idea links all classes in societies that achieve this condition and provides the animating spirit behind all their productions, from their arts to their practical wares. A line from *The Trembling of the Veil*, a memoir Yeats wrote in 1920, records his hope that modern Ireland "might be the first [society] in Europe to seek unity as deliberately as it had been sought by theologian, poet, sculptor, architect from the eleventh to the thirteenth century."[74] Yeats's ironic commendation of a poem to the Senate as a "definite asset" in 1925, however, indicates his skepticism about what a poet could achieve in a legislature.

Something of Yeats's attitudes toward the possibility of "Unity of Being" in Ireland, and of the limited role that poetry might play in its achievement, can be inferred from his reflections on Byzantium in *A Vision* (1925): "I think that in early Byzantium, and maybe never before or since in recorded history, religious, aesthetic and practical life were one, and that architect and artificers—though not, it may be, poets, for language had been the instrument of controversy and must have grown abstract—spoke to the multitude and the few alike."[75] This desire for a unified culture (he goes on to describe it as one where "building, picture, pattern, metal work of rail and lamp, seem but a single image") was a projection onto ancient Byzantium of an ambition he had for the society he inhabited since, as he later recalled, his early twenties.[76] However, as the above passage from *A Vision* makes clear, the poet in a modern society had a problem, one that was rooted in the nature of language itself. Poetry was written in the same medium as political arguments and the abstractions of legislatures, and Yeats suspected that the impurity of its materials made it an unsuitable medium for the promotion of a spiritually unified society.[77]

The differences between what Yeats's senatorial role demanded and what his imagination compelled are central to one of the most important poems in *The Tower*, "Among School Children." This long poem was inspired by a 1926 visit that the "sixty-year-old smiling public man" paid to a school, St. Otteran's in Waterford, as part of his work on a Senate committee that was tasked with investigating primary education in the Free State. In its opening lines the speaker seems fully engaged with a nun's account of the systems that modern thinking has decreed are best for education: the poem's protagonist hears how the children learn "To cut and sew, be neat in everything / In the best modern way."[78]

In the first stanza of "Among School Children," however, there is a hint of something dissociative in this senatorial behavior: after all, the speaker's description of himself as "A sixty-year-old smiling public man" indicates that he is seeing himself not from his own perspective, but from the point of view of the children in the school he is visiting. As the poem continues, the speaker's dissociation from his location in time and place increases. The first stanza break signals a leap in perspective as his public duties are forgotten and the interior world takes primacy:

> I dream of a Ledaean body, bent
> Above a sinking fire, a tale that she
> Told of a harsh reproof, or trivial event
> That changed some childish day to tragedy[.][79]

What follows is an associative chain of images relating to the poet's inner tumult over Maud Gonne, combined with a lifetime's questions over the nature of memory and reality. This digressive poem is in stark contrast to Yeats's Senate contributions to the debates around the School Attendance Bill, in which there was nothing fantastical or abstract. The legislative concerns of the Irish Free State are evident in this poem, which Yeats started in May 1926, the same month that the School Attendance Act of 1926 passed into law.[80] In the early years of the Free State, the reform of primary education was a lively issue in the Senate. Though Yeats was sympathetic to the Montessori model of education practiced by the nuns of St. Otteran's, the chief adviser to the Irish government on educational matters, Timothy Corcoran, SJ, was strongly opposed to its exploratory ethos and instead stressed the need for discipline in schools. The same tensions between what is required through duty and what comes from the free play of the imagination are part of the poem and part of the Senate debates in which Yeats participated. In Yeats's Senate speeches on education he shows himself to be a particularly passionate advocate for the improvement of primary education for children from all social backgrounds.[81] Yeats's adoption of a public role came at the same time as his increased interest in discontinuous selfhood, and the poem "Among School Children" dramatizes the gulf between his social and imaginative selves.

The differences between Yeats's artistic and social selves can be seen in the different responses in his Senate record and his poetry to the same conditions. In the Enforcement of Law Bill of 1923, the Free State government legislated to increase the powers of the army and police to enter private property. Yeats, in one of many Senate interventions in which he asserted the importance of individual liberty, initially spoke out against this bill. However, he eventually signaled his capitulation to government plans by telling an anecdote that centered on how a process server who visited his tower needed the protection of seven or eight Free State soldiers.[82] Part 5 of "Meditations in Time of Civil War," "The Road at My Door," describes a similar (or possibly the same) event. In this poem, the tower-dwelling protagonist is visited by a "brown Lieutenant and his men," representatives of the Free State army. Though the interests of Yeats the legislator are in protecting the innocent and keeping the peace, the envious response of Yeats the poet to these soldiers is very different:

> I count those feathered balls of soot
> The moor-hen guides upon the stream,
> To silence the envy in my thought;
> And turn towards my chamber, caught
> In the cold snows of a dream.[83]

The tumult of the world beyond the tower is represented in this poem by soldiers and storms, hail and rain. Yet rather than deplore these unsettled conditions and the unfortunate necessity for repressive measures that they entail, as he does in his Senate contributions, the speaker of the poem envies the men of action and imagines himself in their place. His description of himself turning toward his chamber "caught / In the cold snows of a dream" reflects the chilly solitude of the writing life and also, perhaps, his own daydreams of being out and exposed to the elements as the soldiers are. The divergences between the uses to which Yeats put his experiences as a legislator and as a poet give us the opportunity to reflect on his full human complexity and contradictoriness.

The Tower was written during a period in which the legal structures in which Irish society operated fell and were built again, and it reflects both of these phases. In particular, Yeats's ambivalent attitude to his new role as a legislator contributes to the volume's strong thematic preoccupation with divided, multiple selfhood. *The Tower* is not just a lament for a former time, but a paean to the very fact of change; it is not only a hymn to self-assertion, but a reflection on just what a fugitive and fluid thing a self can be. Even if Unity of Being was impossible in the modern state then, as "Among School Children" shows, Yeats's renewed consciousness of division within himself enabled him to make remarkable poetry out of a state of disjunction.

2

Jurisdictions of the Past

Austin Clarke

In the notes to "The Young Woman of Beare," a poem in his 1929 volume *Pilgrimage, and Other Poems*, Austin Clarke observes that the new Irish Free State was a jurisdiction in which "the immodesty of present-day female dress is denounced in virile Pastorals and Parliament passes laws against temptations."[1] When he wrote this note, Clarke might have had in mind several recent pronouncements of the Irish Catholic Church and laws of the Free State. The "virile Pastorals" of the church included one in 1927 that identified "the dance hall, the bad book, the indecent paper, the motion picture, the immodest fashion in female dress" as snares of "the evil one" that had the power "to destroy the virtues characteristic of our race."[2] The temptations that the state's legislature, acting with the blessing of the church hierarchy, passed laws to suppress included those contained in films, books, and magazines. The former were regulated by the Censorship of Films Act of 1923, the latter two by the Censorship of Publications Act of 1929, which was enacted early in the same year as the publication of Clarke's *Pilgrimage*.[3]

The poem that Clarke wrote this note to, "The Young Woman of Beare," can be read as a challenge to the church and state's ideas of what was "characteristic of our race." *Pilgrimage*, the volume in which "The Young Woman of Beare" is collected, was never banned under the Censorship of Publications Act of 1929, unlike Clarke's novels. This reflects a wider pattern whereby fiction was more likely to be censored than poetry.[4] This, however, was not entirely for want of effort on Clarke's part. The protagonist of this poem, "Half clad in silken piles / [. . .] Half in dream," talks of prostitution and adultery and generally offends the strictures on decency that the laws enacted that year were meant to enforce on literature.[5] We can be fairly sure that, had his protagonist appeared in a novel, the outcome would have been different. When the archbishop of Tuam reviewed the catalog of County Galway libraries in 1924, the qualities of the novels that were removed and burned were those that contained "(1) Complete frankness in words in dealing with sex matters; (2) insidious or categorical denunciation of marriage or glorification of the unmarried mother and the mistress; (3) the glorification of physical passion; (4) contempt of the proprieties or conventions."[6] Considering how categorically Clarke's poem offends all these strictures, it seems as if he was deliberately courting the flames:

> [. . .] the President
> of Munster had come back.
> All day, in high and low street,
> His orderlies ran by.
> At night I entertained him
> Between the wine and map;
> I whispered with the statesmen,
> The lawyers that break land.[7]

Clarke's poem is a rewriting of a tenth-century poem, "The Old Woman of Beare." In Clarke's version, he takes this poem about the traditional female sovereignty goddess, expands on the sexually frank elements of the original, and increases her offenses by having her consort with the colonial authorities of early modern Ireland.[8] The pagan past—here in the form of the Cailleach Bhéara, a figure from Irish mythology associated with desire, disorder, and creation as well as with sovereignty—acts as the culture's unconscious and returns to haunt the supposed moral probity of the new Free State.[9]

The challenge that Clarke's poetry offers the Free State is made the sharper by his use of materials from the ancient culture of which the state claimed to be the inheritor and guardian. In Augustine Martin's phrase, the past is a "drawbridge across which he can make the most unexpected and ruthless raids upon the present."[10] By making these sorties, Clarke engages in a project of reclamation and points to the possibility of a different Ireland in the future.

Clarke was not the only writer in the 1920s who was looking to materials from former centuries as models on which to base a radical vision for the new state. In 1923 Sophie Bryant published *Liberty, Order & Law under Native Irish Rule: A Study in the Book of the Ancient Laws of Ireland*. In this work of legal excavation, she contrasted the more progressive model offered by Brehon law on several legal issues to that of the English-based common law that the new state had inherited.[11] Bryant, in the early 1920s, hoped that ancient laws on divorce, relationships between nonmarried partners, and married women's property rights might inspire the emergence of a more tolerant state from the revolutionary period. As the decade progressed, though, it became increasingly clear that the Free State's gaelicized legislative program would not bring with it a more liberal approach in social matters. Nevertheless, the hope that the Brehon system might provide an alternative pattern for independent Ireland's laws lived on among some in the conservative jurisdiction that emerged from revolution.

As late as 1940, jurist James C. Meredith speculated hopefully on whether the Brehon-influenced decisions of the republican courts of the revolutionary period had created binding precedents for their successors in the Irish legal system.[12] A similar strain of future-oriented antiquarianism to the one that animated legal writers in the 1920s is detectable in much of Clarke's poetry set in Ireland's past. However, if writers on law like Bryant and Meredith looked to distant Irish history for models that contemporary Irish lawmakers might emulate, then Clarke held up the country's history as a distorting mirror. The former Irish eras he wrote of are, in places, satirical worlds of opposites from the Ireland that developed in the 1920s and 1930s. For Clarke, distant Irish history was a quarry of former mores, laws, and practices from which he could extract and fashion counterweights to the new laws that came into being in his own time.

The eponymous first poem in *Pilgrimage* announces its writer's intention to set sail for a country that is at once new and ancient, as a ship's keel grinds ashore in a world that seems refreshed and renewed. The vision that emerges from the crosshatched rhyming pattern of "Pilgrimage" is highly colored and dramatic:

When the far south glittered
Behind the grey beaded plains,
And cloudier ships were bitted
Along the pale waves,
The showery breeze—that plies
A mile from Ara—stood
And took our boat on sand[.][13]

Clarke opens his volume in a fashion that is no less ringing than Yeats's announcement at the outset of *The Tower*, published the previous year, that he had set out for Byzantium. Like Yeats, Clarke used historical materials to create an imaginary realm in poetry and used this otherworld as a space in which to negotiate with both the possibilities and the inadequacies of the actual. However, whereas Yeats in the mid-1920s made a shadow Ireland by imagining the wineshops, mosaic makers, and lords and ladies of ancient Byzantium, Clarke created a mosaic in the shape of a former Ireland out of the fragments that he had assembled from the country's past. Both Yeats's and Clarke's alternative, imagined, jurisdictions resembled the actual Ireland of the 1920s in that both were undergoing periods of transition. Yeats pictured his Byzantium of the mind as it was passing between being a classical and a Christian society, "a little before Justinian opened St. Sophia and closed the Academy of Plato."[14] The Irish monks and churchmen that Clarke envisaged were in the process of abandoning insular rites and embracing European models.[15]

This turn toward Europe is partially acknowledged in the term Clarke retrospectively used to characterize some of his own poetry from this time. The tenor of Clarke's *Pilgrimage* is set by the handful of poems in it that evoke the Christian Ireland of around eight hundred years earlier, a period Clarke came to label with the term "Celtic Romanesque."[16] In characterizing his poetry in this way, he appropriated an architectural term for a form of building that flourished for more than a hundred years from the early twelfth century.[17] This style is characterized by a newly decorative and sculptural approach to church architecture and represents an aerial leap from the dark, corbeled, and earth-hugging mode of religious building that preceded it. The new spirit that was manifested in ecclesiastical building had an intellectual concomitant, as the Irish church was at the time remodeling its forms of worship and structures on Roman ones. The "Romanesque" element of Clarke's thinking—the fact that he set so much of his poetry in a time when the Irish church abandoned its native rites and looked outward across Europe—raises interesting implications for how we read work that is not typically celebrated for its outward-looking breadth of vision.[18]

What inspired Clarke was not so much the heaviness and solidity of the many-layered carved stone piers with round arches of Ireland's Romanesque churches, but the manuscripts that were produced in the same early Christian monastic settlements. His prose picture in his novel *The Bright Temptation* (1932) of a medieval Irish scribe illuminating a manuscript with "fantastic birds" shows an ideal of intense, almost ritualized, concentration and imaginative freedom: "He turned minute circles, the quatrefoils and interlacing lines around themselves, tracing through remarkable convolutions those fantastic birds and beasts whose claws are no less entangled than their many-times-twisted necks and legs, contracting those richly colored creatures of his imagination until their lengthened tongues were trumpeted around their tails and they had been lettered to their last extremities."[19] Taking his inspiration from artworks like the one he imagined his monk working on, Clarke created a world as sinuously subtle, richly varied, and highly colored as the illuminated letters in monastic books. His description of the beguiling intricacies of a tortuous, coiling style also reflects his own artistic techniques, recalling the remarkable assonantal patterning by which he created sounds that are as delicately interlaced as the images of birds he imagined his monk creating in ink.

On a superficial level, the projects of Clarke and the Free State have strong similarities. In the years around the publication of Clarke's *Pilgrimage*, the Free State sought to claim and propagate the artistic inheritances of the Celtic past, issuing banknotes, coins, postage stamps, and even an official handbook that featured the same intricate knots and interlacements that Clarke had imagined a monk creating in a scriptorium.[20] In one reading, Clarke's imagery can be seen as an endorsement of that of the state; in another, it can be seen as a reclamation of it. Against what was produced in ersatz form as the imagery of the state, Clarke posits an ideal of artistic freedom, in which reality can be refashioned in accordance with the imperatives of the creating imagination. By critiquing the Irish Free State using imagery from the centuries of Celtic Christianity, Clarke puts a very different inflection on what had effectively become the house style of the new dispensation. He wrote that the Censorship of Publications Act proved that the Free State was in the hands of a new breed of "gloomy, self-righteous Gaels."[21] The "Celtic Romanesque" world that Clarke imagined, where "rainfall / Was quiet as the turning of books / In the holy schools at dawn," was an alternative to the "gloomy, self-righteous" one he perceived in Ireland.[22] It was also a place from which he issued some of his most uncompromising judgments on contemporary Ireland.

The "Celtic," not the "Romanesque," elements of Clarke's work characterized it in the minds of his contemporaries, and Clarke paid a high price in the 1930s and 1940s for the antiquarian aesthetic that he shared with the framers of the apparatus of the Free State. When W. B. Yeats compiled his *Oxford Book of Modern Verse, 1892–1935*

(1936), he declared in the introduction to this collection that he "tried to be modern."[23] This may have been among the reasons, though he found room for poems by James Joyce and Thomas MacGreevy, he excluded Clarke, a poet whose visions of the Irish Christian past may have seemed uncomfortably close to the antiquarian preoccupations of his own early work.[24] Samuel Beckett, in a 1934 piece in which he criticized his contemporaries for "delivering with the altitudinous complacency of the Victorian Gael the Ossianic goods," pilloried Clarke in particular for retailing "the fully licensed stock in trade from Aisling to Red Branch Bundling."[25] Patrick Kavanagh, perhaps remembering "The Country of Two Mists" section of Clarke's 1925 book, *The Cattledrive in Connaught*, labeled a grotesque composite of Clarke and some contemporaries "Paddy of the Celtic Mist" in his 1949 excoriation of his peers, "The Paddiad."[26] The past-facing orientation of Clarke's subject matter, more than any of his poetry's other features, conditioned the responses of his contemporaries to his work. It also meant that the innovative and subversive potential of his ancient imagery has been given less than its due.

Clarke turned from the myths and legends of prehistory to the medieval world in his collection *Pilgrimage*, published twelve years after his first volume of poetry. Looking back from the 1960s, he variously described the genesis of his interest in the "Celtic Romanesque" period to his generation and schooling and to youthful conversations about Irish church rites that he had with poet F. R. Higgins.[27] In the retrospect of more than thirty years, he cast the historic orientation of his poetry from this period as a sort of hobbyist indulgence. His interest in earlier centuries, he implied, was a turn away from the state, a reflection of how promising the development of the new polity seemed in the 1920s. He wrote that the years 1925 to 1929 were ones "when the future of our new State seemed so hopeful that Irish writers could delay for a while in the past. Turning from our early myths, I wanted to explore imaginatively a little of the Celtic

Romanesque era and historical periods neglected and almost forgotten except by Gaelic scholars and other specialists."[28] This surprisingly soft-edged account of the conditions of the early Free State suggests, perhaps, the steely presence of irony underneath. Reading Clarke's poetry from this time using the terms with which he supplies us might lead to our overlooking its full implications. A close reading of Clarke's language and the imagery of this volume suggests that his framing of his writing as a carefree turn away from wider developments in "the new State" is not entirely candid.

Clarke's difficulties with the dominant church of the new state, deep though they ran, were just one aspect of his relationship with it. He credited his schooling with his preoccupation with the early Irish church, and, indeed, school magazines from his years at Belvedere College show how this institution saw itself as the heir and propagator of the cultural glories of the pre-Reformation Celtic church.[29] While Clarke could never reconcile himself with the form that the church took in his own time, considering it to be overbearing and grandiose, the monks, scriptoria, and churches that feature in his poetry and fiction from the mid-1920s onward indicate a lingering fascination with the early centuries of Irish Christian culture.[30]

Clarke's preoccupation with Ireland during this golden age of the Catholic Church might initially give the erroneous impression that the volume is in accord with the ethos of the country's new legislators who, at least rhetorically, looked to early Christian Ireland for inspiration.[31] Indeed, in the eponymous opening poem of *Pilgrimage*, Clarke appears to pay tribute to the Celtic church, painting a ravishing picture of a world as highly colored and visually fascinating as the initial letters in illuminated medieval gospels, or the painted carvings on the round arches of Ireland's Romanesque churches, or the sinuous, dazzling figures in Harry Clarke's stained-glass windows:

> Brighter than green or blue enamels
> Burned in white bronze—embodied
> The wings and fiery animals
> Which veil the chair of God.[32]

A blazing excitement at the rediscovery of the cultural glories of the Celtic Romanesque era is audible here. However, there are energies that coil around these lines that suggest that, alongside these forces, certain untrammeled, pagan, ideas are also at work. *Pilgrimage*, like Clarke's publications in the 1930s, reflects a complicated relationship with the dominant church of the new state. Though Clarke's imagery might appear to endorse the official Ireland of his time, it often subverts the received implications of this imagery. At a time when images of early Catholic Ireland were being co-opted into a discourse of obedience and conformity, Clarke presents this historic period as one in which ideas of submission and rebellion, the Christian and the pagan, twisted around and interlaced with each other in mutually reinforcing tension.

The ambiguous final lines of the poem "Pilgrimage," which begins so hopefully with the arrival of a ship on a glittering coastline, do not give the impression that their author has lost himself in the glories of the past. Rather, desolation and religiosity come to the fore, as the ship sets its course past "a barren isle / Where Paradise is praised," and the ship's crew hear hermits pray "Until our hollow ship was kneeling."[33] The description of this place, where the prayers of Culdees—a form of early Christian hermit—are so potent that they seem to cause ships themselves to kneel, carries readers' thoughts to the Ireland of Clarke's own time. The poverty of the barren island that expects a future paradise is thrown into relief by the gorgeous opulence of the church that is depicted in the poem's central stanzas. Clarke's poetry from the 1920s and 1930s suggests, in spite of his own statements on the matter, that the Ireland of the past was not a place he approached in a state of relieved carelessness. Rather, his poems are vibrant with a knowledge of where power in the new Ireland lay, of the vast influence of the Catholic Church on the society and laws of the new state, and with an unsettled consciousness of the necessity of submission before this power.

Clarke's combination of fear and fascination in relation to the church does much to set the tone of his poetry in the first decades of Irish independence. "The Confession of Queen Gormlai" (*Pilgrimage*,

1929) is not about a figure from the twilight world of prehistoric pagan Ireland, but about a historic personage born in the ninth century. A passage from this poem shows the continued presence in Clarke's work of the verbal inventiveness, sonic intricacy, and vivid evocation of landscape and weather that all characterized his earlier work that centered on the pagan past. However, it also shows a potentially subversive responsiveness to new conditions in Ireland.

Issues of marriage and divorce were both of personal significance to Clarke and matters of national contention at the time. Clarke's ten-day marriage to Lia Cummins in 1920 was emotionally (and, he believed, professionally) disastrous.[34] Later in the same decade, divorce law would come to occupy a highly symbolic position as the Free State asserted its legal distinctness from the earlier dispensation. Although an assertion of the indissolubility of marriage was not written into the 1922 Free State constitution, some of its drafters agitated for the inclusion of such a provision. Instead, the Oireachtas, as the legal successor to the Parliament of the United Kingdom, became the authority to which petitions of divorce were submitted. By 1924 three parliamentary private bills for divorce awaited its consideration. The next year the Free State government, while not officially making divorce illegal, did so in practice by declaring that such bills would not be considered in the future.[35] In mid-1925, the tenor of debates on divorce was set by interventions from bishops and the *Catholic Bulletin*.[36] Reflecting the increasingly confessional nature of the new state, divorce was finally declared unconstitutional in the Constitution of Ireland in 1937.

The complicated marital history of Queen Gormlai (she declares to her confessor in the poem "I have lain in three beds / and many have blamed me") ran counter to ideals of life in the newly revivified Christian state that many of its legislators wished to bring into being.[37] As part of her "confession," Gormlai tells a monk how one of her three marriages ended:

Our marriage was annulled,
The Mass bell rung by force,

The flesh that was made one,
Divided and divorced.[38]

Whereas Yeats had been at pains to declare the right to divorce one of the historic inheritances of Ireland's Protestant minority, Clarke pictures it as being a part of life in ancient Ireland.[39] In doing so, he shows divorce not to be contrary to old Irish tradition, but a part of it. Under Brehon law, which was in operation in parts of Ireland until the sixteenth century, a woman could divorce her husband for a number of reasons.[40] Clarke's poem, like other poems in the collection, suggests that he did not just see the "Celtic Romanesque" period as a mystical, dreamy otherworld in which he could "delay" while the Free State ineluctably fulfilled its promise. Rather, it was alive and signaling; it held out the possibility of being an alternative source of values than the Roman Catholic ideas that were driving the legislative program of the Irish government in the 1920s.

As well as representing a reflection on legislation banning divorce, *Pilgrimage* is in some ways a response to censorship. Though the act that brought in the censorship regime that would govern what was legally available to read for decades to come became law in 1929, it was preceded by several years of legal maneuvers that were designed to bring it into being. In 1926, Kevin O'Higgins formed the Committee of Enquiry on Evil Literature, whose task was to investigate and report on whether it was necessary "to extend the existing powers of the State to prohibit the sale and circulation of printed matter."[41] This was followed by the innocuous-sounding Industrial and Commercial Property (Protection) Act of 1927, which linked the protection of commercial interests with that of morals. It had, deep within it, a passage that disquieted W. B. Yeats, acting in his role as senator.[42] This passage, though couched in obscure language, compelled writers who were resident in Ireland to publish their work in Ireland, either solely or simultaneously with foreign publication. The practical effect, as Yeats realized, would be to make any productions anywhere in the world by writers resident in Ireland subject to whatever censorship regime was then in effect in the Free State. Yeats argued against this provision vigorously in the Senate: his four speeches on this matter, perhaps misleadingly, appear under the heading "Copyright Protection" rather than "Censorship" in his *Senate Speeches*.[43] Though the proposal was eventually dropped, its existence is evidence that, by 1929, the year *Pilgrimage* was published, the noose had been tightening around free expression in Ireland for several years.

When Clarke and Yeats are thought of together, it is most often because the younger poet is seen as plowing the same nationalist and Celticist furrows that the older poet did in his early work. However, there is another significant way in which the two are linked. The kind of deliberate affront that some of Yeats's late work—"Leda and the Swan" and the "Crazy Jane" poems among them—offered to state-sponsored notions of decency looks similar to the kind of baiting of the Irish state in which Clarke was engaged in poems like "The Young Woman of Beare" and "The Confession of Queen Gormlai." In the case of both writers, this was not mere dissent for its own sake. Rather, challenging the prevalent legal climate seemed a necessary act if Ireland was not to be infantilized. The current common-law test for what was legally available for circulation was that it must not contain anywhere in it passages that could not be read by the smallest child of reading age.[44] Ireland's writers were quick to point out the stultifying effects of this policy. Seán O'Faoláin warned in a 1936 article that, inter alia, condemned the banning of one of Clarke's novels, the effect of the censorship laws would be to "bring into disrepute, and to limit, not the growth of the author, but the growth of the nation."[45]

In 1932 Yeats made Clarke a founding member of the Irish Academy of Letters, a body that he formed as a pressure group against censorship. Yeats observed with grim satisfaction in a later article that opposition to censorship had brought about what had seemed a vain hope: the uniting of all the intellectuals and artists of Ireland.[46] Edna Longley has noted the long-lasting effects of these developments, observing that "solidarity against the new state's censorship made most Irish writers see themselves as a kind of alternative regime or clerisy: a self-perception that persists."[47] Along with Frank

O'Connor and Seán O'Faoláin, Austin Clarke was one of the notable early members of the Free State's dissenting clerisy. Decades later, he was still agitating against censorship, as in his 1953 article for the *New Statesman and Nation*, "Banned Books": "The present state of Irish letters may be summarised in a single sentence: the majority of modern Irish writers are on the banned list and certain works of theirs cannot be read in Ireland except in the Six Counties."[48]

Clarke's poetry of the late 1920s and 1930s is an early example of spreading disenchantment with the Irish Free State. Mary Colum framed this phenomenon memorably, writing that, by this time, the revived gods that had perched on the "historic hills, enchanted mounds and ancient ruins" earlier in the century had "fluttered their wings and fled."[49] Seán O'Faoláin wrote of the gradual feeling of "a tide receding" that he sensed as he attended the successive dinners of the Irish Academy of Letters in the 1930s.[50] Cultural historian Terence Brown observed of the 1930s that "once more Dublin was a place to leave."[51] There are ways in which Clarke's 1936 *Collected Poems* (a premature title for a poet who would publish for another four decades) appears to be not so much a product of its own time as a remnant of the recently departed heroic era in Irish cultural history. This is not just because it contains work published as early as 1917: with its dedication to AE, its introduction by Padraic Colum, and its long opening poem set in the Connacht of Queen Maeve, it is a book in which the last golden traces of the Celtic Twilight linger.

However, the new poems that Clarke published as part of his *Collected Poems* also face the discontents of their own time, written as they are in a newly mordant register that sinks its teeth into the political life of Free State Ireland. The disillusioned 1930s are strongly in evidence when Clarke considers legal developments in a group of short poems titled "Six Sentences." Hitherto, Clarke's critiques of the state had been notable for their long historical reaches; this one is a short-range attack, as he takes aim at the newly respectable conservative ex-revolutionaries who made up the Irish political class. Recalling the violent early days of the Free State, he raises the ghost of the republican Rory O'Connor, whose execution during the Civil War was the subject of a legal controversy:

> They are the spit of virtue now,
> Prating of law and honour,
> But we remember how they shot
> Rory O'Connor.[52]

The pun in "sentences" is apparent: it is not just a syntactic unit; it reflects the sentence of death passed on the man whose name makes up the poem's final line. This short poem also passes a judgment of its own, in this case on the death warrant on the republican leader that was signed by Kevin O'Higgins, the Free State minister for justice and external affairs, in late 1922. William Cosgrave's justification for this action in the Dáil was that it would show those involved in republican attacks "that terror will be struck into them." Those who were troubled by the revanchist nature of Cosgrave's words were further unsettled by the fact that the death sentence that was passed on O'Connor was of dubious legality. Neither O'Connor nor the other men executed by the Free State on the same day had been tried or convicted, and as prisoners they could not have been involved in the assassination for which they were executed in reprisal. Furthermore, their execution violated the ex post facto principle, which forbids a punishment for a crime that is harsher than the sentence that was prescribed by law at the time that crime was committed.[53] In light of contemporary controversies, the poem's line about how the state's current ministers prate "of law and honour" rings with piercing irony. In passing his own crisp, laconic, "sentence" on the sentence of death that was passed on the prisoners, Clarke counters the legal authority of the Free State with an alternative authority of his own.

Before his turn to the early centuries of Irish Christianity in his volume *Pilgrimage*, Clarke, like his fellow revivalists W. B. Yeats,

Augusta Gregory, and F. R. Higgins, explored the landscape of an earlier time: the mythical territory of the pre-Christian pagan centuries. The publication of Clarke's early martial epic narratives set in this period, *The Vengeance of Fionn* (1917) and *The Sword of the West* (1921), coincide with the revolutionary years in Ireland.[54] His next book, *The Cattledrive in Connaught, and Other Poems* (1925), though it was published early in the history of the Free State that arose from these tumultuous times, evinces a detectably dissident position in relation to the new polity. It is the first, though far from the last, of his volumes in which poems set in the distant Irish past comment on and critique the present-day jurisdiction.

The protagonist of one poem from *The Cattledrive*, "The Pedlar," makes a survey of a troubled and restless Ireland during a journey that takes in "twenty-six counties" of the island. The pedlar's exact itinerary is unclear; the significance of the number of counties he visits is not. Though Clarke's pedlar whips through an archaic landscape on a donkey and cart, the lineaments of the terrain he moves through clearly follow those of the recently founded Free State. After disrupting the round of daily life in the towns of the twenty-six counties that he passes through, the mysterious pedlar reports strange sights and occurrences that bode ill for the future of this fretful jurisdiction:

> Torchlight, in Tara,
> Had armed the rampart at night
> And I heard the harp and crowds dancing
> For a queen that had been married,
> But the cold rain blew them away
> [. . . . .]
> Where no farmer has strayed from the market
> The berries, grown black in the moonlight,
> Hurry us onward.[55]

In rhythms as freewheeling and troubled as the pedlar's journey, Clarke presents an allegory for the Ireland of his time. In light of the poem's earlier reference to "twenty-six counties," it does not take a great leap of imagination to associate the armed rampart of Tara where people are "blown away" with the heavily fortified Government Buildings in Dublin during the Civil War of 1922–23. The rumor-swept state of the country in this poem suggests that its future is an ill-starred one, and the pattern of assonances that twist and interlace through this stanza serves only to intensify its doom-laden atmosphere.[56] "Tara" chimes with, among other words, "armed," "rampart," and, the new state's seal, "harp." These sounds echo in the last word of the poem's final ominous phrase, "Hurry us onward." In writing in this way, Clarke continues in the complex, assonantal style that his former tutor, Thomas MacDonagh, identified as the "Irish mode" in his *Literature in Ireland* (1916).[57] However, not only the aesthetics but the irredentist republican politics of the piece owe something to MacDonagh's example. The poem, for all its imagery of the Irish past, acknowledges the compromises and tensions of immediate post-treaty conditions and responds to them with baleful portents.

Several scholars have traced a causal link between the violence of its foundation and the subsequent drive to religious conformity that characterized the early phases of the Irish state's evolution. They have suggested that the bitterness and uncertainty of civil war generated the reactionary conservatism that came to dominate it in the following decades.[58] If *The Cattledrive* responds to the armed and suspicious conditions that followed the foundation of the Free State, then Clarke's next volume, *Pilgrimage*, seems more a reaction to the official Catholic ethos of this new phase in Ireland's history.

Clarke came through the revolutionary period with only one close brush with the Black and Tans; he was more scarred by the developments that preceded and followed this time.[59] His volumes of poetry and autobiography that address the 1920s and 1930s show clearly that he felt the reverberations of the state's Catholic ethos sharply on his own still-painful psychic wounds. In his memoirs he documents the role of his strongly religious upbringing in exacerbating a sexual guilt that at times overwhelmed him, and he held a lifelong belief that he was forced to leave his job as a lecturer at University College Dublin because his marriage in a civil ceremony and its subsequent breakdown offended the institution's unwritten, but powerful, Catholic code of ethics.[60] During the 1930s, two of his novels were banned under Ireland's draconian censorship regime, instilling in Clarke a sense of persecution that was only heightened by the fact that the chair of the committee that recommended their prohibition, Professor Robert Donovan, had been his superior during his brief tenure as a lecturer.[61]

Night and Morning (1938) frequently, though to a lesser extent than *Pilgrimage*, goes back to Ireland's historic periods to critique the present day. The tone of Clarke's work has changed by this point, being at once more occluded and more lurid, more intellectual and more febrile, than hitherto. The poem "Martha Blake," like much of the volume, grapples with the claims of revealed religion in an individual life, presenting the religious observances of a devout woman. It contains one of the volume's many references to that ambiguous emotion "pride."[62] Although this word can refer to an inwardly directed sense of fulfillment, in Catholic doctrine it is chief among the deadly sins. The infernal place of pride in the poem's protagonist's cosmology is clear:

> The flame in heart is never grieved
> That pride and intellect
> Were cast below, when God revealed
> A heaven for this earth[.][63]

The kind of religious belief that might enable one to reject "pride and intellect," or that might permit one to obey and not ask questions, is one of *Night and Morning*'s chief preoccupations.[64] However, the lowering of the lamp of intellect is contrasted with its opposite, the burning torch of thought, in the same volume. As is so often the case in Clarke's work, what illumination there is comes from another era.

In "The Straying Student," a poem set in the years of the Penal Laws, an unnamed, anarchic, female figure appears in a church; from her the poem's protagonist "learn[s] the prouder counsel of her throat," his "mind [. . .] growing bold as light in Greece."[65] Pride and outward-bound intellectual striving are, here, raised up rather than "cast below." The volume's preoccupation with these qualities has been linked by Vivien Mercier to Stephen Dedalus's struggles for self-definition.[66] While there are certainly analogies between Clarke's and Joyce's attempts to dramatize the location of an intellectual base beyond the one provided by revealed religion, there are perhaps even closer links between Clarke's preoccupations and the presentation of pride and intellect in the 1920s and 1930s work of W. B. Yeats.

Clarke's resistant stance might be traced in part to that of Yeats in the Senate in the previous decade. In Yeats's most notorious contribution to Senate business, ideas of pride and intellect were central. He associated them with his own Anglo-Irish lineage: "I am proud to consider myself a typical man of that minority," he told his fellow senators, before informing them that this group had "created the best of [Ireland's] political intelligence."[67] By the time these emotions took the form of a lyric poem, "The Three Monuments" (*The Tower*, 1928), Yeats identified pride and intellect as having come under attack from the "popular statesmen" who insisted that "intellect would make us proud / And pride bring in impurity[.]"[68] In this poem, as in Yeats's Senate speech, ideas of pride and intellect are central to a vision of how Ireland might develop. Though the connections between Yeats and Clarke most often center on revival themes, read alongside Yeats's poem, Clarke's "Martha Blake" can be read as, in part, an after-echo of Yeats's protests in the Senate in the 1920s.

The poem "Penal Law," like so many of Clarke's works, uses an earlier time to point up the illiberal conditions of the present-day Free State. It is named after the coercive measures against Catholicism that were largely introduced in the seventeenth century. However, the "Penal Law" he writes of turns a title that provokes thoughts of anti-Catholic oppression in a former era of Ireland's history to one that draws attention to the oppression practiced by the formerly persecuted institution in contemporary Ireland:

> Burn Ovid with the rest. Lovers will find
> A hedge-school for themselves and learn by heart
> All that the clergy banish from the mind,
> When hands are joined and head bows in the dark.[69]

This poem's collapsing of different eras, strikingly, conflates the earlier repression of the Catholic Church with contemporary oppression *by* the Catholic Church. As in "Six Sentences," Clarke is invoking, though with a more indecent pun, a more enduring law than that wielded by the Free State government. "Burn Ovid with the rest" has a particular resonance in the 1930s, when it was published. Historian Senia Paseta notes how, in the 1930s, various church figures backed campaigns against "imported literature."[70] Though this was aimed at English newspapers (which were indeed burned in sporadic incidents in the 1920s), this desire to eradicate pagan printed matter from abroad that addressed sex would, taken to its logical conclusion, extirpate great classical literature as well. In the poem's cavalier opening instruction that Ovid might be burned, there is a proud disdain for what this illiberal use of the law might achieve.

"The Jewels," which ends *Night and Morning*, like so much before it in the volume, reads as a condemnation of clerical obscurantism:

> The sanctuary lamp is lowered
> In witness of our ignorance;
> Greed of religion makes us old
> Before our time. [. . .][71]

In spite of the ways in which the laws of the Ireland in which Clarke published it are criticized in *Night and Morning*, it acknowledges the strength and binding force of religious belief. This has led some critics to characterize it as too implicated in the foundational myths of the state to constitute an effective critique of it.[72] However, Clarke's polysemous language leaves open other possible interpretations. If "The Jewels" and, by extension, *Night and Morning* acquiesce to the ideology of the state, then it is acquiescence of such an ambiguous kind as to be indistinguishable from dissent.

In the new phase of his career inaugurated by *Ancient Lights* (1955), Clarke's first volume of poetry in seventeen years, he engages with Irish law more openly than ever before. He criticizes the state for its overcautious legislation on health care ("Mother and Child," *Ancient Lights*) and mocks its censorship laws ("Early Unfinished Sketch," *The Horse-Eaters*, 1960).[73] He also, again, excoriates the Irish state for the execution of its republican enemies. The opening poem of *Ancient Lights*, "Celebrations," takes a jaundiced look at the public festivities that accompanied the 1932 Eucharistic Congress decades earlier, calling the statue of Justice that stands over the entrance to Dublin Castle "The blindfold woman in a rage" who "Condemns her own for treason."[74] Even in the 1950s, the legal controversies of earlier decades continued to haunt Clarke. One of the legislative acts of the 1920s relates to the treason that Clarke imagines the enraged statue of Justice wielding was the Treasonable Offences Act of 1925. This defined treason as, among other things, "levying war against Saorstát Éireann." This was one of a series of legislative attempts by the Free State government to secure their power in the aftermath of the Civil War by ensuring that the harshest punishments could be used against any subsequent republican militants.[75] In a poem that examines the combined operations of the church and the state in the early years of the latter's existence, the former is shown to be complicit with draconian authority.

Though the title of *Ancient Lights* might refer to the illumination provided by former times, it has a modern legal meaning as well. The right to "ancient lights" allows the owners of buildings to forbid the construction of other buildings that would deprive them of access to light that they have previously enjoyed. These words are a means of legal defense and are written under windows in warning to others. During the 1920s and 1930s, Clarke saw the grandiosity of the church and the authoritarian leanings of the new state looming darkly on the landscape. His use of Celtic Romanesque and early modern elements in his poetry from the 1920s and 1930s might, long before he used those words, be seen as his giving notice of his own ancient lights, condemning the obscurantism of the church that allied itself to the Irish state, and presenting alternative jurisdictions as models for the future.

3

Sounding Justice

Rhoda Coghill

Poet, composer, and musician Rhoda Coghill's first full poetry collection, *The Bright Hillside*, was published in 1948. In it are thirty-two poems that powerfully evince, among other qualities, a sense of the symphonic possibilities of landscape and sky, water and weather.[1] Though above all her poems are illuminated by a sense of the beguiling variousness and multiplicity of life on earth, they also communicate, at times, strong lunar and subterranean energies. Coghill's Christian beliefs are an element of both the light and the dark of her poems—she was a practicing member of Ireland's Quaker minority, and her work communicates a profound interest in both spiritual love and, as Anne Fogarty has discussed, eschatological bleakness.[2] To Coghill, every sound on earth, from the quietest to the loudest—from the wing beat of a moth to the crash of the surf against sea cliffs—is part of the score of grand symphony that is animated by an invisible conductor:

> And every little movement taps a drum.
>   A moth's pale, inaudible wing
> Teases the heavy-drowsing senses till
>   It seems a fretful, noisy thing.
>
> Loud as a sudden sportsman's bullet-shot
>   A round-nosed rabbit bolts for home,
> Above the steady, shouting cliffs that toss
>   Away white sheaves of whistling foam[.][3]

The world that Coghill depicts in her poems, in which light can be heard, birds swim like fish through the rainy air, and bushes branch like coral, is a markedly impressionistic and synesthetic one. However, Coghill's painterly music is not poetry of fey charm or local color: shadows of uncertain origin frequently pass across her changeful, wakeful, landscapes. No exact equivalence can be drawn between the events through which a poet lives and their artistic achievements: as John Redmond has argued at book length, yoking poems and public contexts together too readily is a hazardous activity.[4] It is nevertheless intriguing to read Coghill's poetry in light of the wider forces—both official laws and law-like strictures emanating from other sources—that were at work in the Ireland of her times. Read in the context of these laws, Coghill's preoccupations with themes of criminality, subterfuge, violence, and female guilt show the marks that were made on poetry by the restraints that were placed on Irish women.[5]

"In Wicklow," the inaugural poem of *The Bright Hillside*, communicates a lively, energized natural world through its imagery and in its insistent and compelling internal rhymes. In its depiction of mourning trees and streaming wind, there is a sense of stored energy being summoned, as if the power of a silent grief is suddenly waking and finding expression.

> The high trees grieve, like the sea's water.
> The sad sky crouches on Carraig and Slaughter;
> And a crude donkey, from the windy quarter
> Calls up the rain[.][6]

In this ostensibly bucolic work, there is a faint sense that human battles are not too far beneath the troubled surfaces. This is underlined by the fact that these landscapes and the weeds and flowers that cover them are poised for attack and defense. In this poem, the hilly terrain south of Dublin is a place

Where twilight-bannered, elfin nettle
And the fool's-parsley's starry clusters battle
For kingship of the lane.

The quiet whisperings of foliage are represented by the dissonant rattle of the half-rhymes "nettle" and "battle," as the landscape itself speaks of struggle, force, and fear. Alongside a love of nature, in this poem are elements of grief and dispossession, a brooding sense of conflict, and a sense of calamitous change. As a poem, it shows in compressed form the preoccupations and techniques that are in evidence in the rest of the volume.

The same uneasy qualities that seethe in the language of "In Wicklow" are a part of all four country-landscape poems that open the collection *The Bright Hillside.* The other three poems are titled "Summer in Sheephaven," "Burren, Co. Clare," and "Afternoon by the Lake at Clogherrevagh." These four poems together constitute a sort of tour of the island, respectively depicting landscapes in the provinces of Leinster, Ulster, Munster, and Connacht. This circling of the territory creates a structural statement that Ireland is the landscape of her imagination, while also carrying an echo of the warring ancient kingdoms that foreshadowed the territorial divisions that continue to play such a marked role in the island's history.

Coghill's attunement to conflict is also audible in the Ulster landscape of "Summer in Sheephaven," where "stealthy running waves are threading fringes / In secrecy along the strand," while "Muckish keeps a moody peace."[7] Another poem, set by the Liffey in Coghill's native city of Dublin, sees an "Avenue of serene, Ascendancy swans" alongside the "Trail of the single gunman cormorant."[8] By the time this poem was published in a book in 1948, decades had rolled under the bridge since the swans of the former Ascendancy were menaced by gunmen with any regularity, as they had been in the revolutionary period 1919–23. There is a suggestion in these, and other, lines that the traumatized and traumatizing years of revolution still colored how Coghill saw Ireland years later. It is as if the peace that settled on the landscape in subsequent decades created a space in which the violence that had once occurred there could be perpetually imaginatively re-created and reenacted by the changing light, weather, and seasons.

These poems transmit a lively if occluded political consciousness in relation to not only Ireland's violent past but also the status of women. In the Sligo poem "Afternoon by the Lake at Clogherrevagh," something of these energies vibrates through the lines:

> A night's snowfall, a purge of green, has covered
> the high-set tomb of Maeve. Winter returns,
> a puppet government in April's state.

Maeve was a legendary warrior queen of Connacht, and many of the stories around her traditionally stress her strength and indomitability. For this symbol of female power to have her tomb, and the surrounding green, covered up by a "purge" suggests that more than a cairn has been covered over by a swirl of mountaintop April snow.

Born in 1903, Coghill's transition into adulthood was coterminous with the Irish public sphere becoming a less congenial place for women. A Dublin poet, she worked for the state broadcaster as an accompanist for many years. It was not even a given that she could perform music on the radio: Richard Pine, in a chapter on Coghill, records how the Irish government sought to dissuade her employer, the national broadcaster Radio Éireann, from employing women. She was exempt from the station's practice of paying women at a standard rate that was 80 percent of that of their male colleagues.[9]

The year 1922 was a significant one for Coghill, in which she gained her bachelor's degree in music from Trinity College Dublin; it also saw the establishment of the Irish Free State.[10] She saw this violence and chaos in Dublin: in an interview, she describes seeing the ashes from the burning Four Courts after a music exam, as fragments of a thousand years of historical records drifted on the winds over Dublin.[11] According to Heather Ingman, the year that saw this snowfall of ashy records also marked an adverse turning point for Ireland's women. Once the dust had settled, the landscape that was formed following these eruptive years had a new and difficult shape for women artists:

> Irish women after 1922 experienced a gradual erosion of their political rights. In 1925 the government sought to bring in restrictions on women's employment in the civil service, thus excluding women from having a voice in shaping policy on economics, health and welfare. [. . .] The Juries Act of 1927 [. . .] exempted women from jury service and thus ensured only one gender's voice was heard in the legal process. At stake was women's right to participate in the public life of their country. Were women to be allowed to be full citizens or were they to be confined to the roles of wives and mothers which was what the State seemed to be offering?[12]

It is hard to know exactly what effect these new laws had on Coghill's work and reception. What is clear is that Coghill's two volumes of original lyric poetry, published eight years apart, represent a far more abbreviated and neglected body of work than their quality would indicate is just.[13]

Like the sublimated violence that troubles her landscapes, a low-key dissidence is at time audible in her work. As Kathy D'Arcy has observed, Coghill, "treats astutely and [. . .] subversively of women's experiences."[14] In Coghill's poem "The Robin" (*The Bright Hillside*, 1948), the bird's song gives a "light counterpoint" that challenges louder and more powerful voices. At this time, the question of whose voice would be heard, and in which contexts, was one of lively concern to women writing in Ireland.[15] Coghill's "The Robin" is an example of how her imagery from nature has varied significances, some of them with radical possibilities.

In this fairy tale–like poem, a mythologized robin perches at the window of a country church as a Mass is sung inside. Perhaps it is more folk than fairy tale: it has all the appealing pastness and knotty intricacy of the medieval fable in which it has its origins: in legend, the robin gained its red breast as a mark of honor after pulling a thorn from the suffering Christ. However, this bird is significantly positioned "Outside the church." In spite of this suggestion of exclusion, it is free of the sense of guilt that oppresses the human congregation. From its elevated position, it sings out as joyously as Hardy's thrush or Keats's nightingale:

Outside the church
What did you hear? A rusty robin chinked
His tiny fiddler's change, and came to perch
In a red-fruited rowan-tree that tried
To comb the open window with its leaves.

He cocked his head and pertly peered inside,
And shook his body with a song. His eyes,
Blacker than ivy-berries, never blinked.
No creeping guilt befouled his Paradise[.][16]

This poem could, on a first reading, be interpreted as a paean to the inherent holiness of nature, as represented by the sheltering rowan leaves at the church window and, of course, the vividly realized robin at the poem's center. It could also be read as an exemplar of the romantic trope of natural piety: in comparison to sinful humanity, the shining-eyed bird gives voice to its immaculate state in full-throated ease, as the earthbound humans sit inside the church, dutifully praying in order to expiate their mundane sins.

However, these lines have further possible meanings that emerge under pressure of rereading. The bold robin and red-berried rowan might, instead of icons of Christian holiness, be seen as exemplars of a certain pagan vitality that counters the kind of dark, life-denying religious strictures that hold the poem's congregants in thrall. (It is probably for this reason that it was rejected from inclusion in *The Capuchin Annual* in 1945.)[17] This impression increases as the poem continues. The robin, we are told, sings so loudly that it rivals even the solemn voice that intones the Mass. Rather than being melodic or soothing, it drowns out the words of the priest with a challenging, irruptive, acoustic:

> Through the grave, holy rite the happy bird
> Drove a light counterpoint. The celebrant's word,
> Subtle and fugitive as the altar fires,
> Was lost in bubbles, loops and freaks and gyres[.][18]

The fact that a bird linked in myth to Christ drives its song through a Catholic church service suggests something that runs counter to official Ireland in the 1940s, where the church had something close to hegemonic power in relation to social life. There looks to be a hint of the kind of casual anti-Catholicism that was common in midcentury Irish Protestant communities in the description of the priest's words as "subtle and fugitive," spoken from amid infernal "altar fires." These words raise the ghosts of historic Protestant fears and prejudices about the casuistry of the priesthood. However, there is much more than mere sectarian suspicion at work in these lines. Just as the institutions of law might promote ideas that run counter to justice, this poem suggests that the institutions of religion might be inculcating ideas that are opposed to holiness. The voice of the bird introduces a new outsider's note into a place where only one voice is heard.

The dissenting tone of this poem is heightened by the fact that the birdsong described here, with its "bubbles, loops and freaks and gyres," has a notably contemporary, even jazzy, sound. As Coghill was a pioneering composer of avant-garde music, the style of the bird's song is significant. Musicologist Laura Watson describes Coghill as one of the women "who led the vanguard of modern composition in Ireland during the first half of the twentieth century."[19]

In mid-twentieth-century Ireland, innovative art, and in particular music, was the subject of significant suspicion.

Jazz music was the center of a church-endorsed moral panic in Ireland in the decades leading up to the 1940s. It was represented by its opponents as antinational and as misdirecting the people of Ireland from their true Gaelic selves.[20] From the 1920s the Gaelic League, backed by the church, led campaigns against the national broadcaster playing jazz music. The renewed 1934 campaign was particularly vehement, and historian Johannah Duffy writes how "in the early 1940s, the Minister for Posts and Telegraphs [banned] 'jazz and crooning' from the airwaves, as if it was only the false allure of popular music which was preventing Irish people from appreciating their true heritage."[21] In a jurisdiction where genres of music were banned from the national broadcaster, the song of Coghill's robin issues a challenging clarion call. To write a poem about a creature whose music disrupts the sound of a church suggests the role of a musician and poet like Coghill herself in introducing a subtly dissident sound in a strongly clerically dominated Ireland.

The robin is not the only bird in *The Bright Hillside* who raises its song to the heavens. In another poem, "free birds are singing their own songs."[22] In yet another poem, from a "blurred, blinding loudspeaker sky / Comes pouring like sunlight the lark's noisiest music."[23] These effusions of joy are linked to audibility: she writes in the title poem, "The Bright Hillside," "With a gull's beak I cry, / And mount through strong resistance."[24] Coghill lived in a society where women were expected to keep their voices to themselves and where those who did not, like the bird she wrote of, faced "strong resistance." The joyfully singing and soaring birds that rise up to view in her poems represent a dream of a different kind of existence.

As the dissident robin suggests, outsider status is one of Coghill's preoccupations. As an unmarried woman who made her living from art, and who published poetry at a time when very few of her contemporaries were doing similarly, she placed herself on the outside. There are normative processes through which societies align their outsiders with criminals. In many societies racial minorities are the objects of significant suspicion, while sexual minorities are criminalized.

Criminality is a prominent theme in Coghill's first collection. In her poem "The Murderer Watches the Dead Detective's Funeral," a chillingly defiant killer asks "*Who are the police anyway*?" In another poem, "The Chestnut Tree," the central image is so strongly figured as both a woman and a convict that the reader might suspect that it stands in for that first female transgressor, Eve:

> What crime did she,
> The chestnut tree,
> Commit, that she must bear
> The stigma of disgrace,—must wear
> (When first her gummy buds unfold
> To show the leaves they can no longer hold)
> Green convict's arrows? All in Nature
> Obeys an iron legislature,
> And the proud chestnut, like her neighbour,
> Serves, every year, a year's hard labour;
> But she alone, of all
> The trees is branded criminal.[25]

Ideas of criminality are introduced into the poem by the similarity between a natural phenomenon and a symbol of incarceration. Chestnut leaves have rows of parallel veins that form the shapes of arrows; traditional British prison uniforms featured prominent broad arrow patterns. By linking these two things, the poem raises the unsettling idea that the onset of female maturity brings with it an imposed stamp of criminality.

The central conceit of the poem, like that of "The Robin," links a being from nature to human ideas of culpability. Whereas the robin offends by drowning out a celebrant, the tree shows its guilt by developing along the inevitable lines that nature has dictated. The idea of detecting inherited, inherent sin by the markings on a tree's leaves is so absurd, it leads to thoughts of why anything in creation should be judged or condemned for being what it is. Why should women, this poem subtly implies, via their progenitor Eve, be burdened with the guilt for sins that they have never committed?

The chestnut tree in Coghill's poem shows the leaves its buds "can no longer hold." There is an irony here that is so quiet it is easy to miss: Why would a tree want to hold onto its unblossomed state? The leafing of a tree is synonymous with the ineluctable changes of nature. However, to Coghill, this natural progression only reveals her "Green convicts' arrows." This is a poem that seems ironic and insinuating about the misdirected values of Coghill's society. What crime did she, the chestnut tree, indeed? The stage that succeeds childhood innocence can be its opposite "experience"; to Coghill, what succeeds this phase of innocence is guilt.

Pioneering scholar of Coghill's work Kathy D'Arcy notes that this poem is conscious of Irish state ideology with regard to women, in that the chestnut tree at the center of the poem follows the Irish state's prescribed life cycle of a woman, "flowering and giving fruit" until, at last, she is stripped of her foliage and twigs, a "hag" who "drinks the winter sun."[26] This prescribed life cycle that was proposed to Irish women was not one that Coghill, who never married, followed. However, the imaginative weight of these pervasive societal expectations can be glimpsed in the preoccupations of her poems. This is part of the uneasy biopolitics that are at times visible in *The Bright Hillside*. In one of her poems a kind of shadow of mortality falls on the landscape that she writes of, and it brings with it thoughts of "sterility":

> [. . .] So the afternoon moves onward,
>
> then dulls, and grows a universal shadow.
> The sun falls, the life-seed, frustrate, into
> A barren cloud-womb, to sterility.[27]

These words seem to envision the menstrual cycle through an image of the changing light of sunset. This low-key acknowledgment of the female body makes this work very unusual in Irish poetry of the 1940s.

This preoccupation is visible elsewhere in the collection: one of the poems, which is full of images of fruit and ripening, is titled "Lamenting a Sterile Muse."[28] Another poem, "Hail, Posterity," focuses on the future. This poem, whose speaker has "sowed no acorns," begins with an epitaph from Sappho in which the subject is promised only oblivion in the hereafter: "But thou shalt lie ever dead nor shall there be any remembrance of thee then or ever." It goes on to consider the idea of immortality through progeny, as the narrator reflects that she has not

> [. . .] forged a strong link in the chain
> that grounds the anchor of heredity
> in distant Genesis, have sowed no acorns
> to furnish future forests with proud wood;
> [. . . .]
> No one will seek my grave, or mark the date
> when I shall leave the world [. . .][29]

David Wheatley has noted a similar preoccupation with natality and sterility in the work of Coghill's contemporary Samuel Beckett. Wheatley roots Beckett's bleak preoccupations in the conditions of the Irish Free State (1922–37), the polity in which both he and Coghill lived some of their most formative years. In his articles, Wheatley reflects that the "sexual puritanism" of this state has much to answer for: "All this comic anti-natalism, I would like to suggest, is born of Free State Ireland and its shaping, or warping, effect."[30] Though Coghill's approach is mostly far from comic, something similar might be said for her poetry.

There were no Irish laws that stated that women had to marry and have children. However, insofar as these expectations could be encoded in the laws of a western European democracy in the 1930s, they were. Article 41.2 of the 1937 Constitution states, in clauses that were controversial even when they were drafted,[31] that

> 1. In particular, the State recognises that by her life within the home, woman gives to the State a support without which the common good cannot be achieved.
> 2. The State shall, therefore, endeavour to ensure that mothers shall not be obliged by economic necessity to engage in labour to the neglect of their duties in the home.

These words are in the foundational document of the state, the origin from which the other laws of the state in theory grow and against which they can be tested. As such, they sway the development and direction of subsequent laws and court judgments. The clauses of the Constitution that are quoted above are among the very few that mention women at all.[32] They carry an implicit devaluation of non-maternal and non-home-based roles: the gender stereotyping of this clause means that Coghill, by pursuing a life dedicated to music and writing, and not a husband and child rearing, was withholding from "the State a support without which the common good cannot be achieved." She was not committing a crime, but neither was she following the state's normative expectations as expressed in its fundamental legal document.

The linkage between guilt and a covering of leaves that is at the heart of "The Chestnut Tree" is part of its preoccupation with clothing and female roles. The leaves with their arrows that indicate criminality eventually fall away to reveal a new, ascetic role.

> [. . .] quite burnt out, she stands
> Nunlike, amazed, and raises stiff gloved hands;
> And then, when in her rusty frame

No queenly flame,
No ripened-apple flush of sunset lingers,
Comes Surgeon Frost to amputate the fingers.

At the moment when the tree is stripped of her leaves, the poem takes on a peculiar force and power. The preoccupation of this poem with clothing and coverings brings thoughts of other strictures on women in twentieth-century Ireland. These, like the prohibitions on jazz, were not statute law, but nevertheless had a law-like force. A campaign originated in the Mary Immaculate Teacher Training College in Limerick in the late 1920s that, according to Caitríona Beaumont, laid down precise rules on dress, including exact minimum lengths for dresses and sleeves.[33] These "laws," of course, were unenforceable in any court and had been ratified by no parliament. Nevertheless, these church-sponsored rules powerfully regulated what women could wear. Under these conditions, the leaves of a chestnut tree signaling its "crime" had a particular resonance. What joins this poem and "The Robin" is the theme of guilt. In "The Robin," the bird represents the joy that might be attained in freedom from imposed ideas of culpability. In "The Chestnut Tree," though, the ascription of guilt is explicitly linked to ideas of womanhood, punishment, and imprisonment.

Coghill's two original volumes of poetry are slender monuments to both conflict legacies and to the low point that the middle decades of the twentieth century marked for Irish feminism. For a poet to be prolific takes the active permission, support, and promotion of many people. In the world in which Coghill lived, in which serious poets, like judges, or most politicians, or most jurors, were men, this support was not available to her. Though Coghill did not enjoy anything like the same level of recognition of her male peers, either during her lifetime or after, her work was appreciated by some of her contemporaries. In her papers, preserved by her family, is a carefully kept clipping from a short review in a Belfast newspaper that grants that she "writes with distinction, in modern verse forms." There is also an exultant telegram of congratulation from novelist Kate O'Brien.[34]

Poet and critic Kathy D'Arcy titled a piece on Coghill "Why Uncomplicated Recovery Is Not Enough." One way in which the recovery of Coghill's work can be complicated is by attempting to view it alongside the laws and norms of the society in which she wrote it, acknowledging the barriers to publication that she faced. Rhoda Coghill's poetry suggests that her consciousness of the state in which she lived was ambivalent. With its expression of transgression, guilt, and criminality in relation to the nonhuman world, her poetry suggests a process of internalization that itself reflects the discouragement of women's voices in the mid-twentieth-century Irish public sphere.

4

The Civil Servant as Poet

Thomas Kinsella

From the late 1940s until the mid-1960s, Thomas Kinsella worked as a civil servant, and his poetry from these years often carries distorted reflections of the values and language of his workplace. Kinsella's poetry and other writings from this time, like the civil service documents on which he worked, powerfully evince the necessity of an international outlook and a break with tradition. The increasingly international nature of Kinsella's civil service work was one manifestation of a change in ideas that was stirring in the country at the time. In light of the last chapter, on Rhoda Coghill, it is worth pointing out that as a man he had opportunities to influence and to observe the high-level workings of the country in which he lived in a way that was generally unavailable to women. During this transformative period in Ireland's modern history, Kinsella was in its crucible.

Though *Butcher's Dozen: A Lesson for the Octave of Widgery* (1972), an indignant satire on the British judicial inquiry into Bloody Sunday, is his best-known engagement with law (one I go into further in the next chapter, on Seamus Heaney), Kinsella's earlier life brought him into close contact with the machinery of the state. From around 1960, he was private secretary to head of the Department of Finance T. K. Whitaker, a civil servant who has often been called "the architect of modern Ireland."[1] In an interview, he talked about how his work in the civil service changed as the 1950s and early 1960s brought an increased consciousness of the world beyond Ireland's shores.[2] The department where Kinsella worked from around

1950 was pursuing a program that involved internationalizing Ireland in many ways, including planning for Ireland's membership in a European free-trading bloc, promoting Ireland as a destination for foreign investment and expertise, and creating an export-based industrial economy.[3] These ideas, it was hoped, would rescue the country from what looked like the real possibility of terminal economic stagnation, unemployment, and depopulation.[4] There was a change in direction, and this worked its way not just into government policies but, arguably, into Kinsella's imagination.

Kinsella is part of a tradition of male poets in the Irish civil service that is older than the state itself. Prominent members include modernist and former Land Commission employee Thomas MacGreevy (b. 1893) and Customs and Excise official Dennis O'Driscoll (b. 1954). Between these two were neo-revivalist Customs and Excise official Padraic Fallon (b. 1905) and diplomats Denis Devlin (b. 1908) and Valentin Iremonger (b. 1918). Kinsella himself (b. 1928) joined the Land Commission in 1946, before moving to the Finance Department in the early 1950s. It is possible only to speculate on why so many poets have worked as civil servants, but it is perhaps related to the fact that, in the midcentury, with emigration high and secure jobs hard to come by, the civil service could take its pick of talented candidates.[5]

However, once employed, not all civil servant writers were treated equally: all the poets listed above published under their own names, while many prose writers (including Conor Cruise O'Brien, John Girvan, and, famously, the satirist known to the civil service as Brian Ó Nualláin) published under pseudonyms.[6] Just as poetry was less likely to fall afoul of the censorship regime than other kinds of writing, poets in the civil service were granted freedom to publish under their own names that distinguished them from other kinds of writers.[7] The indulgence shown to poets was perhaps born of respect for the art form and, perhaps, out of knowledge of its limited readership. Through Kinsella's poetry, as through Brian Ó Nualláin's pseudonymously published prose, readers are able to see the developing lineaments of midcentury Irish bureaucratic modernity.

The civil service in which Kinsella worked embodied some of the dominant ideas that lay behind the new state. As Justin Quinn has pointed out, in the decades that followed 1922, "the patriotic heroism of the Republic was transformed into bureaucratic zeal."[8] Michael Hartnett made the same point, but with a greater degree of asperity, noting that the foundation of the Free State encouraged "the noble art / of writing forms in triplicate" and, ultimately, ushered in a dream of an orderly, bureaucratic nirvana: "we entered the Irish paradise / Of files and paper-clips."[9] Poet Theo Dorgan made a similar point in passionate terms in his 2012 essay "Law, Poetry and the Republic":

> Our infant republic, at the handing over of power, could have chosen differently, could have looked beyond the inherited practice of civil administration, the inherited apparatus of law and its customs of governance; but of course we did no such thing. We took on, unquestioned, the burden of the common law as it had evolved in Britain, with all its precedents and preconceptions, never once asking if this was an appropriate tradition of our people, in our time. Never once asking if this was the proper frame for our future.[10]

Kinsella's poetry reflects how the "inherited practice of civil administration" that Dorgan writes of having been handed from the former British administration to its Irish successor was an ambiguous legacy for the new state.

It is not fanciful to connect the civil service's famed devotion to order with the preoccupation with order and method that runs through Kinsella's work. He acknowledged how working methods that he first learned from Whitaker in the civil service still shaped how he worked more than a half century later: decades after leaving his office job, he moved work from left to right across his desk in the approved civil service manner.[11] An in-tray to the left and an out-tray to the right is hardly an image that readily accords with any received ideas of poetic composition; it does, however, tie in with an ideal of order that Kinsella's poetry often seems to be striving toward.

This ideal, which was fostered in the civil service, is complicated in Ireland by its associations with Victorian colonial governance. Kinsella himself intuited this, as is evidenced in a note that preceded his volume *Nightwalker, and Other Poems* (1968). "Victoria," he wrote, "was the proximate parent of the New Ireland."[12] The words "the New Ireland," which the speaker of the eponymous poem "Nightwalker" sees in capitalized form on a discarded paper, underwent one of their periodic revivals in the early 1960s.[13] The phrase had a special resonance for Kinsella, as it was the title of a 1966 speech (produced in book form in the same year) by his former mentor, T. K. Whitaker. Whitaker's speech *The New Ireland: Its Progress, Problems and Aspirations* was delivered in Brussels in May 1966. This speech set out for a European audience the ideals of free trade, industrialization, and inward investment that were first propagated in his *Programme for Economic Expansion* (1958). However, the words "the New Ireland" suggested something broader than the economic reforms advocated by Whitaker: they pointed to a more generally international outlook, the beginnings of youth culture, and new forms of mass entertainment, such as the opening of the state television station in 1962. More broadly still, it indicates the loosening hold of the traditional narratives of nationalism and religion on Irish life.[14] In short, it meant the stirrings of a society moving away from the preoccupations of its own dominant ex-revolutionary generation. Kinsella's surprising ascription of the creation of "the New Ireland," at least in part, to the queen-empress, demands a very different narrative of the development of modern Ireland to any typical account.

A passage in Kinsella's "Nightwalker" in which a statue of the Virgin Mary is compared to one of Victoria seems linked to his mysterious note that "Victoria was the proximate parent of the New Ireland":

> The Blessed Virgin smiles from her pedestal
> Like young Victoria. Celibates, adolescents,

> We make our vows to God and Ireland thankful
> that by our studies here they may not lack
> Civil Servants in a state of grace.[15]

In these lines Kinsella hints at the centrality of Victorian ideals to the new state's civil service and, by extension, to the state itself. In these lines there is a hint that the expected religious devotion of the cohort of novice-like new civil servants is of a piece with, and perhaps a replacement for, the Victorian imperial sense of mission that would have been inculcated in an earlier, preindependence, generation of Ireland's administrators. Kinsella's suggestion that there is a lineal descent from Victoria to the present-day Irish state is an oddly countercultural one, particularly in light of the famine with which she is often associated in popular memory. However, the conflation of the Marian and the Victorian that Kinsella makes in "Nightwalker" is perhaps more explicable in light of the conservative social legislation of independent Ireland. This was a polity in which, as Margaret Scanlan has observed, "Victorian family values [were rewritten] as traditional Gaelic purity."[16]

The continuity of the professional civil service founded in Victorian times after the foundation of the Free State has been widely noted by historians and cultural critics, including by historian J. J. Lee, who wrote that "Irish public administration closely and consciously imitated the English model."[17] Joseph Brooker, similarly, describes the decades after independence as ones in which "a rhetoric of national renewal was accompanied by the persistence of pre-revolutionary processes and institutions."[18] Queen Victoria's appearance in the poem in association with the new recruits to the civil service suggests Kinsella's consciousness of the persistent shaping power of colonial ideas and procedures in the state.

A note Kinsella made as he prepared "Nightwalker" shows that he saw the survival of the same "Victorian" ideas that he apprehended in the civil service in himself: "Today the *positiveness* of the Victorian mind survives in Ireland (in me . . .) after the catastrophes of W.W. II & Hiroshima. And who will say this is not an enrichment, rather than an impoverishment? To be able to face the contemporary world, with the positiveness (marginal, yet there) of commitment to structure, meaning, purpose, giving, maybe, a means of dealing with a monster of formlessness & malignity."[19] In Kinsella's ponderings on the potentially restorative nature of his own Victorian qualities to a world ravaged by war and nihilism (a very specialized form of Irish export), the countercultural cast of his ideas becomes clear. The idea that Ireland's people were suited by their history to offer illumination to a benighted world was a common trope in the decades before Kinsella wrote the above note, but the people who deployed it tended to focus less on Victorian Ireland and more on the Christian golden age of the seventh to the ninth centuries.[20] The fact that the author of *Butcher's Dozen* (1972) and many translations from Irish focuses on the potential of his own "Victorian mind" suggests the complex cultural dynamics at work in Kinsella's imagination; it suggests he recognizes the role played by the systems and ideas that he critiques in his own formation. Kinsella's thoughts of Victoria may have been quickened by the removal of a large statue of her from his workplace, Government Buildings, in 1948, two years after he started working there, and the same year as the passage of the Republic of Ireland Act, by which twenty-six counties of Ireland left the Commonwealth to become a republic in the following year.[21] The tense and tortuous relationship with the past that is such a significant element of Kinsella's writing is something he apprehended in the Irish state for which he worked.

Kinsella's early poetry shows evidence that he was haunted by the symbols and images of the state from the outset of his career. The title poem of his collection *Another September* (1958) begins with its half-asleep speaker's imagination roving over the dawn-lit countryside beyond his bedroom and ends with a nightmare image of the entry of destructive forces in the guise of symbols of enlightened, constructive civic governance. In contrast to the *aisling* form, where a beleaguered woman who represents Ireland appears to the poet, the figures that arrive are the sculptured ideals that adorn the summits of public buildings. Indeed, in Dublin, an eighteenth-century allegorical figure of Lady Justice stands over the main entrance to Dublin Castle, a place occupied by both the pre- and post-1922 civil service.

> [. . .] It is as though
> The black breathing that billows her sleep, her name,
> Drugged under judgement, waned and—bearing daggers
> And balances—down the lampless darkness they came,
> Moving like women: Justice, Truth, such figures.[22]

In an interview, Kinsella has downplayed the significance of the menacing figures that appear in the poem, claiming that they are part of the kind of vision that arises just before sleep. However, a Jungian reading, in which dreams are interpreted as links to shared archetypes, might follow the resonances of this imagery.[23] The sword and scales that the figure of Justice traditionally holds are here reimagined as "daggers / And balances." In this way, a statue intended to be representative of fairness and equality before the law is reimagined very differently.[24] The "balance" held by Justice, seen in light of this poem, seems part of the kit of a trader; the dagger seems more suitable for foul play than equitable dealing. The fact that Justice, in particular, appears armed in this poem, and comes out of the darkness, makes her seem more like a mugger than an exemplar of equity. For all Kinsella's recognition of his own "Victorian mind," his representation of these figures is in keeping with a long-held conception of justice in Ireland, where what was seen from the colonial metropolis as enlightened and just is perceived closer to home as oppressive, where what counted in official eyes as legal ownership was equated more locally with rapacity and theft.[25] If Victorian positivism is acknowledged by Kinsella as one element of his inheritance from Ireland's colonial past, the nightmare vision with which this poem concludes suggests he is the inheritor of other, darker, legacies as well.

In the mid-1950s Kinsella painted a portrait, perhaps a self-portrait, of a smoking, unbuttoned, after-hours attic dweller in his poem "Baggot Street Deserta."[26] The poem's title, poised between downbeat Dublin irony and an acknowledgment of abandonment and desolation, gives a good indication of its subject matter. In among the associative chain of imagery that is summoned by the speaker, a curlew appears: a bird of the twilight in more ways than one. It has been identified by art historian Karen E. Brown as one of the elements of "the type of scene that appealed to poets of the Irish Revival."[27] However, amid these faintly Audenesque, enervated, lines, the appearance of this storied bird merely sparks a consciousness in the speaker of his own exhaustion:

A cigarette, the moon, a sigh
Of educated boredom, greet
A curlew's lingering threadbare cry
Of common loss[.][28]

The consciousness of depletion and the exhaustion that is such a feature of this poem were diagnosed as a chronic condition of post-"Emergency" (as the Second World War was officially designated) Ireland by Seán O'Faoláin, who wrote that Ireland emerged from the cataclysms of the mid-twentieth century "a little dulled, bewildered, deflated."[29] Another friendly commentator thought that the Irish state, around the time this poem was published, was at risk of "implosion upon a central vacuity."[30] This is one of Kinsella's first poems that is set amid the recognizable—albeit fantastical—geographic coordinates of the Republic, with sites that include a fairy bog, border marches, and Baggot Street itself. Coming at the end of a poem that contains so much of the country's geography and history, albeit in imagistic guise, the speaker's ejection of a quarter inch of cigarette from his window suggests a casualness, a kind of who cares, in the face of the "threadbare" imperatives to serve order and the state.

It was increasingly a consensus at Kinsella's employer that wholesale change was necessary after the exhaustion of the sustaining power of earlier ideas. This is at the core of the keystone document that was produced by the Department of Finance during Kinsella's time there, the *Programme for Economic Expansion*, published in 1958.[31] This was a wide-ranging attempt to imagine and plan a way out of the economic stagnation of the time, a vision of a future credit-based, market-driven, internationalized, export-based Irish economy.[32] Though an official document, this government publication has curious affinities with literary ones. It has what looks, for an official document, suspiciously like a story line, following an arc of crisis and redemption. The document strikes a grim note at its outset, warning of high levels of unemployment and the prospect of a falling population owing to large-scale emigration.[33] However, it promises hope through comparisons with other countries that had overcome similarly unpromising beginnings and calls on "the initiative and enterprise of private individuals and groups and on the determination of the nation as a whole to overcome natural handicaps."[34] To this end, it sets out a series of measures, including the reduction of direct taxation, the encouragement of exports, and the promotion of Ireland as a target for foreign investment. It was sold for a price appropriate for a novel, two shillings and sixpence. This was the blueprint for "the New Ireland," and the language of this report percolated into Kinsella's poetry, where it remains as a monument to a moment when ideas that were to become a form of Irish economic orthodoxy were new and surprising.

"A Country Walk" in *Downstream* (1962), Kinsella's last volume of lyric poetry written entirely during his time as a civil servant, recounts a dusk walk during which the speaker broods over both historical dispossessions and the present-day venality and shabbiness of the country around him. It begins with what looks like distaste for the country's turn from the heroic ideals of 1916 and toward the mercantile. (The speaker notes on his walk "MacDonagh and McBride, / Merchants; Connolly's Commercial Arms.") The poem ends, however, with what could be read as a more hopeful note. The speaker's walk is illuminated at its terminus by a distinct change in mood; as he stands on the bridge, considering a river whose waters recall the destructive flux of history, a new light comes over him:

And grimly the flood divided where it swept
An endless debris through the failing dusk
Under the trembling span beneath my feet.

Venit Hesperus.
In green and golden light.
Bringing sweet trade.[35]

John Goodby writes of these lines that "at its conclusion the debris of the poem achieves a brief coherence, flashing briefly and epiphanically from his scattered self-communing at the point where road and river meet."[36] The language and coloration of the epiphany that Goodby has identified are significant. The evening star arrives amid a "failing dusk," but it gives the poem an entirely new tone, one that mingles Virgilian language with the colors of the Republic. There is, however tentatively, even ironically, it is expressed, some idea of redemption from failure that is framed in national terms here, and it is connected with the prospect of "sweet trade."[37]

Kinsella's influential mid-1960s essay "The Irish Writer" also suggests, like the *Programme for Economic Expansion*, that a break from tradition is necessary. There is a sense in this essay, as there is in the *Programme*, that a radical rupture with what has come before is necessary for future development: "Is there then any virtue for literature, for poetry, in the simple continuity of a tradition? I believe there is not. A relatively steady tradition, like English or French, accumulates a distinctive quality and tends to impose this on each new member. [. . .] [F]or the present it seems that every writer has to make the imaginative grasp at identity for himself, and if he can find no means in his inheritance to suit him, he will have to start from scratch."[38] What Kinsella is arguing for here is the existence, in Ireland, of a paradoxical tradition of discontinuity. This piece reflects formal changes in Kinsella's own work and was written during the same years during which he increasingly embraced a poetics of process.[39] The chief qualities that Kinsella identifies as being the condition of the Irish writer bear marked similarities to those that are attributed to the Irish economy in the *Programme for Economic Expansion*. Both documents evince a consciousness of an inheritance that is insufficient to create a viable future and of the necessity of individualism and a revolutionary break with the past.

All this is context for ideas of progress and development in Kinsella's long late-1960s poem "Nightwalker." This poem pictures, amid the bureaucratic props of papers and umbrellas, the fissures and contradictions at the heart of the civil service's projects. Its business-attired protagonists

> [. . .] wait at the station, assembled for the day's toil,
> Fluttering our papers, palping the cool wind,
> Ready to serve our businesses and government
> As together we develop our community
> On clear principles, with no fixed ideas.[40]

The language of multinational capital was becoming a part of Irish life during this time, and this poem, with its references to a "transitional period," "clear principles," "community," "development," and "productive investment," shows that Kinsella did not think it was unworthy of integration into poetry.[41]

Kinsella was not the only poet to tune into these new frequencies. John Montague's *The Rough Field* (1972) identifies the early 1960s as a turning point and features fragmentary bulletins to illustrate this, in the filmic style of a montage of headlines: "In 1960/1 Irishmen attained many high positions abroad and the national economy, for the first time in history, showed an upward trend"; "a trade expansion of 5 per cent?"; and "From 1960 the Gross National Product . . ."[42] These consonances between the two poets' works are evidence of how the language of international trade and capital permeated the imaginations of Irish writers in the early years of the 1960s. However, "Nightwalker" does not present these developments as unambiguously welcome ones:

> Robed in spattered iron she stands
> At the harbour mouth, Productive Investment,
> And beckons the nations through our gold half-door:
> Lend me your wealth, your cunning and your drive,
> Your arrogant refuse. Let my people serve them
> Holy water in our new hotels,
> While native businessmen and managers
> Drift with them chatting over to the window
> To show them our growing city, give them a feeling
> Of what is possible; our labour pool,
> The tax concessions to foreign capital[.][43]

A change of point of view has occurred since *Downstream*, possibly one connected with Kinsella's departure from the civil service. The poem's depiction of "native" servility and the possibility of exploitation from abroad suggests that Ireland, in its attempt to escape economic stagnation, might be on the verge of willingly replicating the worst elements of the former colonial dispensation. The condemnatory attitude of this passage is apparent; however, it also contains a subtle acknowledgment of the central aim of the Irish government's plans, which was, in short, to slow the rate of emigration.[44] When Kinsella conjures a figure who appears like an Irish Statue of Liberty welcoming inward investment at "Our gold half-door," he is both summoning the half door of Irish vernacular cottage architecture and referencing a then recent book, George W. Potter's *To the Golden Door: The Story of the Irish in Ireland and America* (1960). In Potter's long view of Irish emigration to America, he contrasts centuries of legal discrimination suffered by the Irish people at home with the wealth and opportunity available to them in the United States.[45] Kinsella's co-option of the title of a book about emigration to the United States is an acknowledgment of why the *Programme for Economic Expansion* was written in the first place: to gain income from exports and inward investment that would enable Ireland to slow the exodus of its people. Despite the fact that the thrust of the lines quoted above is contemptuous, we cannot attribute a solely polemical motivation to Kinsella's poem. As with his references to Queen Victoria, there is a complex intersection of recognition and rejection at work in it. This poem, like so many others by Kinsella, brims with an ambiguous consciousness of the changes that shaped Ireland in the past and those that were reshaping it as he wrote.

Near the end of "Nightwalker," as the eponymous walker roams in a neighborhood beside Dublin Bay, he hears a sea mew speak words from Ireland's legendary first bardic poet, Amergin. The bird's imagined cry of "*I will become a wind on the sea again. / Or a wave of the sea, / Or a sea sound*" suggests the immemorial idea of the supernatural authority of the poet.[46] These lines, however, contain destabilizing hints of comic self-deprecation. This both-ways positioning is characteristic of Kinsella's stance in relation to Ireland and Irish history.

The word "productive" appears frequently in the *Programme*. The Department of Finance document explains that "productive" expenditure is "productive in the sense of yielding an adequate return to the community in competitive goods and services" and that, further, this kind of expenditure "must receive a greater priority than at present in the public capital programme."[47] Fairly early in the document, it becomes clear that what is meant by "productive" expenditure is the opposite of social expenditure, an opposition that subtly creates the implication that welfare spending is somehow "unproductive."[48]

Kinsella's role in the civil service put him at the center of the contested ideas that have formed Irish modernity, and his poetry bears the marks of the imperatives of this time and place as well as of his reactions against them. In particular, his poetry witnesses the arrival of language and ideas that went with the development of postwar multinational capitalism and evinces a knowledge of both the possibilities these ideas brought and their regressive, dehumanizing potential. Kinsella's poems from this time, with their imagist combination of lofty abstractions and up-close specifics, and with their often hierophantic tone of pronouncement and adjudication, are gravid with unseen forces.

5

Unwritten Laws

Seamus Heaney

"I abide by statutes utter and immutable— / Unwritten, original, god-given laws," claims Sophocles's heroine Antigone in Seamus Heaney's version of the play, *The Burial at Thebes* (2004).[1] With these words, Antigone asserts the jurisdiction of a very different supreme legal authority than the one that holds sway in the kingdom, Thebes, to whose laws she is subject. Her statement could have been spoken by Heaney himself. In a writing career of more than a half century, he consistently questioned the bounds of what was "just" and "legal," taking these concepts beyond the realms of courts and legislatures and applying the tests of a higher court, that of "the republic of conscience."

In this play, Antigone places herself outside the official laws of the kingdom, as promulgated by King Creon, by performing burial rites over her outlawed brother, Polyneices. On coming to power after a civil war, Creon declared that one nephew, Eteocles, was a loyal servant of the kingdom, while the other, Polyneices, was its enemy. In doing so, he had laid down the law as to right and wrong, hero and criminal. However, to Antigone, her duty is equally straightforward: there are higher laws to which she is obedient and to which the laws of the kingdom are a dispensable impediment. She must fulfill her obligation to a member of her family and carry out the customary ceremonies for one who had died. The tragic conflict that Antigone instigates, with its clash between official authority and familial loyalties, rings loud with echoes from Heaney's Northern Ireland.

The law as ordained by King Creon is akin to positive law: that is, his ban on honoring the dead Polyneices has been enacted by the recognized lawmaking power in the land and exists independently of its ethical status. Antigone's stance can be more readily identified with the natural law tradition, with which positive law has often been set in opposition.[2] Natural law has been conceived of as universal and independent of specific times or jurisdictions, having, instead of any temporal, earthly power, its basis in human reason.[3] In light of which network of ideas should the burial rites that Antigone has performed be seen?

In titling his version *The Burial at Thebes*, Heaney places issues of what is "legal" and "illegal" at center stage. The burial, after all, is the "illegal" act that sets in motion the bloodshed that follows; it is the act that is either criminal or commendable, depending on the angle from which it is viewed. The most passionate speeches of the play decry the separation of the enforcement of positive law from the demands of natural justice. At one point Antigone tells the tyrannical king, Creon, her reasons for disobeying his ban on burying her brother:

> I disobeyed because the law was not
> The law of Zeus nor the law ordained
> By Justice, Justice dwelling deep
> Among the gods of the dead.[4]

These lines can be read in light of a quote from Hegel that Heaney uses in a 2004 lecture, "Title Deeds: Translating a Classic." In it, Heaney quotes the opposition that the philosopher posited between subterranean "Instinctive Powers of Feeling, Love and Kinship" and "the daylight gods of free and self-conscious, social, and political life."[5] The deep-dwelling gods that Antigone cites as her ultimate judges are associated with the former, the laws of Creon with the latter.

In this speech, Antigone expresses a capacious idea of what law can be; she rejects the notion that the making and enforcement of laws is the preserve of the state, as legal sociologist Georges Gurvitch was to do centuries later. Rather, Antigone points to rights that are antecedent to positive law, the traditions of respect for the dead that have been inherited from previous generations and ratified by long custom. Alan Hunt, in a book chapter on Gurvitch, summarizes his ideas as follows: "The legitimacy and effectiveness of law is to be found in the active life of communities which create law by their activities."[6] Heaney's Antigone suggests that "laws" are not just codes laid down by authorities and policed by the threat of force; they are in fact much more shadowy and amorphous entities, ones that are formed and operate beyond the control of those that would insist on a monopoly on their definition and enforcement. In Antigone's insistence that "unwritten" laws take precedence over written ones is the potentially radical suggestion that the disobedience of official laws can, at times, be in the interests of justice.[7]

The title of Heaney's 2004 lecture "Title Deeds: Translating a Classic" neatly encapsulates both its legal and its literary themes.[8] In his lecture, Heaney describes the combination of artistic decisions and historical circumstances that led to his writing a version of *Antigone* for the Abbey Theatre in Dublin. Though the play was first performed in 2004, part of its root system grew in the Northern Irish prison hunger strikes of the early 1980s. In this lecture, Heaney parallels the story of Antigone with the disturbance in the waiting crowd when the body of hunger striker Francis Hughes was handed over by the Royal Ulster Constabulary (RUC).

Heaney goes on to discuss how, in the context of his native Northern Ireland, Antigone's words take on new resonances and cites an influential linkage between the Greek heroine and the province by Conor Cruise O'Brien in a piece, titled "Views," that was published in the *Listener* in late 1968.[9] At the time O'Brien wrote this article, the legal injustices suffered by Northern Ireland's Catholic minority included gerrymandered constituency boundaries, discrimination in employment and the allocation of council housing, and routine harassment by the enforcers of the law, the RUC, as well as by special constabularies and loyalist militias.[10] In O'Brien's analysis, Creon was like the unionist establishment that flagrantly misused the apparatus of the law to reinforce existing imbalances of power, Antigone was seen as being in an analogous situation to the province's wronged Roman Catholic minority, and Antigone's rebel brother was compared, in his determination to bring about change through violent action, to Northern Ireland's nationalist paramilitaries.

In this influential article, O'Brien declared that even peaceful protests against this unjust state of affairs seemed certain to provoke a violent reaction, raising the question of whether they could be justified. After some deliberation—in fact, almost in spite of himself—he comes to the tentative, cautious, view that Antigone and, by extension, Northern Ireland's civil rights protesters had right on their side:

> Creon's authority, after all, was legitimate, even if he had abused it, and the life of the city would become intolerable if citizens should disobey any law that irked their conscience. [. . .] We should be safer without the trouble-maker from Thebes. And that which would be lost, if she could be eliminated, is quite intangible. [. . .] In losing it, man might gain peace at the price of his soul.[11]

By the time he came to reprint the article in 1972, O'Brien went back on this concluding idea, suggesting the protests were not worth their cost. The two versions of O'Brien's essay are vivid snapshots of the dilemmas that arose in a time and place—Northern Ireland in the late 1960s and early 1970s—when the onset of widespread violence led to a chasm opening between the two traditional aims of law enforcement: serving justice and keeping the peace.

In the speech by Antigone quoted above, not for the first time in his writing, Heaney invokes the concept of "unwritten" laws.[12] This idea, among the robes and pillars of the play's ancient Theban setting, might suggest uncodified, universal standards of conduct with regard to the burial of and respect for the dead. Heaney had previously deployed the phrase in the mid-1980s, in a poem that he wrote following a request from the Irish chapter of Amnesty International, "From the Republic of Conscience" (*The Haw Lantern*, 1987). In this poem, as in *The Burial at Thebes*, Heaney writes of the importance of "unwritten law" in this utopian fantasy polity:

> At their inauguration, public leaders
> must swear to uphold unwritten law and weep
> to atone for their presumption to hold office[.][13]

Nathan Wallace has written that "Heaney's oath of office to 'uphold unwritten law' also evokes the history of the human rights idea, which springs from the natural-law tradition."[14] This idea of uncodified and inalienable human rights is indeed one element of the phrase "unwritten law," but the idea also has a separate lineage in Ireland.

As Heather Laird has explored in her book *Subversive Law in Ireland*, "unwritten law" was the name for the popular justice that was administered within agrarian societies in eighteenth-, nineteenth-, and twentieth-century Ireland, distinct from and, indeed, running counter to the "written" system of official law.[15] A central tenet of this law was that access to land and means of subsistence were fundamental rights that took precedence over the rights to land that were asserted and recorded in official, "written," laws.[16] It is typical of Heaney's work that its meliorative, peaceable, ideas are inextricable from more radical and subversive ones that are drawn from Ireland's complicated legal history.

In *The Burial at Thebes*, as elsewhere in his writing, Heaney's knowledge of Irish legal history is part of what shapes his engagement with justice, and injustice, further afield. The phrase "unwritten laws" takes on yet another significance in the play as Creon speaks, at times, with the accent and idioms of George W. Bush. His regime was accused, at the time of the play's first performance, by Heaney among many others, of ignoring international standards of human rights in prisons like Abu Ghraib and Guantánamo Bay.

Heaney's work, especially from the mid-1970s, is notably concerned with the condition of being caught between a network of official and unofficial jurisdictions and with weighing the claims of both positive and natural law in response to this condition. Heaney's poetry is a record of the dilemmas faced by a poet who, at various times in his career, had to negotiate the rival demands of existing administrations, militant republicanism, and his own conscience and sense of justice.

His poem "Punishment," for example, centers on questions of culpability and retribution, linking the imagined death of a prehistoric woman with the punishment by the IRA of women whom they suspected of associating with British soldiers. His confession that, in the face of the Provisional IRA's version of "justice," he suspected he would merely "connive / in civilized outrage" has attracted much critical comment.[17] This is a notable example of a strange but characteristic tendency in Heaney's poetry: his recourse to legal language when questions of unofficial allegiance are raised.

Examples of this tendency proliferate in his work: in a poem about a sectarian murder, Heaney describes the inhabitants of his district as "Slow arbitrators of the burial ground"; he asks of a man killed while breaking an IRA curfew, "How culpable was he / That last night when he broke / Our tribe's complicity?" A stone thrown at a Protestant ancestor of his who had married a Catholic is called "exonerated, exonerating."[18] Heaney's employment of legal language—"connive," "arbitrators," "culpable," "complicit," "exonerate"—gives an indication of the seriousness with which community boundaries are policed and of the gravity of the consequences of breaking the unofficial "laws" that relate to them. It also hints that, in Northern Ireland, official law is just one kind of law and that the power of unwritten laws still had to be heeded. Decisions about what was "legal" were, for Heaney, not merely the preserve of the courts.

In matters of justice and law enforcement, for almost all of his writing life, Heaney faced difficult decisions about when to speak out and in what manner. This was true even before the outbreak of widespread sectarian violence in Northern Ireland. In 1968, in the wake of the attacks by police on civil rights marches in October 1968, Heaney wrote a short ballad-form protest piece that was performed on Irish radio. It ended with an ironic encomium to the Northern Irish minister for home affairs, William Craig, which acted as a savage condemnation of him:

> They'll cordon and they'll baton-charge
> they'll silence protest tunes
> They are the hounds of Ulster, boys,
> sweet William Craig's dragoons.[19]

The gulf that has opened by this point between what is lawful and what is just is clear: Heaney's most intense engagement with the law came after the people tasked with preserving the peace broke it. The late 1960s, the time of the civil rights marches, were a turning point for Northern Ireland. The breakdown of RUC discipline in their policing of Catholic areas, particularly in Derry, and of civil rights marches in 1968 marked the end of the broadly peaceable, if heavily policed, conditions in which Heaney had grown up.[20]

The following year, in August 1969, the army would be deployed alongside the RUC, showing that civil policing had largely collapsed.[21] However, it took a few years before Heaney registered the end of these conditions in the volumes he published with Faber and Faber. There are no overt references to policing in his volume *Door into the Dark* (1969), published the year after the march he described in "Title Deeds," nor are there any in *Wintering Out* (1972). It would be nearly seven years before his 1975 volume, *North*, contained direct references to the actions of the police at the time of the civil rights marches. For insights into Heaney's attitude toward the enforcement of "law and order" in Northern Ireland between 1968 and 1975, readers must look to his less widely circulated writings, like "Craig's Dragoons."

The publication history of this 1968 radio piece matches that of other early works by Heaney that are explicitly critical of actions by the police and army. According to Karl Miller, "Craig's Dragoons" circulated anonymously for several years before Miller himself published it in the autumn–winter 1971–72 edition of the *Review*.[22] The same oblique dynamics can be seen in the publication history of Heaney's poem in response to Bloody Sunday, the name given to the day in January 1972 when British soldiers killed thirteen and shot and injured a further thirteen unarmed civilians during a Northern Ireland Civil Rights Association march.[23] Heaney's poem in protest at this event, "The Road to Derry," is an unambiguous condemnation of injustice. "And in the dirt lay justice like an acorn in the winter / Till its oak would sprout in Derry where the thirteen men lay dead."[24] Its conclusion, which evokes both the bodies of the dead and the possibility of new life, is poised between anger at what has happened and hope for revolutionary change. Here, unambiguously, "justice" is shown not to be on the side of those tasked with preserving "law and order."

As in the case of "Craig's Dragoons," the fugitive publication history of this poem is indicative of Heaney's hesitations about engaging directly with issues of law and order in Northern Ireland at this time. Shortly after he wrote it, Heaney sent it to singer Luke Kelly with the suggestion that he sing it to the tune of the republican ballad "The Boys of Mullaghbawn." However, the song was never recorded, and its words went unpublished until Heaney sent it to the *Derry Journal* in 1997. But 1997 was not 1972, and by this time, three years after the IRA cease-fire, the cutting political edge of the piece had been considerably dulled. In the publication histories of "Craig's Dragoons" and "The Road to Derry" we can see the same desire not to condone or exacerbate violence that lay behind Heaney's decision in around 1972 to stop reading his "Requiem from the Croppies," a poem commemorating the dead of the 1798 rebellion, aloud in public.[25] Though the Troubles, and in particular the house burnings inflicted on Northern Ireland's urban Catholic population, are recalled in Heaney's 1972 volume, *Wintering Out*, nothing in the collection matches the directness of what is in his uncollected works.[26]

Looking at the decisions made by Heaney's contemporaries shows the fine judgments that public speech at this time required. Thomas Kinsella's long 1972 poem on Bloody Sunday is commonly known as *Butcher's Dozen*, but it was published with the subtitle *A Lesson for the Octave of Widgery.* In naming the *Widgery Report* in its title, critic Brian John observes, Kinsella positions his work not so much as a response to the events of January 30, 1972, but as a rebuke to the judicial inquiry that exonerated the soldiers responsible for the shootings.[27] Kinsella's pamphlet publication acts as a counterweight to this report, giving voice to a series of ghosts who contradict, either flatly or satirically, Widgery's findings:

> The news is out. The troops were kind.
> Impartial justice has to find
> We'd be alive and well today
> If we had let them have their way.[28]

Later, Kinsella traced his use of ghostly protagonists directly to another Irish poetic engagement with the law: the spectral figures that plead their cases in Brian Merriman's eighteenth-century poem whose title, translated from Irish, is *The Midnight Court.* In matters involving law, there is a lineage of poetic as well as legal documents that converse with and develop from each other.

An extraordinary response to Kinsella's poem was published the following year: an anonymous pamphlet issued by the British and Irish Communist Organisation titled *Kinsella's Oversight.* This strange palimpsestic intervention follows Kinsella's own poem word for word, changing only enough elements to redirect its outrage away from the British Army and justice system and toward the IRA. So, a critical reference to the British Army in Kinsella's poem, for example, is replaced with one to Seán Mac Stiofáin, Provisional IRA chief of staff. Reading the above passage from Kinsella's poem alongside its corresponding one in *Kinsella's Oversight*, it becomes apparent how both British and republican claims to uphold "justice" could be critiqued in this unstable jurisdiction:

> The news is out. Mac Stiofan's [*sic*] kind
> Impartial justice has to find[.]
> We'd be alive and well today
> If we had let him have his way.[29]

This series of overwritings (Widgery by Kinsella, Kinsella by the anonymous author of *Kinsella's Oversight*) gives an indication of the quasi-judicial status of poets. As an officer of the midnight court of poetry, a distinct, parallel, place of judgment, Heaney knew that he could not make one false step.

Heaney vividly explores the condition of Northern Ireland's Roman Catholic minority before the law in "A Constable Calls" (*North*, 1975). In this poem, set in the broadly peaceable but menaced jurisdiction of mid-twentieth-century Northern Ireland, a member of the overwhelmingly Protestant RUC comes to the family's farm and records information on what crops the family has been planting. The policeman's visit is, on the surface, routine and administrative, but the evident power politics of observation mean the poem is shot through with anxiety. This is evident from the description of the policeman's bicycle at the beginning of the poem, whose dynamo might be mistaken for a gun:

> Heating in sunlight, the "spud"
> Of the dynamo gleaming and cocked back,

The pedal treads hanging relieved
Of the boot of the law.

The representative of the law who visits the Heaneys' farm is represented not as an upholder of justice but as a threat, a symbol of force and coercion used against a minority who might harbor different political aspirations from those held by the majority. "The arm of the law" is a phrase that suggests the reach and persistence of the organizations charged with punishing criminality. Here, though, the law is represented by a blunter image: a boot.

An early prose version of "A Constable Calls" (*North*) strongly hints that enforcers of the law could not always be trusted to behave lawfully. It was first published in prose form in Padraic Fiacc's anthology of poetry from Northern Ireland, *The Wearing of the Black: An Anthology of Contemporary Ulster Poetry* (1974); the next year it was published in Heaney's own volume *North*. The line Heaney removed before the poem's second publication in *North* is italicized here:

[. . .] I assumed small
guilts and sat imagining the black hole in the barracks.
"Well, I'll have to be beating on."
He stood up, shifted the baton case[.][30]

Though "beating on," an Ulster phrase meaning "making tracks," may well have been cut from the *North* version because non-Ulster readers would not know what it meant, it also may have been cut because of its allusion to police brutality. If this is the case, then, with the loaded reference to the policeman "beating on" removed, the version in *North* engages less openly with the widespread breakdown in police discipline in the late 1960s than the version Heaney published in Fiacc's anthology.

Different kinds of publication demand different registers. What could be written of directly in a ballad like "Craig's Dragoons" or

"The Road to Derry" was a matter of allusion and obliquity in the poems that Heaney included in the Faber-published volumes that were intended for a wider audience.

Heaney's continuing preoccupation with the violent events of the summer of 1969 is seen in the poem "High Summer" in *Field Work* (1979). This poem, in both its title and its subject matter, covers similar ground as an earlier poem, "Summer Home," in *Wintering Out*. Both involve memories of stays in hot climates, and both include the horrifying discovery of a swarm of maggots. By 1979, however, Heaney explicitly links finding the maggots (bought for a fishing trip and then forgotten) with the legal system of Northern Ireland:

> On the last day, when I was clearing up,
> on a warm ledge I found a bag of maggots
> and opened it. A black
> and throbbing swarm came riddling out
> like newsreel of a police force run amok,
> Sunspotting flies in gauzy meaty flight,
> the barristers and black berets of light.[31]

In these lines, the ghastly multitude of flies and maggots, disturbed from their somnolent state and swarming into the air, is a reminder of the violence that was unleashed in the wake of the civil rights protests. Conor Cruise O'Brien, in an article with which Heaney was familiar, described the pre-1969 situation in Northern Ireland as "one of frozen violence," writing that "any attempt to thaw it out will liberate violence which is at present static."[32] Heaney's poem, which describes disturbing a bag of maggots and, in doing so, illustrates the gruesome consequences that can arise from a sudden awakening from a state of neglect and forgetfulness, seems to come from a similar point of view to O'Brien's article. However, by comparing the swarming flies to the army and lawyers, "barristers and black berets," Heaney represents these figures not as keepers of the peace or seekers after truth, but as an integral part of the reanimated violence of Northern Ireland.

Images of policing haunt Heaney's poetry from the outset of the Troubles, but from the mid-1980s there are glimmerings of an attempt to reimagine it.[33] The red lamps that Heaney remembered the police using at roadblocks are subtly invoked in the title poem of his volume *The Haw Lantern* (1987), named for the crimson winter-ripening fruit of the hawthorn tree. Heaney, in the volume's title poem, conflates this bright-red fruit with the lantern carried by Diogenes the Cynic, a philosopher who, according to legend, roamed the streets of Athens in the fifth century BC searching for "one just man":

> it takes the roaming shape of Diogenes
> with his lantern, seeking one just man;
> so you end up scrutinized from behind the haw[.][34]

Diogenes, in his lamp-lit search for justice, bears an odd similarity to a Northern Irish policeman in one of Heaney's earlier depictions. In his poem "The Ministry of Fear" (*North*), Heaney writes of policemen who "Swung their crimson flashlamps, crowding round / The car like black cattle."[35] Neil Corcoran writes that "being stopped regularly at roadblocks by RUC patrols" was a feature of Heaney's life before he left Northern Ireland, and Heaney himself describes moving around Northern Ireland as a matter of "delays measured in hours, searches and signings among the guns and torches."[36] These red lamps were such a feature of police patrols that they could be used to trick the unwary, as Heaney imagined happening to his second cousin Colum McCartney before he was murdered in 1975: "What blazed ahead of you? A faked road block? / The red lamp swung, the sudden brakes and stalling," Heaney wrote in his elegy for McCartney.[37] In the title of *The Haw Lantern*, there is an attempt to take an image—the inquisitorial red lamp—of what Heaney considered to be a tool in an unjust situation and to imagine it again in the context of a search for justice.

Heaney was no less preoccupied with prisons than he was with the police, and they held a similarly ambivalent place in his poetry. Long Kesh, later HM Prison Maze, held the hundreds of prisoners who were arrested with the introduction of internment in August 1971. It appears in both Heaney's 1972 and his 1975 Faber volumes.[38] Initially a ramshackle collection of corrugated iron huts and barbed-wire-surrounded compounds on a former Royal Air Force base, this camp eventually grew to become a vast prison complex of twenty-two compounds.[39] It is hardly surprising that Heaney refers to this prison in both *Wintering Out* and *North*: the Northern Irish prison population rose dramatically during the three years that separated the two volumes and carried on rising to a peak of three thousand inmates in 1979. By the end of the 1970s, the province had the highest prison population per capita in Western Europe.[40] In fact, both *Wintering Out* and the poem "Whatever You Say, Say Nothing" in *North* contain the same passage on the prison. In these repeated lines, a roadside that was once familiar has become a sight that is reminiscent of a weird, eerie war film:

> This morning from a dewy motorway
> I saw the new camp for the internees:
> a bomb had left a crater of fresh clay
> in the roadside, and over in the trees
> machine-gun posts defined a real stockade.
> There was that white mist you get on a low ground
> and it was déjà-vu, some film made
> of Stalag 17, a bad dream with no sound[.][41]

In the unreal, alienated, dawn light of these repeated lines, a nightmarish vision of the failure of civil law unfolds. References to machine-gun posts, bombs, and, most of all, a notorious Second World War German prison camp would all be out of place in a poem that describes the enforcement of civil law. Heaney's lines suggest that this is not a peacetime situation, in which criminals are arrested, but is a wartime one, in which prisoners of war are captured.

The differences between these two ways of seeing prison inmates during the Troubles would be, for the prisoners who starved themselves during the hunger strikes of the early 1980s, a matter of life and death. Heaney's poetry from the 1970s onward reflects contemporary legal arguments regarding how prisoners should be categorized. This issue is at the heart of "Visitant," a prose poem about a German prisoner of war in his pamphlet publication *Stations* (1975). This collection of prose poems was issued, as is the case with much of Heaney's more politically inflected work, in a very limited run.[42] In keeping with the supernatural connotations of its title, its protagonist of "Visitant" is imagined as a liminal figure, at once a mundane and an otherworldly visitor. Though officially an enemy combatant, the prisoner is described as a Sunday-afternoon visitor to the family, who first appears like

> a ghost with claims
> on us, precipitating in the heat tremor. Then, released
> from its distorting mirror, up the fields there comes
> this awkwardly smiling foreigner[.][43]

At the time that Heaney was writing this poem, hundreds of nationalists were being held in makeshift camps similar to the one in which the poem's wartime protagonist was imprisoned. At this time, the way in which prisoners in Northern Ireland might be conceptualized and categorized was of central importance to political discourse. Initially, internees in camps like Long Kesh were detained without a formal prison regime, did not have to wear prison uniforms or carry out work, and were free to associate with each other and elect their own officers to negotiate with prison staff.[44] This was to change dramatically with the introduction of a policy of "criminalization," which was intended as a propaganda blow against the IRA. The ideas behind this shift were summarized by Margaret Thatcher in a speech she gave in Belfast in March 1981, by which time the policy had existed for several years: "There is no such thing as political murder, political bombing, or political violence. There is only criminal murder, criminal bombing, and criminal violence."[45] In 1974, "full responsibility for law and order" was handed from the army to the RUC (although in practice the two were to operate in tandem), internment without trial was stopped from February 1975, and prisoners sentenced after March 1, 1976, were denied what was, for all practical purposes, the prisoner-of-war status they had previously held.[46]

Heaney's poem about a German prisoner of war is alive with the same questions that haunted his later version of *Antigone*. What measure of humanity is owed to the outlawed? Who is "the enemy," and who is practically a member of the family? In "Visitant," a man who might have been considered "the enemy," a captured member of the forces making war against the state, merely appears as gentle and insubstantial. The heat shimmer amid which he appears parallels the equivocal status he occupies. The poem suggests, very subtly, the ambiguous and shifting relationships that attempts to create hard-and-fast categories of prisoners could disguise.

The removal of special-category status for paramilitary prisoners in 1976 led to the first "blanket protests" by Republicans, in which prisoners refused to wear their uniforms and were confined to their cells. The "dirty protest" followed and then the hunger strikes of the early 1980s.[47] In both Heaney's poems and his subsequent comments on this terrible time in Northern Ireland's prisons, a note of self-reproof is consistent. It is audible in a poem from *Station Island* (1984) that recounts the story of Russian dramatist and doctor Anton Chekhov's journey to the prison island of Sakhalin. Written in the wake of the hunger strikes, it presents the sound of a glass smashing as being as piercing and discomfiting as the playwright's consciousness of his own freedom:

> It rang as clearly as the convicts' chains
> That haunted him. In the months to come
> It rang on like the burden of his freedom[.][48]

Commenting on this poem to Dennis O'Driscoll, Heaney said that "if I had followed the logic of the Chekhov poem, I'd have gone to the prison, seen what was happening to the people on the hunger strike and written an account of it."[49] However, he did not visit the prison, and the burden of Heaney's freedom can be seen in several of his other poems from *Station Island*. He alludes to the situation in the prisons in "Away from It All," a poem with a title that suggests absconding from responsibility but that pictures a sunset that is, in a portentous choice of image at a time of hunger striking, "a fine graduation between / balance and inanition."[50]

Inanition also haunts "Sandstone Keepsake," a poem in which Heaney recalls an evening when he went out for a walk along a beach in County Donegal, picked up a stone, looked at the towers of the prison camp across the water in Northern Ireland, and was himself observed through binoculars by security forces as he stood peaceably with his new keepsake. The beach Heaney looks across the water at is Magilligan Strand, the site of a 1972 anti-internment protest that took place the week before Bloody Sunday. At this protest the British Army used barbed wire to close off part of the beach and attacked protesters as they approached this makeshift barrier. While this was happening, a significant verbal confrontation took place between nationalist leader John Hume and a British soldier. Their encounter, which was captured on film, has an emblematic quality:

> HUME: Under what law? [. . .]
> [. . . .]
> SOLDIER: It has been prohibited by your government.
> HUME: Whose government?
> SOLDIER: The government of Northern Ireland.
> HUME: Not our government.[51]

This repudiation under pressure of the official law of the land by Hume is an echo that haunts Heaney's poem. Heaney wryly references his own earlier work "Exposure," a poem in which he imagines himself in a parallel life, hurling a stone for "the desperate."[52]

The title of "Sandstone Keepsake," as well as referencing the "stone" of militant republicanism that Yeats describes as being "in the midst of all," also contains within it the surname of Northern Ireland's most famous hunger striker, Bobby Sands.[53] The "Sands" nested in "Sandstone Keepsake" suggests the existence, spectral but present, of alternative codes: both the one that would permit violence and the code by which Sands starved himself to death.

Heaney imagines a conversation with the ghost of another hunger striker, Francis Hughes, in the title poem of *Station Island.* This direct engagement with the hunger strikers is an unusual one for him in his 1980s poetry. The ghost tells his protagonist that he was a "hit-man on the brink, emptied and deadly. / When the police yielded my coffin, I was light / As my head when I took aim."[54] For the most part the prisoners and their plight are more subtly present in Heaney's poems in the first half of the 1980s. During the years that followed the hunger strikes, Heaney became increasingly associated with Amnesty International.[55] His poem "From the Republic of Conscience," written in 1985 after a request from the Irish chapter of Amnesty International, opens with the protagonist hearing a curlew high above the runway when he lands in this imagined ideal republic. Though Heaney later traced this image to his memory of what he heard when a plane he was in switched off its engines after landing on Orkney, the line also suggests the humanizing impulses behind Yeats's poem "Paudeen," a touchstone poem for Heaney.[56] In this poem Yeats's protagonist, on hearing curlews calling in the "luminous wind," remembers that there is not a "single soul that lacks a sweet crystalline cry."[57] The same belief in the inherent value of every life informs Heaney's attitudes to prisoners.

The full complexity of Heaney's engagements with the law is only beginning to come to light now, with the opening to researchers of his letters and occasional draft and uncollected writings.[58] By reading these documents alongside his more widely circulated works, the skillfulness with which Heaney played, in Bernard O'Donoghue's phrase, a "wary and socially accomplished game," reflecting on the experiences of an overlooked minority in Northern Ireland while not endorsing the violence committed in their name, becomes clear.[59]

Among the correspondence that Seamus Heaney archived at Emory University in Atlanta, there is evidence in a file containing documents that "Settings, xiii," one of the poems in his collection *Seeing Things* (1991), is an oblique response to the killing of three Provisional IRA members in Gibraltar in 1988. In the same file of correspondence there is evidence of Heaney's tangential involvement in the publication of two republican poetry pamphlets, one by Bobby Sands and one by Jack Mitchell.[60]

"Settings, xiii" has, hitherto, not been associated with the Troubles, but lines from the poem that Heaney sketched on the back of a piece of paper that he eventually filed in a folder of correspondence from January 1989 suggest this context for the poem. The page is in a file in which three linked documents are kept: a long protest poem about the "Death on the Rock" killings titled *GiB: A Modest Exposure* that Heaney had been sent in January 1989; a letter from the poem's sender, Republican activist Niall Farrell (the brother of, depending on which facts one prioritizes, the thwarted perpetrator of a bombing in Gibraltar or the victim of a shooting there, Mairéad Farrell); and a draft of Heaney's careful response to both the letter and the poem.[61] Receiving this poem in draft form, along with a request for his help in publishing and promoting it, put Heaney in a delicate position. Though he did not speak of receiving this poem, he explained to Dennis O'Driscoll that, during the 1980s, "the IRA's self-image as liberators didn't work much magic with me. But neither did the too-brutal simplicity of Margaret Thatcher's 'a crime is a crime is a crime. It is not political.'"[62]

Mairéad Farrell, along with two other members of the Provisional IRA, was killed on March 6, 1988, by British troops in Gibraltar in an incident that became known as the "Death on the Rock" killings. This name comes from the title of a controversial Thames TV documentary that aired in April 1988, a month after the killings. In it, Jonathan Dimbleby summarized the troubling question at the center of the documentary: "The question which goes to the heart of the issue is this: Did the SAS [Special Air Service] men have the law on their side when they shot dead Mairéad Farrell, Daniel McCann and Sean Savage, who were unarmed at the time? Were the soldiers acting in self-defense, or were they operating what's become known as a shoot-to-kill policy[?]"[63] At the time, "shoot-to-kill" was shorthand for a controversial tendency among security forces to kill suspects rather than arrest them.[64] This had been investigated by policeman John Stalker, who, early in 1988, stated that "I never did find evidence of a shoot-to-kill policy as such; there was no written instruction, nothing pinned on a noticeboard. But there was a clear understanding on the part of the men whose job it was to pull the trigger that that was what was expected of them."[65]

In the "Death on the Rock" documentary, barrister George Carman set out the position in law: that force was legal only when it was reasonable in the circumstances. In light of his comments, evidence from witnesses that two of the IRA members had died with their hands in the air, while another was shot while running away, strongly suggested that the soldiers who killed them acted unlawfully. Though the three who were shot were unarmed, they were almost certainly scouting in advance of a car-bombing mission. The inquest that September decided by a nine-to-two majority that the soldiers' use of force was not excessive and that the killings were lawful.[66]

The lines that Heaney sketched on the back of the paper waver in and out of legibility, but the final words are clear enough:

> a gorged cormorant on the rock
>   at noon
> Exiled and at home in ~~the~~ a big glitter.[67]

A clue as to the approximate date that he wrote these words can be found on the draft letter that he wrote to Niall Farrell, which is dated January 17, 1989. Heaney's papers are peppered with notes-to-self like the above, records of times when he, while busy working on something else, caught a glimpse of a promising handful of words and scribbled down a few lines. The stray phrases and sentences that appear in his notebooks and nowhere else show that many of these ideas remained in germ form. Others, like the ones quoted above, germinated, becoming part of a poem, "Settings, xiii," in *Seeing Things* (1991). Like so much of Heaney's writing, these lines take simple, easily grasped images whose meanings radiate and ramify under the pressure of attention.

The poem in which they eventually appeared, one of the twelve-line works in the "Squarings" section of *Seeing Things*, is the first in the "Settings" subsection of this long sequence. As such, it does much to give this subsection its tone, communicating simultaneous impressions of both brilliancy and secrecy. The first nine lines of this poem are:

> Hazel stealth. A trickle in the culvert.
> Athletic sealight on the doorstep slab,
> On the sea itself, on silent roofs and gables.
>
> Whitewashed suntraps. Hedges hot as chimneys.
> Chairs on all fours. A plate-rack braced and laden.
> The fossil poetry of hob and slate.
>
> Desire within its moat, dozing at ease—
> Like a gorged cormorant on the rock at noon,
> Exiled and in tune with the big glitter.[68]

The poem, like much of the "Squarings" sequence, is honeycombed with references to light and water, and these elements give it, for all its slabs and slates, a certain disembodied airiness. The aerial aesthetic of this sequence is intensified by the fact that these poems begin with numbers rather than titles, a feature that means that the reader must take what bearings they can from the poems' imagery. In the case of "Settings, xiii," from the clues of "whitewashed sun-traps" and "hedges hot as chimneys," it seems the poem is set in a hot climate. The reader might wonder whether Heaney is remembering visits to Spain or the Basque country, as the poems he set there, too, vividly evoke punishing heat. The poem shares other features with Heaney's earlier works set in these hot places: it communicates a sense of torpor and a deep but unspecific unease, as if something latent and sinister were basking in the sun.[69] Though earlier critics who wrote about "Settings, xiii" sensed its oppressive, troubled atmosphere, no one has connected the poem to the "Death on the Rock" killings.[70]

Gibraltar is not the only backdrop to this work. A version of "Settings, xiii," with a few small differences from the published version, is on display under the title "Bothar Buí" at the dwelling of the same name. This place is a unique and scenic holiday home on the Beara peninsula in West Cork, a group of traditional farm buildings and modernist structures that was designed by architect Robin Walker in the 1960s.[71] However, the archived pages on which Heaney sketched some of the lines from this poem suggest it has links to the infernal as well as the idyllic. For example, in light of the draft letter to Farrell, the words "Like a gorged cormorant on the rock at noon" take on new meanings. "The rock" is a nickname for the Crown colony of Gibraltar. The hot climate in which the poem is set and the "big glitter" could indicate the Mediterranean, while the fact that the "suntraps" are "whitewashed" suggests both the appearance of southern Europe and the concealment of incriminating facts. Reading this poem again in light of the file of documents in which draft lines from it can be found, several of its elements indicate an ambush in the offing, including the references to "silence," "stealth," something "athletic" on rooftops, and, above all, the cormorant—the swift, dark, hook-billed predator known proverbially to anglers as "the Black Death."[72] There is, of course, a limit to what the context can tell us about the poem. The reference to exile, for example, is not readily explicable in light of the context in which the lines were most likely written. Rather, Heaney's poem seems to offer an oblique, imagist response to the bloody events in Gibraltar.[73]

The version of the poem that Farrell had sent to Heaney, titled *GiB: A Modest Exposure*, named "Paul Macdonnell" as its author; it was later published under the name "Jack Mitchell." Full of furious anger against the British legal system, one of the main targets of its ire is the two-week inquest of September 1988. At this inquest, the central issue of contention was whether the British Army's Special Air Service had used excessive force against the three Provisional IRA members. The poet's view on this, despite the inquest's findings, is uncompromising. To him, invoking "law" to justify the killings was mere hypocrisy:

> It's sickening to hear them jaw
> Of human rights and rule of law;
> Their favourite view of human rights
> Is through a loaded Browning's sights
> And as for rule of law, by God,
> Whose law ordains a murder squad?[74]

The four-piston propulsiveness of the poem's rhythm contributes to its power and is shared with that of balladic poems that protest the use of government-supported force in Northern Ireland. These include Thomas Kinsella's *Butcher's Dozen* (1972) or Bobby Sands's *Prison Poems* (1981) and even Heaney's own uncollected protest ballads "Craig's Dragoons" (1968, first published 1971) and "The Road to Derry" (1972, first published 1997). The rhythmic and rhyming patterns of *GiB* contribute to its momentum, underscoring its unswerving line of argument. This argument is foreshadowed in its introduction, written by Séamus Deane (fada in original), in which he writes that it is "the legal system that is at the heart of the matter," because unjust actions by Crown forces were "concealed in the language of law and order, of justice and morality."[75]

Some clearly expected that, on this occasion on which the distance between law and justice appeared to have swung wide, Heaney would fulfill the historic function of an Irish poet and wade in. In his draft reply to Farrell's letter, however, Heaney gently parried Farrell's request that he provide an endorsement of the long poem. However,

Heaney praised *GiB*, writing that it was "full of good things and goes along with a terrific zest and intelligence." He also noted "its head-on energy and its terrible subject matter and its general mixture of fierce feeling and elegant technique" and gave advice on how the poem might be published. On the subject of providing an endorsement, though, Heaney was firm: he wrote that, while he was "happy to facilitate its circulation," he was "not prepared to 'plug the thing.'" He went on to advise that

> the optimum force would be achieved by having a joint publication in Britain *and* Ireland. When Bobby Sands's poems were being prepared for publication, my suggestion was that they be placed with a London or Dublin publishing house. That way many people—reviewers, editors, broadcasters—would have had a chance to approach the subject neutrally (so to speak). If the thing appears from a politically aligned address or organ, many people would take it as propaganda rather than outrage, and the moral force of the thing would be blunted or deflected by the suasion of the "propaganda" label. You'd get the public attention—in reviews *etc*—of the "converted" whereas the point here would be to raise the consciousness of the half-committed.[76]

This letter contains both more and less surprising elements. Less surprisingly, it shows Heaney's famed instinct toward inclusiveness in his idea that the volume be given both Irish and British publication. There are other ways of reading this letter, too, however. By expressing a wish to "raise the consciousness of the half-committed," it looks as if Heaney is making the point that better propaganda could be had from the poem if it did not look like it was propaganda.

His answer, too, reveals a surprising involvement in the publication of republican poetry, showing that he provided at least one suggestion on the publication of *Prison Poems* by Bobby Sands, who had died eight years earlier.[77] There is a blog post by former Sinn Féin publicity director Danny Morrison that contains an account of how Heaney may have supplied his suggestion. In this post, Morrison recollects meeting Heaney on a train and Heaney's agreeing to read the poetry of Bobby Sands (which was later published as *Prison Poems*).[78] He further remembered that he sent Heaney the poems and that Heaney brought them back to the Sinn Féin offices a week or two later with "a message for me in which he said that the trilogy 'The Crime of Castlereagh' read like or was derivative of Wilde's 'The Ballad of Reading Gaol.'"[79] Morrison says that was the extent of his contact with the poet.

Heaney's account of meeting Morrison in his poem "The Flight Path" (*The Spirit Level*, 1996), and subsequently in the collection of interviews *Stepping Stones*, indicates a much more terse engagement. Heaney recalls shortly rebuffing a request from a republican that he "write / Something for us" in "The Flight Path" (*The Spirit Level*, 1996); he later identified his interlocutor in this poem as Danny Morrison.[80] The letter he wrote to Farrell, however, goes some way to corroborating the claims that Morrison made on his blog post. Heaney never publicly stated that he had been in any way involved in the publication of Sands's poetry, nor that he had given any advice on the publication of *GiB*. As he put it in *The Redress of Poetry*, he could not endorse the "violent means and programmes of the Provisional IRA."[81] Perhaps it would be fair to conclude that, though Heaney was resolute in not promoting violence, and though he never endorsed the actions of the Provisional IRA, he was willing to be involved, at least at arm's length, with the poetic productions of those who both endorsed and committed acts of violence.

During the 1980s Heaney was photographed standing next to the South African law professor Kader Asmal, who had notably investigated the shoot-to-kill policy in Northern Ireland. Both were protesting against apartheid outside Dunne's Stores in Dublin, which at the time sold South African goods. In 1988 Heaney published a poem titled "New Worlds" in *The Prison of His Days*, a miscellany to mark the seventieth birthday of Nelson Mandela. Though he never collected this poem in any of his volumes, it has strong thematic similarities to two of his poems that are concerned with Irish prisoners, "Sandstone Keepsake" and "Away from It All." All three poems share a self-accusatory, burdensome knowledge of privilege:

> In the country poetry has deserted,
> In a language tonic as their swimming pools,
>
> There are many poets, all insisting
> Their poetry brings new worlds into being.[82]

This poem presents the world as it is seen through sunglasses. In the world that Heaney conjures, screened off by its plate-glass doors, the art of poetry is deader and more sterile than if it were not practiced. In this grimly denatured and deracinated cityscape, the potential triteness of poetry is laid bare. The poem's final acidly ironic assertion that "poetry brings new worlds into being" refutes a very ancient argument for the value of poetry, one that such famous sonneteers as Philip Sidney and William Shakespeare expressed in different ways: that poetry has the power to remake the world in a better and brighter form.[83] The fourteen lines of Heaney's poem, chopped into unrhymed couplets, are a hollow echo of the sonnet form. This is a significant move for Heaney, to whom the sonnet form meant so much. The guilt and implied self-castigation that are such a significant part of Heaney's poetry from the years that immediately followed the 1980–81 hunger strikes are strongly present in his poem for this famous South African prisoner.

"New Worlds," published in 1988, allows us to consider again the lines from "Settings, xiii," "Like a gorged cormorant on the rock at noon / Exiled and in tune with the big glitter," which he likely wrote not long after, in early 1989. Though the context in which Heaney wrote these lines suggests that the cormorant represents the soldiers who killed the three members of the IRA unit in Gibraltar, Heaney's repeated tendency during the 1980s to link poetry with ideas of glut and satiety opens the possibility of other readings. His writing about prisoners and the mistreated is inseparable from his preoccupation with his own privileges and freedoms.[84] In other words, when "Settings, xiii" is read in light of Heaney's other poems from this time, it becomes possible to read the "gorged cormorant" as, in part, a reflection on himself.

Heaney's poetry from the time of *The Spirit Level* (1996) shows a new openness about acknowledging what he called the "life-waste and spirit-waste" of the previous quarter century.[85] From the time of the cease-fires of the 1990s, Heaney would write more unsparingly, and with unflinching specificity, about people who were held prisoner in Northern Ireland in the 1970s and 1980s. It is as if these poems are meltwater in an imaginative thaw that followed the cessation of widespread hostilities. For example, when he wrote in *The Spirit Level* that the "gaol walls all those months [that is, the months of the dirty protests of the late 1970s] were smeared with shite," the graphicness of these lines is at odds with the allusive metaphor making and troubled sense of physically comfortable, mentally discomfited, separation that characterizes his 1980s poems that reflect on Northern Irish prisoners.[86] The years after the mid-1990s can be counted as a distinct period in Heaney's work, at least so far as prisoners are concerned.

Heaney's late poem "The Wood Road," which pictures a militiaman neighbor, exists in two different versions—the first printed in 2006 in the poetry magazine *Magma*, the second in his last collection, *Human Chain* (2010). A different impression of this enforcer of the law is given in the poem with a small circulation from the one in his Faber-published volume, and, as such, it is a late example of his double-edged approach to law in Northern Ireland. The Faber version pictures the neighbor as follows:

> Roadblocking the road,
> The rest of his staunch patrol
> In profile, sentry-loyal,
> Harassing Mulhollandstown.[87]

The earlier version of this poem contains a crucial difference from the later one: in it, the final line of the section quoted above is "Guarding Mulhollandstown."[88] The original word Heaney chose, "harassing," suggests the condition of Northern Ireland's Catholic minority before the law and is also redolent of the word's original meaning: "to attack or lay waste to." As with the two versions of "A Constable Calls," one version points more toward the police and militia being enforcers of the law, the other toward their being aggressors who acted in support of injustice.

There have been several instances in Heaney's career, as here, of his issuing poems in different versions for small-scale and widely circulated publications. However, what makes the instance quoted above different from earlier ones is that, in 2010, the more disaffected voice (the one that says "Harassing Mulhollandstown") is in the Faber-published version that is intended for wider circulation. This constitutes a reversal to what had been Heaney's practice for the best part of thirty years. Perhaps the advent of the peace initiatives that would result in the Good Friday Agreement of 1998, and the resumption of something closer to the operation of ordinary civil law in Northern Ireland, changed what Heaney could publish.

In his 2004 lecture "Title Deeds," Heaney explicitly connected the suicide in prison of Antigone, the heroine of his translated play *The Burial at Thebes*, with the deaths of the hunger strikers. In the same lecture he spoke of how making this connection between Northern Ireland and Thebes became his own authenticating "title deed" to the canonical work.[89] However, Heaney's version of *Antigone* confused audiences who may have thought that, in the Abbey, Ireland's national theater, *The Burial at Thebes* would be the de facto national poet's imprimatur on the ongoing Northern Irish peace process. Instead, at the end of the play, the audience witnessed the horrifying spectacle of the corpse of Antigone, who hangs herself in captivity, rising before them. A survey of contemporary reviews suggests that Heaney may have dashed critical expectations. Helen Meany, writing in the *Irish Times*, complained that "the setting and context are vague, contributing to a sense of dramatic vacuum." Neil

Corcoran wrote in the *Guardian* that "this version is less transparent to specific political instance than *The Cure at Troy*."[90] Critics and audiences in post-peace-process Dublin were, understandably, not thinking of the hunger strikers of the early 1980s when they came to the theater to see this play in 2004. However, as Heaney's poetry and prose works show, this period and these people were still much on his mind after the peace agreements. Peace in the political sphere is not necessarily reflected by similar conditions prevailing in the imagination; indeed, the opposite can be true.

At the end of his lecture "Title Deeds," Heaney rounded on the grotesque mistreatment of prisoners by the powerful that was one of the results of the West's "War on Terror" that followed the 9/11 attacks. He condemned the rush to "trample down human rights and civilized standards and international law, to perpetrate torture, to proceed with clandestine renditions, with the scandal of Guantanamo, the offences in Abu Ghraib, and a multitude of other locations."[91] Heaney's speaking out about these injustices against prisoners matches a statement he made in a 2008 piece for the *Irish Times*: "If we know the way society is unbalanced, we must do what we can to add weight to the lighter side of the scale."[92] For Heaney, as "New Worlds" shows, poets who were not troubled by injustice were not worthy of the name of poets at all. Throughout his life, Heaney's poetry responded in both apparent and less apparent ways to the administration of laws—particularly laws that regulated societies in ways that held the powerful to account or held violence in check.

The thaw in the politics of Northern Ireland after the peace agreements of the 1990s did not lead to Heaney forgetting the injustices that took place in the past in the name of keeping the peace and enforcing the law, but it did mean that he inflected his memories of them differently. Heaney's publication of a poem whose different versions show law-enforcement agents "guarding" and "harassing" his district is a suitable epitaph for his engagements with law enforcement in his work. From the anger of "The Road to Derry" to the whisper-quiet suggestion of disaffection at the "Death on the Rock" killings in "Squarings," Heaney addressed the state's role in violence in Northern Ireland with differing degrees of intensity and directness throughout his career. It was his way of living with the rival, incompatible, claims of multiple jurisdictions, including British, Irish, republican, and, above all, those of what he termed "the republic of conscience."

6

Legislators of the Unacknowledged

Paula Meehan and Paul Durcan

A statue of the Virgin Mary stands in a niche carved into the side of a rocky escarpment that rises at the edge of Granard, a small town in County Longford in the Irish midlands. This silent, isolated, object is given a voice by Paula Meehan in her poem "The Statue of the Virgin at Granard Speaks," in her 1991 collection, *The Man Who Was Marked by Winter.* When the statue speaks in the poem, it is to air a traumatic memory, as she laments her previous failure to say anything when she witnessed a terrible birth. At the point in her narration when she reaches this event, the poem's long lines shorten, as if indicating the difficulty of speaking about what she has seen:

> [. . .] though she cried out to me in extremis
> I did not move,
> I didn't lift a finger to help her,
> I didn't intercede with heaven,
> Nor whisper the charmed word in God's ear.[1]

As the poem's title and the above passage from it suggest, ideas of speech and silence are central to it. It has its origins in the fate of Ann Lovett, a teenager whose death, after she walked from her school and gave birth alone in front of a shrine on a wet afternoon in January 1984, became a cause célèbre in Ireland. In the public outcry that followed Lovett's death, the issue of speaking out became central. Though it was strongly disputed, several sources claimed that Lovett's pregnancy was known about in the town, but that no one had talked to her about it. An anonymous back-page piece in *Hot Press* in March 1984 linked Lovett's death to a wider societal tendency to stay quiet when faced with uncomfortable matters: "Everybody knew, but nobody did anything," the journalist wrote.[2] These words were echoed almost exactly in the refrain of a song Christy Moore released on an album in 1989, "Middle of the Island": "Everybody knew, nobody said."[3] It is unlikely that the *Hot Press* journalist had heard the song before writing the article: it was not released on an album until several years after the article was written. It is also unlikely that the song was inspired by the March *Hot Press* article: its lyrics indicate that it was written only a week after the tragedy, months before the article was published. Rather, the consonances between Moore's song, the *Hot Press* piece, and Meehan's poem suggest that the circumstances of Lovett's death awoke a general desire to trouble the depths beneath the placid surfaces of Ireland's silences. Though Meehan's poem focused on a single, imaginary, failure to speak out, it touched on matters of knowledge and silence that reverberated far beyond Granard.

This poem, which focuses on an agonized choice to remain silent in the face of a terrible reality, resonated strongly with the Irish public. This is attested to by Andrew Auge, who notes that it is "the Paula Meehan poem most familiar to the general reading public in Ireland" in a 2009 article.[4] Its status was confirmed in 2015, when it was one of ten poems short-listed in a vote organized by RTÉ to find Ireland's favorite poem of the past century.[5] Its impact might be related to its depiction of a strange contemporary phenomenon: in the summer of 1985, statues of the Virgin Mary were seen to move at various locations around the country. In an article on the moving statues, Karen Steele reports that those who witnessed the apparitions frequently interpreted what they saw as a sign of celestial distress or a warning over the direction the country was taking.[6] The legal controversies of the 1980s helped to stoke this sense of crisis: Auge wrote of how both Lovett's death and Meehan's poem were connected by readers with "the cultural crisis in 1980s Ireland occasioned by the fierce legislative battles that were fought over contraception, divorce and abortion."[7] Though the poem has been associated with legislation, its relationship to it is an implicit one: after all, no laws are mentioned in the poem, just as no laws were broken in the deaths at the poem's center.[8] Nevertheless, responses to Meehan's "The Statue of the Virgin at Granard Speaks" were, at some level, also responses to Ireland's laws.[9] The fact it was illegal to buy contraception without a prescription, and unconstitutional to obtain an abortion, had helped to force the things that could have saved Lovett's life beneath the surface of the sayable.

The 1980s was a decade of multiple crises in Ireland, both economic and social, and these factors forced reckonings that would not have been necessary in more settled times. Eavan Boland said the "Ireland of the eighties—the decade from which the poems in [Paula Meehan's] *The Man Who Was Marked by Winter* come—was a quicksand for a poet. No ground was safe; no assumption was solid."[10] During the 1980s the imagery of Ireland's most prominent poet, Seamus Heaney, changed radically, as the textures of the contemporary—with its aerosols, jumbo jets, punks, and rolling news coverage—made their way for the first time into his work.[11] Heaney also responded to the contemporary world in his public statements: he signaled his dissent from the direction the Constitution was taking in an open letter to the *Irish Times* in 1983. This was in response to the proposed Eighth Amendment, whose eventual passage into law reinforced the existing ban on abortion with a declaration of the equal right to life of fetuses and the people who carried them. Heaney, perhaps surprisingly for a poet who had written so frequently about his right to an Irish identity, wrote that the prospect of the outcome of a referendum made the possession of this identity less appealing. In the past, he wrote, he had been "embarrassed to be called British," but if "the proposed amendment to the Constitution is passed, a significant number of people from this State are likely to be even more embarrassed to be called Irish."[12]

This was far from the only legal or constitutional controversy of this decade in which a poet became publicly involved. Brendan Kennelly, interviewed in *Hot Press*, reflected on the 1984 Kerry Babies case as being "like some medieval witch-hunt with the victims burning at the stake and the crowd dancing around the fire," as the mistreatment of an unmarried woman by the police after the body of a baby was found highlighted the vulnerability of women in the legal system.[13] Ireland's poets, as Meehan's, Heaney's, and Kennelly's writings all show, often imagined and gave voice to lives outside the parameters of what was officially sanctioned.[14] During this decade, the country's law-enforcement agencies came under question as never before, and legal challenges and referendums made the constitution a battleground in which different visions of Ireland's future were fiercely contested.

Throughout the 1980s Paula Meehan's older contemporary Paul Durcan's poetry combined whimsy with an angrily countercultural position. Like much Irish poetry from this anxious and fractured time, his often has a dissonant, rebellious, offbeat feel. His collections written wholly or partly in the 1980s evince an anarchic style in which outrage toward the powers of Irish society, including those responsible for making and enforcing Ireland's laws, is a key element.[15] Perhaps his compulsive engagement with law can partially be explained by his personal circumstances: he is the son of a judge father and a mother who trained as a solicitor as well as the brother of two lawyers. He briefly studied law during his first, short-lived, stint at university.[16] The compulsive excoriation and ridiculing of the agents of the law in Durcan's poetry are matched by his urge to deform and reshape the fundamental constitutional documents of the state. A particular target of his satire has been Article 41 of the Irish Constitution, which holds that the state recognizes "the Family as the natural primary and fundamental unit group of Society."[17] In one of Durcan's poems, an imaginary judge opines that the television is the "basic unit" of the family. A woman who smashes it is, therefore, in one of Durcan's many courtroom scenes, dealt with harshly:

> Justice O'Brádaigh said wives who preferred bar-billiards to family television
> Were a threat to the family which was the basic unit of society
>
> As indeed the television itself could be said to be a basic unit of the family
> And when as in this case wives expressed their preference in forms of violence
> Jail was the only place for them. [. . .][18]

On first reading, this poem, in which a woman is jailed for damaging a domestic object, is ridiculous. However, reading this poem in conjunction with the Constitution suggests that the idea of unjust but legally sanctioned physical confinement for a woman was not so very fantastical. Article 41.2 of the Constitution states that "In particular, the State recognizes that by her life within the home, woman gives to the State a support without which the common good cannot be achieved."[19] Though some have argued that this is not prescriptive, legal scholar Yvonne Scannell writes how it was deployed by the Irish courts in ways that discouraged mothers from working outside the home, pointing to two cases in the 1980s in which Article 41.2 was used by the courts to justify tax discriminations against unmarried women and lower social welfare payments. Commenting on Article 41.2 (which follows on from the section of the Constitution that Durcan quotes), Scannell writes that it "can be rationalized by an attitude of romantic paternalism which, as a famous American judge has said, 'in practical effect puts women, not on a pedestal, but in a cage.'"[20] Durcan's poem shows the punitive confinement of a woman but, in doing so, draws attention to how physical limitations placed on women are enshrined in the legal foundations of the Irish state.[21]

Durcan's collection *The Berlin Wall Café* (1985) is highly engaged in developments in Irish law. In particular, the Eighth Amendment debates of 1983 made a deep impression on his work. The titles of the poems in this collection—including "Archbishop of Kerry to Have Abortion" and "Catholic Father Prays for His Daughter's Abortion"—indicate as much. In the second of these poems, Yeats's prayer for his daughter is referenced, but it is not for her future prosperity or beauty that the speaker prays. Rather, he asks that, if his daughter should for any reason dread the prospect of being a mother,

> I pray that she may find a nursing home
> Tended with compassion by nursing nuns
> In which she will be given the abortion that is her due.[22]

The end-stopped rhythms and tonal solemnity of this poem mimic features of prayer. The defiance of taking an activity associated with the church and using it to make a point so contrary to church teaching is in keeping with the disaffected tone of the volume, which contains some of Durcan's angriest political interventions. Part of his task as a poet is to delegitimate acknowledged powers.

Attention to the silent roles often played by women in Irish life is also central to Paula Meehan's poetry from the 1980s, as "The Statue of the Virgin" indicates. In 1983, the year before Meehan's first collection of poetry was published, only 11 percent of books published in Ireland were by women.[23] Meehan's first three collections, written in whole or in part in the 1980s, look deep into a hidden Ireland: the prisons of Northern Ireland and the Republic, heroin addiction, and domestic abuse all form part of her subject matter.[24] A decade younger than Durcan and educated partly in the United States, Meehan's cultural referents are different, and her poetry shows the influences of ecology and Buddhism to a greater extent than that of the elder poet. However, she shares many of Durcan's preoccupations, most notably with the lives of marginalized women. This ties in with an even more powerful preoccupation in her work: one with the working-class, inner-city Dublin of her childhood. From the time of Paula Meehan's first volume, *Return and No Blame* (1984), the vanished sights and sounds of this midcentury environment have provided some of the most vivid threads in the fabric of her work. In her 1980s volumes much of her poetry is set in the rain-swept streets of Dublin in the 1950s and 1960s. The sounds of children playing and street traders, conversations in tenements, the feel of tanners and florins, the smells of canals and of the river that pulses through Dublin's center all feature prominently.[25] In her early volumes she repeatedly focuses on the conditions and constraints of women's lives in this place, both in the present day and in previous decades. Although, as "The Statue of the Virgin" shows, her engagement with society is more elliptical than Durcan's satirical swipes, she shares with him a desire to search out the hidden places in Irish life. At times, this expresses itself as a search for how the country's founding documents can shape, or have failed to shape, everyday life at even the smallest scales.

In a 1998 interview, Meehan described how women had been granted an un-asked-for status as "icons" in the Irish state and said that the silence that was expected as part of this role was both subtly culturally conditioned and brutally enforced: "It is much handier to have the women as icons than to have to deal with the bleeding, emotional, living reality of the women in front of you. If you could just keep them behind their icons. [. . .] And if they step out, put them in the mental asylum, put them away, give them Valium. That's a much easier way to cope with the women. But they are also citizens of your country."[26] As discussed, Article 41.2 of the Irish Constitution describes a passive role for women within the home. Meehan's focus on women as "citizens" is, therefore, a more active one than the Constitution's idealization of women as wives and mothers. According to the *Oxford English Dictionary*, a citizen is a "legally recognized . . . national of a state . . . having certain rights, privileges, or duties."[27] However, the implications of this word, as Meehan recognizes, go beyond this definition. Both the notion of citizenship and the rights that come with it are particularly powerful ones in the Irish state's foundational documents. The Proclamation states that the "Republic guarantees religious and civil liberty, equal rights and equal opportunities to all its citizens," while the 1937 Constitution linked citizenship and speech, guaranteeing "the right of the citizens to express freely their convictions and opinions."[28] The disjunction between the interests of women and the roles that were expected of them had been addressed by feminist campaigners in Ireland during the 1970s: the Irish Women's Liberation Movement held consciousness-raising exercises in which women spoke about sex, childbirth, and other taboo subjects without being interrupted.[29] In a way, the speaker of "The Statue of the Virgin at Granard Speaks" engages in a form of this activity, giving voice to a previously undiscussed trauma. Meehan's poetry, like other feminist writing in Ireland at the time, drew attention to the fact that all citizens of Ireland, regardless of their sex, had the right to be heard.

Meehan's knowledge of Ireland's foundational documents, and what they represent, is evinced in her poetry. "Ard Fheis" (*The Man Who Was Marked By Winter*, 1991) is a poem that takes the imagery and rhetoric of a political party's annual gathering and intersperses it with the daydreams of a female delegate who, significantly, is disconnected from the proceedings. In this poem, the image of a copy of the Proclamation of 1916 that has been locked away in a "chilled vault" takes on a central importance. The poem's protagonist drifts off as the political speeches around her become "sub-melody, sonic undertow":

> The room pulses in, then out, of focus
> and all this talk of the people, of who we are,
> of what we need, is robbed of meaning[.][30]

The woozily drifting state that Meehan describes is not without political significance. In an interview, Meehan highlighted the gender politics that are present in this work, saying of it that "the poem is about a woman at a political meeting. While the men talk at this annual political meeting she is just dreaming away and goes through all her life, *her own life*, from school on. It is the men who talk. She is just dreaming away."[31] Daydreaming is what people do when they are not engaged in what is around them; it is what people do when no one is listening to them. The protagonist's account of being put into this fugue state by political statements about "what we need" is in itself a political statement. The powers in the land are named and enumerated in this poem too, imagined in a "cobwebby state, chilled vault / littered with our totems"; these totems include a "bloodstained Proclamation." This introduces an element of irony into the poem: this foundational document of the Irish Republic states that it was addressed to "all [Ireland's] men and women" and that it guarantees them "equal rights and equal opportunities." However, the poem indicates that this document has been banished to a cold subterranean afterlife in a "chilled vault," just as its ideals of equality were put on ice and replaced by dozens of measures that helped to drive women from public into exactly the kind of private, enclosed, life that the speaker experiences.[32]

If the Constitution is the blueprint for the official Ireland, the 1916 Proclamation that Meehan mentions in "Ard Fheis" has had a more ambiguous afterlife. The Proclamation was initially a symbol of rebellion and idealism but acquired an ambiguous role, both central and unfulfilled, in the Irish state established after 1922.[33] Its adoption by the Irish state makes it, to Durcan, part of the coercive apparatus of power. Its ideal of "cherishing all children of the nation equally" recurs in his poetry, often appearing to acidly satirical effect. One, a meditation on power relations and economic inequality, is accompanied by a negation of one of the Proclamation's central statements: to Durcan, Ireland is a country "where all the children of the nation / Are not cherished equally."[34] In another poem, a security guard who is invited to take off his uniform is asked, "do we not cherish all children of the nation equally?"[35] Durcan's approach to the established authority of the Proclamation has two very different effects: On the one hand, it is part of his postmodern emphasis on breaking down the kinds of grand narratives that the state exemplifies. On the other hand, the presence of the Proclamation in Durcan's imagination more than sixty years after its publication is a testament to this document's continuing power and the continuing hope of transformation that it symbolizes.

Throughout the 1980s Durcan frequently depicted an irresponsible legal system and a wronged but quiescent public in his poetry. He did this so obsessively that it is as if the Irish legal system came, for him, to symbolize all power imbalances and all injustice. A poem published in 1980, "This Week the Court Is Sleeping in Loughrea," begins with "perplexed defendants" watching helplessly from the dock as the court officials doze around them:

> solicitors in suits, and barristers in wigs and gowns,
> Snoring in their sleeves,
> Whilst, up on high, upon the judge's bench
> His lordship also snores[.][36]

In another poem from the same volume, a defendant is on trial for the circumstances of his conception. His barrister begs "My Lord, and Ladies & Gentlemen of the Jury, / I beg that you show clemency to / The boy who was conceived in the *leithreas*."[37] This poem—at a time when the sale of contraceptives had only just been legalized—seems to be a sharp comment on how matters of conception were of interest to the law.

Legal inquisitors appear so frequently in Durcan's poetry that when Derek Mahon came to write a friendly pastiche of his work, it naturally culminated with a courtroom scene.[38] His family connections to the legal system alone cannot explain why he devotes so much energy to making Ireland's legal authorities—legislators, judges, and policemen—look ridiculous.[39] As these lines suggest, his poetry has a strong anarchic streak, an overriding feeling that the powerful must be cut down to size. His long poem *Ark of the North* (1982) culminates with the cross-examining of "the Accused," described as "a selfconfessed hack and poet to boot" by a demonic counsel for the prosecution.[40] When it comes to earthly authority, of which courts are a powerful symbol for Durcan, poets are always on the wrong side: the unacknowledged criminals of the world.

Durcan was carrying on a long tradition of dissent by Irish twentieth-century poets, but he did so with the idiom and imagery of his time.[41] The punk sensibility, with its aggression, irony, and impatience with existing authorities, was pervasive. As Fintan O'Toole wrote, during the 1980s in Ireland, "tradition could be used only ironically."[42] This disaffected youth culture in rebellion against dominant societal powers is a central part of Durcan's *Jesus, Break His Fall* (1980), a volume named for a line in his elegy for Sid Vicious, or the titles of his poems, like "Fuckmuseum Constance" and "A Funk in Obelisk."[43] There is something of the formal dissonance of punk in Durcan's 1980s poetry. His poems from this time are studded with nonsensical tags and singsongy repetitions, lines go on too long and must be awkwardly accommodated on the page, poems come to an end midthought or midsentence, and it is clear that sense is not always the main concern. In one fairly typical poem the speaker advises the addressee as follows:

> [. . .] enroll in that university correspondence course in law
> And tort. I have always thought that tort is the sort of sport
> To interest a girl like you. [. . .][44]

Here, not just the agents of law but the study of law is seen as ridiculous, and the blunt rhymes suggest the silliness of the pursuit: "tort," "thought," "tort" (again), and "sport" are all in one line. It rhymes, but in the same way that the clang of a gate that is banging in the wind rhymes with the next clang. This characteristic technique contains humor, but a humor that is based in a kind of savagery. It is a blunt denial of the possibility of progress, a subsuming of meaning to the random chimes of words, a clangorous rejection of elegant shapes and euphonious sounds, a refusal, if not to make sense, then to *prioritize* sense. Anarchy, of course, is a mode of representation, but with its roots in the Greek for "without a ruler," it is a stance toward legal authority.[45] Poetry is an art form whose name derives from the Greek verb "to make," and its associations with creation link it to a desire to see something new and different in the world. Because of this, perhaps poetry is of necessity oppositional to the status quo. In any case, Durcan's anarchic imagery and forms are of a piece with the ridiculous courtroom scenes and kissing policemen that appear in his work from this time. His poetry is, in its form and subject matter, anarchy in the Republic of Ireland.

Durcan's poem "The Divorce Referendum, Ireland, 1986" registers his support for a constitutional amendment to remove the ban on divorce that had been enshrined in the 1937 Constitution.[46] The chief emotion of the poem, though, and one that links his aesthetic to Meehan's, is one of distressed silence. Divorce was on Durcan's mind before the referendum, a fact that can be seen in the notes toward his 1980 collection that are lodged in the National Library of Ireland. Scrawled on a piece of lined A4 in a file of notes are the words "New Book." There follows a short list of themes for *Jesus, Break His Fall*, among them "Marriage." The word that follows this is unclear, possibly "Chains"; the words after that are very clear: "& Divorce."[47] This is personal business: Durcan was himself to divorce four years after the appearance of this book.

"The Divorce Referendum, Ireland, 1986" is one of Durcan's most considered contributions to a legislative debate: draft after draft are filed in the National Library of Ireland. In it, the speaker listens in anger as a priest advises his flock on how to vote: "I could feel my breastplate tighten and my shoulderblades quiver." The language is one of violence: breastplate, blades, and quiver create an image of the poet going into battle. For all its belligerent imagery, though, the entire poem passes without its angry protagonist saying a word: he *imagines* reprimanding the priest and, seeing a child, silently wishes her "as many husbands as will praise her."[48] This is a report of an interior monologue: something felt and reasoned through in the mind and not spoken aloud, putting the speaker in the same category as the citizen who watches from the dock as the court sleeps around them in "This Week the Court Is Sleeping in Loughrea." This is a published poem: Durcan had more opportunity to speak out than most. However, what he is describing here is a cultural rather than a personal condition, as he calls into question the authority of those who are listened to and gives voice to one person—himself—whose opinions were, at least temporarily, concealed.

Ireland's laws on homosexual acts also engendered legal controversy in the 1980s. Homosexuality had long been a matter for silence, as the Offences against the Person Act of 1861 (inherited by the Irish state and retained after homosexual acts were decriminalized for men over the age of twenty-one in England and Wales in 1967) penalized sexual acts between men. This law was confirmed by two court cases in the early 1980s: first, the Irish Supreme Court threw out a legal challenge to the state's laws in 1980; then, in 1983, the High Court rejected a request for a declaration that the laws affecting relations between consenting adults were unconstitutional.[49] The Constitution was central to the outcome of these cases: in the second case, the court declared that laws "had existed for hundreds of years prohibiting unnatural sexual conduct which Christian teaching held to be gravely sinful," and judges cited the preamble to the Constitution that stated that Ireland was a Christian country.[50]

Durcan wrote a poem that protested both the application of law to private affections and the setting up of the sexual orientation of a majority as a universal standard. His poem "The Martyrdom of Saint Sebastian" is named for a saint who has traditionally been associated with homosexuality, but it also contains a nod to "Sebastian Melmoth," the pseudonym of Oscar Wilde during his postfall exile. Wilde's imprisonment, and the authority of the law, is represented through an image of the speaker's judge-father's locked bookcase:

> We dwell in a conspiracy of keys.
> I gawp through the panes at the spines
> Gazing out at me through their prison bars,
> Especially your own two heroes' spines,
> Oscar Wilde and Roger Casement[.][51]

The speaker does not just look at the books: the books gaze out at him, standing in silent judgment on the present. Wilde's situation was, of course, not of merely historical or literary interest at the time Durcan wrote his poem. The law that remained in force after the court cases of the early 1980s was the same one under which Oscar Wilde had been convicted in England almost a century earlier.[52]

Censorship, too, is an element of "The Martyrdom of Saint Sebastian," with its image of locked-away books. Though the Censorship of Publications Act of 1929 had been used to ban books by authors as diverse as Aldous Huxley and Edna O'Brien, by 1990 (when Durcan's poem was published) almost all of these bans had lapsed after a rule limiting bans to twelve years was introduced in 1967. Though the tide of censorship slackened in the 1980s, a book on Irish censorship that was published in 1990 noted that an "examination of the *Register of Prohibited Publications* for the past ten years suggests that books with a homosexual content have become a particular target of Irish censorship."[53] This is a feature of other poems by Durcan that center on issues of homosexuality: the same forces that compel silence are part of his poem "I Was a Twelve Year Old Homosexual" (*The Berlin Wall Café*, 1985). This poem recounts a very small-scale incident of censorship, as the speaker recalls that, as a child, his mother, father, and a priest talk him out of exchanging love notes with another boy in his school. The silencing of the speaker of "I Was a Twelve Year Old Homosexual" is paralleled by the locking away of Wilde's books in "The Martyrdom of Saint Sebastian." The reader is left with the impression that the "conspiracy of keys" in the latter poem is also a conspiracy of silence. This was a conspiracy that the penal code and censorship regime both strengthened.

The Northern Irish Troubles continued throughout the 1980s, and Paula Meehan's poems, from the time of her earliest published work, attest to the place of this conflict in her imagination. Meehan's "The Dark Twin" (*The Man Who Was Marked by Winter*, 1991) presents the reader with a strange yet eerily familiar land of dark uniforms and cocked rifles. In this land there is a stranger to whom the reader not only owes a mysterious moral obligation, but is actually closely related: "She is your dark twin. You know you must heal her / The burns from the bombings will ease as you rock her."[54] Meehan's poetry from these years not only frequently addresses Northern Irish violence, control, and surveillance, but also implicates the reader in it, suggesting that no border can be drawn between the individual and their wider situation.

Though the material of the conflict of Northern Ireland is visible in Meehan's 1980s volumes, the psychological world that they create relates to something closer to the home of the Dublin-dwelling poet. This much is evinced by "No Go Area," a dark and portentous fantasy that opens her 1985 volume, *Reading the Sky*:

> In the fifth zone
> it is all sex and experiments.
> Few ever go this far.
>
> In the sixth zone
> you might have trouble in the dark
> knowing if you are beast or offering.[55]

Though "No Go Area" takes its name from the nationalist areas of Northern Ireland in which paramilitaries had established de facto jurisdiction, and from which official law-enforcement agencies were excluded, there is more at work here than an evocation of the northern state. In "No Go Area," the references to sex, fear, and unequal power relations all suggest an atmosphere of secrecy and tension surrounding sexual matters that was prevalent throughout the island of Ireland. Meehan's poetry from these years is a stark testament to the presence of the Northern Irish security apparatus and penal system in the imaginations of citizens of the Republic. It also witnesses how this apparatus was translated into metaphors for issues that were closer to home. In this way, Northern Ireland, in Meehan's poetry, is the Republic's dark twin.[56]

In her first volume, the poem "Borders" focuses on tar, an evocative material in relation to Northern Ireland in more ways than one:

> The difference in a stretch of road,
> The colour of the tar
> Told what state had tarred it,
> Told us of borders
> And the wars between men.[57]

What Meehan's poem describes is how the surfaces of border roads, punctuated by stockades and haunted by soldiers, changed in appearance in the places where the Republic and Northern Ireland met. This was a subtle way in which this meeting point of the jurisdictions was marked: not only did road markings and signs change, but the new rhythm and sound of the road surface beneath the car's wheels let travelers know that they were entering a new jurisdiction. However, tar—a word that is repeated twice in this short poem—reminds the reader of another authority, as does the phrase the "wars between men." With these words, the tarring and feathering of victims of IRA punishments—often women whom they judged to have transgressed by having relationships with British soldiers—are summoned to the reader's imagination. This becomes, therefore, not just a poem about the jurisdiction of two states, but one about the "justice" administered by a third, unofficial, authority. This unofficial legal apparatus cast its shadows across the entire country, and these shadows are visible in Meehan's poetry.

After the declaration of the Republic of Ireland in 1949, "the Republic" kept a second meaning smoldering within it, referring to the unrealized state that encompasses the entire island. This ambiguity of jurisdiction, one of Durcan's poems suggests, makes Irish law a malleable, tenuous code. In one of the most sustained and shocking engagements with the idea of law in his poetry, "Poem Not Beginning with a Line from Pindar" (*Daddy, Daddy*, 1990), the speaker recalls his judge-father's response to the killing of ten Protestant workers by republican paramilitaries in 1976: "'Teach the Protestants a lesson.'" This is followed by a more mysterious statement: "'The law is the law and the law must take its course.'"[58] As critic Lucy Collins points out, this indicates an understanding of "law" that was often kept silent and interiorized or that was expressed only in familial and intimate contexts.[59] Durcan's quotation of a judge's seeming endorsement of an unlawful "law" suggests that, just as "Republic" had two meanings, "law" did as well. There is the law of the land that, as a judge, the speaker's father was tasked with upholding. This law, however, is not the law that the judge states "must take its course." Rather, he speaks of the law of historic cause and consequence: a consciousness of past wrong that demands present-day retributive action, in spite of its official illegality. This "law" is older than that of the Irish state and is analogous to the Old Testament's "an eye for an eye." The continued presence of this dark "law" in Ireland is illuminated in Durcan's poem.

Meehan's poetry about Northern Ireland is testament to the inextricability of events in the news from those in a citizen's inner life. The Troubles were exacerbated by the deaths of ten hunger strikers in the summer of 1981, and Meehan's poem "Hunger Strike" (*Reading the Sky*) begins with a description of the speaker's efforts to tend her garden, but rapidly becomes a meditation on how the face of Bobby Sands, the leader of the hunger strikers, haunted her.[60] In the case of Sands, the famous photograph of his face, smiling, casual, its blurriness an element of its homeliness, became visible all over Ireland during 1981 in newspapers, murals, and TV news reports as well as on posters and (as in her poem) protesters' placards. At the same time, the prisoners who slowly starved themselves behind the high walls of Northern Ireland's prisons took up residence in the country's imagination:

> At the G.P.O. a man held a blown up
> Photo of your face. It was the exact
> Same face that terrorized my childhood
> From the elevated altars of the poor.[61]

These lines suggest both the fear and the veneration that the stricken Sands provoked. The news from Northern Ireland helped to generate the mental weather for the South, and neither the border nor broadcasting laws prevented this shared psychic front from developing. This cross-border communication was one that the Irish state feared: cultural historian Terence Brown described the 1970s and early 1980s as a time during which the authorities of "the Republic of Ireland tended to hope that the Northern Irish problem could be isolated by a mental quarantine."[62] This effort at "mental quarantine" was augmented by Section 31 of the Broadcasting Act (1960), which was designed to forbid the words of paramilitaries and groups linked to them from being broadcast. However, the attempt to conceal information can have unintended consequences, drawing attention to what is muted. The preoccupations of Meehan's and Durcan's poems from these years attest to how central things can become when the law attempts to banish them to the periphery.

Durcan's dissent from his father's opinions matches his dissent from other areas of Irish life and laws that were older than he was. However, generational division is just one aspect of his poetry. Durcan's poem about a day in the early 1960s when his father bought him a copy of James Joyce's *Ulysses* gave him an opportunity to engage with the restrictions of a past Ireland, both legal and unofficial, and to reflect on how they changed. This poem has a much more playful, relaxed attitude to societal restrictions than many of his poems from this time. Part of the humor of the poem comes from the ambiguous legal position the book occupied in its author's homeland, as his father engages with the bookseller in Durcan's poem "Ulysses" (*Daddy, Daddy*, 1990):

> My father asks him if he would have brown paper
> With which to wrap the green, satanic novel,
> Make a parcel out of it.[63]

Ulysses was never banned in Ireland, but only because few bookshops ever attempted to sell it. Therefore, the moment in the poem at which the speaker's father drops his objections to the book and buys it is a strange one, where it is both purchased and hidden. *Ulysses* to Durcan is a symbol of humanistic understanding, and the description of it as a "satanic novel" has a contemporary resonance, as novelist Salman Rushdie lived in fear for his life after publishing the novel *The Satanic Verses* (1988).[64] The speaker later finds the book next to his father's bed, reporting that when "I got to reading *Ulysses* myself / I found it as strange as my father / And as discordant," neatly summing up his father's response to the book and his own response to his father. The poem becomes a hymn to a changing Ireland, showing the loopholes and gray areas of Irish life for better and worse. The moment of harmony and communion with the older generation that this poem celebrates hints at the possibility of a wider forgiveness and the role literature might play in it.

Paula Meehan's "The Pattern," too, suggests how a communion with an older Ireland, formed by a different legal code, might be achieved. In it the speaker pictures her mother polishing a floor: as she waxes and buffs, Meehan imagines her mother trying to catch a glimpse of herself in that gleaming surface: "I have her shrug and go on / knowing history has brought her to her knees."[65] The desire for self-discovery hovers in these lines, as do hints of how this can be thwarted through a confined location and the necessity of constant domestic labor. In spite of this knowledge of limitation, there is hope of change in the image of the children who crowd around the mother at the end, skidding on their socks on the polished floor "as planets / in an intricate orbit about her." In this image of children running rings around their mother, there is an indication of generational supersession.

This takes on a new resonance in the light of a 2008 interview in which Meehan spoke of new literature from Ireland as being one of the unintended consequences of the Secondary Education Act of 1966 from which she (born in 1955) benefited:

> I don't think this was an individual act; I think it was a collective energy bubbling up out of that moment when an underclass of writers who were enabled in childhood to have a middle-class education had taken those middle-class tools and used them to explicate, express, celebrate, critique, an undersong. [. . .] What you're seeing in the '90s is the full articulation of a process that began in the '60s with the free education act and the product of that. [. . .] Whether or not we liked the education, whether or not we used it as the original givers of the gift intended, our generation was enormously empowered.[66]

Legislative history both is a part of and creates history, as the values and ideals of a society are given expression in the rules that govern that society and help to form its future. Though Meehan's work often focuses on women's prisons (whether literal or domestic), it is also preoccupied with the means by which these prisons might be escaped. By the 1980s, not only was Meehan ready to write of the Ireland in which she lived, but as a result of the education laws of the 1960s, there was a newly expanded educated public ready to read what she had to say.

There would have been no unacknowledged world in Ireland in the 1980s had the laws of the land and the life lived within it been congruent: had all women worked in the home, had all marriages lasted forever, had no one been homosexual, had there been no sex outside marriage, had all pregnancies been both within marriage and wanted, had there been no doubt that Northern Ireland was governed justly. This was not the case, and, as a result, whole areas of life existed in shadow worlds. Ireland's laws and Constitution continued to promote a certain version of Irish life at the cost of driving those who did not conform to secrecy. This was the unacknowledged world to which Ireland's poets, including Meehan and Durcan, were drawn and gave expression. While both poets have different methods, a feature their poetry shares is that it constantly returns to those whose lives go unspoken and to what is hidden and underrepresented in the culture at large.

"Poets are the unacknowledged legislators of the world," wrote Shelley, but poet George Oppen corrected this in the 1970s: bearing in mind how poets wrote about hidden areas of life, putting into words what was overlooked because it was hitherto unnamed or undescribed, poets, he wrote, were "the legislators / of the unacknowledged."[67] These words contain a suggestion that poetry can be seen as a form of public utterance that is inherently *at variance* with existing law, a necessary counterbalance and a response to it. The truth of this is indicated by the powerful impact of Meehan's "The Statue of the Virgin," which questions a whole society's silence. Though its opening line acknowledges that "it can be bitter here at times like this," the poem, too, looks forward to a time when conditions might change: it contains the promise of coming spring as "the light swings longer with the sun's push north" and a vision of "riot in the hedgerows / of cow parsley and haw blossom."[68]

7

The Body of the Law in New Poetry

Elaine Feeney, Miriam Gamble, Julie Morrissy, and Doireann Ní Ghríofa

Globally, the most publicized story from Ireland in 2018 was the popular vote to repeal the Eighth Amendment of the Irish Constitution. This vote overturned a provision that had, since 1983, strengthened an existing ban on abortion by ascribing to "the unborn" an equal right to life to that of pregnant women.[1] The thirty-five-year movement that preceded the repeal of this amendment galvanized tens of thousands of marchers, with a demonstration in Dublin in March 2018 stretching for well over a kilometer through the city. Many of the slogans on the protesters' banners and placards were statements of rejection. Signs that read "I am not a vessel" were prominent, alongside ones that stated "I am not a walking womb" and "I am a woman not a womb." These slogans, with their insistence on bodily autonomy, and their assertions of what women were *not*, were the outward and visible sign of an inward and spiritual transformation. They communicated a powerful sense of a mass rejection by Irish women of the roles and expectations that had been projected onto them for generations.

The signs and banners the protesters carried indicated their rejection not just of a specific provision of the Constitution, but of a whole official view of women that had informed the state's legislation since its foundation. The ideals of womanhood and motherhood against which the marchers protested were, as I have written in previous chapters, in significant part encoded in and projected by the laws of the Irish state. The 1937 Irish Constitution, none of whose drafters were women, is extraordinarily prescriptive about women's lives.[2] Article 41.2.1 asserts that "by her life within the home, woman gives to the State a support without which the common good cannot be achieved." The next provision expresses a further aspiration that mothers "shall not be obliged by economic necessity to engage in labour to the neglect of their duties in the home." It is notable that the drafters of the Constitution use the word "woman" in its essentializing singular form and that they elide "woman" and "mother" in these two joined clauses. Historian Caitríona Beaumont tells of how, among the documents of Father John Charles McQuaid, one of Eamon de Valera's closest advisers, there is a paper titled "Rights of Women," which states with reference to the draft 1937 Constitution that "nothing will change in law and fact of nature that woman's natural sphere is in the home."[3] In accordance with this belief, the 1937 Constitution promoted certain restricted models of womanhood and, implicitly, devalued others. It was the sponsoring presence behind other legislation that kept women out of the public sphere. To give just a few examples, it justified the existence of the so-called marriage bar, a law that required women to give up most public service jobs on marriage; it was used to justify discrimination in social welfare payments, and it justified limitations on the ability of married women to sit on juries and stand for public office.[4] Irish women, regardless of their personal inclinations, were steered by the country's laws toward the roles of mother and wife.

From the early 1920s, the control of women's bodies animated much of the legislation of the new Free State. In short, there was an attempt to curtail life trajectories that involved ambitions beyond marriage and child care by law. Even before the ratification of the 1937 Constitution, with its notorious Article 41.2 that pronounced the place of women to be in the home, many laws were passed that had the effect of narrowing the choices available to women. For example, the censorship law that enabled the state to ban certain books was not without its gendered and embodied aspects: as

Beaumont notes, "amongst the books banned by the 1929 Censorship of Publications Act were *Family Limitation* (1914) by Margaret Sanger and *Wise Parenthood* (1922) by Marie Stopes." In 1934, the Criminal Law (Amendment) Act banned the importation and sale of birth-control devices. The 1936 Conditions of Employment Act "gave the Minister for Industry and Commerce the power to control and restrict the number of women working in any given industry."[5] Even if, to McQuaid and many of his generation, the home was women's "natural sphere," the Irish state nevertheless attempted to reinforce its confining power on women with its laws.

The poets whose work is the focus of this chapter—Miriam Gamble, Doireann Ní Ghríofa, Elaine Feeney, and Julie Morrissy—were born in the decade between the end of the 1970s and the end of the 1980s. They came to maturity at a time when laws that related to women's experiences and life trajectories in both Irish and Northern Irish jurisdictions were coming under question as never before. The atmosphere they breathed in their formative years had itself been forming for many decades. The introduction of free universal secondary education in the 1960s both expanded the number of politically active women and created new and receptive audiences for their ideas. The Irish Women's Liberation Movement, founded in the early 1970s, inspired later feminists with high-profile acts of resistance, like the illegal importation of contraception into the Republic on the May 1971 "Contraceptive Train."[6] The decline in the authority of the Irish Catholic Church, which had traditionally supported the idea that the domestic sphere was the natural one for women, also played a part in changing the tenor of the public discussion about women's lives as the twentieth century advanced. The decline in the church's authority was accompanied and hastened by multiple scandals, including ones relating to church-run industrial schools, Magdalene Laundries, and Mother and Baby Homes (which I discuss further in the conclusion in relation to the poetry of Kimberly Campanello). The stories of cruelty that emerged from these institutions contributed to anger at the hypocrisy of an organization that had, in the words of Fintan O'Toole, been "using a narrative of vulnerability to turn children and women into prey, purporting to protect children and women from danger while exposing them to it, and rendering them defenseless by removing them from social and legal supports in the name of defending them from spiritual threat."[7]

Twenty-first-century statistics evidence the transformative consequences of these years. In percentage terms, women's participation in the workforce increased tenfold between 1961 and 2009; a 2011 study found that more women than men were enrolling in third-level education.[8] The artists that are the subject of this chapter grew up in different parts of the island of Ireland, and their work encompasses a wide array of styles and standpoints. However, something that unites the work of all four is an imaginative process of rejection and reclamation.

The work of these poets echoes the challenging stances toward idealized images of womanhood that is such a prominent feature of the poetry of an earlier generation of poets, including Eavan Boland, Paula Meehan, and Mary O'Donnell. In the mid-1990s, Lia Mills pointed out in a powerful article for the *Feminist Review* that the "iconic feminine," that fusion of womanhood and nationhood, was coming under sustained critique by Irish women poets.[9] One example of this kind of writing is Eavan Boland's "Mise Eire" (*The Journey, and Other Poems*, 1987).[10] The speaker of this poem, who disrupts the *aisling* figure of nationalist poetry on whom she is based, begins: "I won't go back to it—." Similarly, in Boland's poem "Anna Liffey" (*In a Time of Violence*, 1994), named for the legendary female embodiment of the river that runs through Dublin, the poet again rejects mythical comparisons: "A river is not a woman," she writes at the poem's outset.[11]

Also in the 1990s, Paula Meehan, in the same spirit as the 2018 protesters, rejects comparisons with the kinds of patriarchal ideals women were expected to emulate in her poem "Not Your Muse" (*Pillow Talk*, 1994):

> I'm not your muse, not that creature in
> the painting, with the beautiful body,
> Venus on the half-shell [. . .][12]

A number of iconic images of women are rejected in these three short lines: muse, figure in a painting, Venus. A number of less exalted images are rejected at the same time: creature, body, oyster. In these assertions by the speaker of what she is not, Meehan creates a sort of anti-*aisling*, subverting a genre of Irish poetry in which a female personification of Ireland typically inspires a male poet with nationalist feeling.[13] Meehan knows, as the protesters who marched through Dublin did, that to be raised to an icon is inseparable from being reduced to a function.

Similarly, a series of poems by Mary O'Donnell in her 1993 collection, *Spiderwoman's Third Avenue Rhapsody*, radically reinterprets another mythical figure: that of Eve. "What gave them the idea / That I was spawned from a rib?" the speaker demands.[14] Later in the same sequence, in "Eve's Maternity," the act of giving birth is overshadowed by "scribbling old men / with scrolls and texts" who bear a strong resemblance to Ireland's predominantly male legislators:

> [. . .] in that moment
> when they split in her womb,
> two selves at war, the future
> disabled by scribbling old men
> with scrolls and texts,
> who would write that this was so,
> and that was so,
> *now and forever,*
> *until the end of time.*[15]

The "scrolls and texts" that these men write are like the myths of Eve and the *aisling*, and like the laws of Ireland: they efface women's lived experiences and impose a male-centered order and structure in their place. Irish women poets of the 1980s and 1990s sought to demolish the identities given to mythical women like Anna Liffey, Eve, Venus, and Kathleen Ní Houlihan and to replace them with ones that they themselves had fashioned.

This iconophobic approach, so visible in the 1990s, has been a strand in Irish writing since independence. It is the central theme of Dorothy Macardle's early short story "The Portrait of Roisin Dhu" (*Earth-Bound: Nine Stories of Ireland*, 1924). Macardle's reworking of Wilde's *The Picture of Dorian Gray* opens with a description of a supernaturally beautiful portrait of an Irish woman who has been painted by a man to represent "that wild, sweet holiness of Ireland for which men die."[16] As the story progresses, the reader learns that the painting's sitter was mysteriously drained of beauty and, ultimately, life as the portrait of her progressed and that she died at its completion. ("How unbeautiful!" the painter cries on seeing her dead body, in a further Wildean twist.)[17] Macardle, writing at the outset of the Irish Free State, was as aware as the women who followed her of the power of icons and idealizations to inhibit, disable, and drain.

As Claire Connolly has pointed out, "Ireland has long been imagined in terms of female images: Mother Ireland, wild Irish girl, gentle colleen, old hag, wise woman."[18] Perhaps in reaction to this trope, the poetry of many women from Ireland who have come to prominence since 1970 has featured a tendency to debunk and reclaim female icons.[19] The poetry of Boland, Meehan, and O'Donnell, especially in the 1990s, displays a tendency to break down existing images and to replace cloudy ideals aimed at nationalistic or religious cohesion with more variegated images that would reflect the complexities and contradictions of women's lived experiences. Late-1980s and 1990s poetry by Irish women introduced themes that can still be heard in the works of their successors decades later.

Unlike many earlier poets, Julie Morrissy is more interested in the legal mechanisms by which patriarchy is perpetuated than in the mythical figures that underwrote the patriarchal order. However, like these earlier poets, Morrissy in part achieves her effects by confronting and breaking up what is already there: she is a poet of montage and collage, reforming extant texts in order to symbolically break down existing authorities and create new forms. Her 2017 poem "Civil Regulations Amendment Act 1956: Retirement of Women Civil Servants on Marriage" is a highly critical response to the law from which it takes its name. It opens with a direct quotation of the decorous legalisms of Section 10 of the act for which it is named: "10 (1) Women holding positions in the Civil Service, other than positions which are declared excepted positions under subsection 2 of this section are required to retire on marriage."[20] The opening is as stark a rejection of the lyric form as it is possible to imagine, but found poetry, even if it is found in a statute book, is still poetry. In this case, it is found at the intersection where decades of ideologically motivated attempts to use the law to curtail women's actions meet the bland, bureaucratic formalisms of the Irish state. This poem is highly conscious of the legal disabilities that earlier generations of women in Ireland faced. Morrissy, a poet from Dublin whose legal training brought her a deep familiarity with the Constitution, is perhaps even more aware than her contemporaries of the provisions that sought to keep the home as the chief sphere of women's activities.

Morrissy's poem swiftly diverges from its source text. In the bricolage that follows, she splinters existing patterns of words and then re-forms them as a mosaic (see fig. 1). As critic Niamh O'Mahony has observed, this kind of collage work is widespread in the less known Irish experimental poetry tradition of which Morrissy is part.[21] It is also an approach with international precedents: here Morrissy is following the practice of the Tobago-born Canadian poet and former lawyer M. NourbeSe Philip. In her work *Zong!* (2008), a long poem that addresses the horrors of the slave trade in previous centuries, Philip restricts herself to the words used in a centuries-old legal text.[22] Philip uses only words from the surviving summary of the case *Gregson v. Gilbert* (1783), a case in which the plaintiffs sought to claim the insurance on slaves who had been thrown overboard and drowned by the crew when the ship on which they were being transported, the *Zong*, ran short of drinking water.[23]

hold women/position women/service women/other women/declare women/except women/require women/establish women/ retire women/ purpose women/section women

Source: Julie Morrissy, "Civil Regulations Amendment Act 1956: Retirement of Women Civil Servants on Marriage."

Philip's decision to "lock" herself into the store of words that is available in the legal summary reflects, in her words, the experiences of the "men, women and children [who] were locked in the holds of the slave ship *Zong*."[24] In Morrissy's work, like in Philip's, a legal text that is deeply imbued with prejudice and exploitation is reclaimed, and new patterns and resonances that were never intended by the authors of the original legal text are created. Smooth legalisms are ruffled and reshuffled into words of compulsion, exploitation, and objectification. Morrissy's work, by reproducing and recasting Ireland's former laws, acknowledges the weight that the past exerts on the present. However, the splintering effects of her collagistic style negate the power of the same weighty documents, symbolically rejecting and repealing them.

The significances of Morrissy's collage poem go beyond employment conditions: the prominence given to the words "section women" is significant. "Sectioning," a euphemism for detaining someone under mental health legislation, has a distinct place in women's history. As both pioneering feminist writer Betty Friedan and poet Paula Meehan have pointed out, women who were distressed or damaged by their experiences were often declared to be insane. Their legitimate troubles were translated into a vocabulary that made them subject to medical intervention, and the structural reasons for their distress were dismissed.[25] Morrissy's deployment of "/ section women" has still darker connotations. The words "section women" and, typographically, the slash that proceeds them suggest cutting. With reference to Irish women, this perhaps evokes, in a shadowy form, the symphysiotomy scandal. This was a procedure that widened the birth canals of women in labor and caused catastrophic long-term health problems for more than fifteen hundred women in Ireland.[26] These events might seem remote from the civil service legislation that gave rise to Morrissy's poem, but the "marriage bar" and symphysiotomy are linked. Both resulted from the kinds of unreflective objectification and instrumentalization of women that Morrissy's poem's staccato orders ("hold women/ position women/ service women/ other women") so chillingly raise.[27] Morrissy's work, by quoting, shredding, and rehashing legal texts, releases the latent energies in words and confronts the reader with the hidden histories that lie beneath the surfaces of Ireland's laws.

The wide popular appeal of the campaign to repeal the Eighth Amendment was linked to the fact that it was not just about abortion rights. The repeal campaign, like Morrissy's poem, was powered by memories of decades of women's legal exclusion from full societal participation and by a sense of having inherited a secondary status as citizens of Ireland. Even when times had moved on, memories of the diminishment of women's rights that were enshrined in the 1937 Constitution and in a host of other laws remained within touching distance in the memories of mothers and grandmothers. The recovery of this matrilineal inheritance is a preoccupation of the Galway-born poet Elaine Feeney, as can be seen in her poem "History Lesson" (*Rise*, 2017).

In this work, Feeney attempts to construct an alternative history to the male-centered narratives that she learned at school and, later, was expected to perpetuate in her job as a teacher. She achieves this through collagistic techniques that have affinities with Morrissy's, stitching together a poem from stories from the lives of the first-person speaker, from her mother, and from her grandmothers. Also like Morrissy, her work reveals a preoccupation with the legislative history that shaped and directed women's lives. Her mosaic approach gives rise to a contrapuntal, fragmentary history that collides with and challenges the instances of official history that pepper the narrative.

As in the poetry of Morrissy, the ways in which laws can classify and categorize are a strong theme in Feeney's work. Italicized lines announcing the passage of certain laws punctuate the poem like bulletins: "*In 1927 women are banned from sitting on juries in Ireland*," and "History lessons. *In 1935 contraception is banned in Ireland*." About two-thirds of the way into the poem, though, the "history lessons" that Feeney writes of touch on the speaker's own experiences of motherhood:

> In 2007 a doctor tells me I have a brain clot,
> I am pregnant, I ask him of the option of a termination.
> He tells me that I will change my mind when I am a mother.
> "I am a mother," I say.[28]

Though the Eighth Amendment purported to enshrine an equal right to life of the mother and the fetus she carried, it meant that women's lives were, in practice, often treated as being of secondary importance compared to the survival of their fetuses. The reader has been prepared for the above encounter with the doctor by the long contextualization that has preceded it. The speaker, who had worked as a history teacher, informs the reader that she had taught the history of the 1912 Ulster Covenant, the 1916 Rising, and the Irish Civil War. The doctor's dismissal of a woman's perspective on her own health and life has been licensed and made possible because women's experiences are, as the reader has learned, not taught as *history*. This exclusion from the narrative has led to the doctor in the poem, unconsciously, not taking the words, and hence the life, of a female patient seriously. Like Morrissy, Feeney highlights how the existence of laws that limit women's choices in one area is linked to all kinds of other diminishments and dangers.

The consequences of overlooking women's words and experiences are presented with unusual force in Feeney's poem. One stark line in Feeney's "History Lesson" reads "Savita Halappanavar dies in October 2012. I cannot stop crying." Halappanavar's name is a resonant one in recent Irish history: she was a thirty-one-year-old Indian dentist who died of avoidable complications relating to a septic miscarriage at University Hospital Galway. As philosophy lecturer Heike Felzmann writes, Halappanavar "was a healthy pregnant woman who had been diagnosed with an inevitable miscarriage at seventeen-weeks gestation, but was denied an early medical termination based on the Irish legal constraints regarding abortion. She died from sepsis that developed while she was waiting to deliver the fetus naturally (subsequent investigations into the case also highlighted substantial shortcomings in her medical care)."[29] As poet Doireann Ní Ghríofa, who has dedicated a poem to her, has stated, Halappanavar "was admitted to hospital while suffering a miscarriage, and despite her repeated requests to terminate her pregnancy, she was denied the procedure that would have saved her life."[30]

The public outcry that followed the death of Halappanavar provided the impetus behind the Protection of Life During Pregnancy Act of 2013. This was the first piece of legislation to outline mechanisms by which women could access abortion in Ireland. As legal scholar Fiona de Londras writes, this represented progress of a highly restricted character, only allowing for "abortion where there is a real and substantial risk to the life of the pregnant person."[31] In the legal history of Ireland, the date of Ní Ghríofa's poem's first publication—September 2013—is significant. It was published slightly more than two months after the signing into law of this act.

The case of Halappanavar resonates with Ní Ghríofa's work more widely: raised in a largely Irish-speaking environment in County Clare in the 1980s and 1990s, Ní Ghríofa is a poet whose works, taken together, form a highly articulate and intricate exploration of absences. Her poems often depict the traces that are left at cleared spaces and see them from unexpected and revelatory angles. "Waking" is set in a maternity ward, though Ní Ghríofa indicates in an interview that it is not an imagining of Halappanavar's last days, but a passionately recalled and transfigured memory of a painful moment in the poet's own life:[32]

> The procedure complete, I wake alone.
> The hospital sleeps. [. . .]
> [. . . .]
> I trace the wound and weep.
>
> The only sound I hear now
> is the retreat of a doctor's footsteps,
> echoing my heartbeat.[33]

Alienation rings through the sonic architecture of this poem: the beeps of machines and the sounds of footsteps are woven into its fabric, as echoes follow echoes: "complete," "sleeps," and "weep" are rounded out at the end by "The only sound I hear is the fading retreat / of a doctor's footsteps, echoing my heartbeat." The tracking of heartbeats is a central feature of this poem; it was also central to Halappanavar's tragic narrative in University Hospital Galway, as the detection of a fetal heartbeat meant that she was denied the treatment that might have saved her life.

This sad poem of miscarriage is also one, as Ní Ghríofa has said, that reflects "the sense of disorientation, loneliness and loss."[34] But there is a further emotional state that comes through strongly to the reader, one that resonates with the fate of Halappanavar: the overlooking and neglect of a female patient. From the loneliness of the speaker on waking up to the sound of retreating footsteps at the end, this is a poem of solitude in which the only person other than the speaker, a doctor, is depicted in the act of walking away. Like Feeney's "History Lesson," this poem carries a strong and chilling sense that Halappanavar's story might have been the speaker's own. In both poems hangs a strong sense of being medicalized and ignored.

The same themes that are found in the work of poets from the Republic have animated the work of women who grew up across the border in Northern Ireland. Miriam Gamble grew up in Belfast in the 1980s and 1990s, and her work combines an eye for the freakish amid the humdrum, an outsider's perspective that informs its thrusts of savage humor. The title of her collection *Pirate Music* (2014) suggests something rollicking and fantastical, but, as the back cover states, the collection in fact "takes its title from unlicensed broadcasting." The question of who is licensed to be heard, and of who has permission to speak, is a recurrent one in this collection. A poem prompted by a speech-recognition machine's failure to understand the speaker's Northern Irish slant on the English language ends, "I swear, Your Honour, it isn't coming from me."[35] This poem, titled "Misrecognition," contains a double pun: in her failure to pronounce a sentence in a form that is acceptable to a machine, she appeals to an imaginary judge whose job it is to pronounce a sentence. In another poem, an incompetent riding instructor is obeyed because "the man's word on all things equine is law."[36] This collection is shot through with a sense that there is legitimate and illegitimate speech and of there being words that, by virtue of the sex of their speaker or the accent in which they are spoken, carry weight and words that do not. In these regards, Gamble shares themes and preoccupations with her contemporaries from across the island of Ireland.

The recurrent idea of being observed and dictated to by the law surfaces in the poem "Bodies" (*Pirate Music*, 2014). Ostensibly about horse riding, it soon settles on ideas of the law that suggest that the horse is an allegory for experiences that are not solely equine. The horse, we are told, must learn

> to take a contact on the mouth
> that's light but present, like the watchful eye of the law
> when one is a fundamentally law-abiding citizen.[37]

The horse learning about the limitations of its world and the forces that govern its actions is joined in a simile to the person who must learn to live under "the watchful eye of the law." This juxtaposition is a telling one, in that it suggests that the law, like the horse's rider, aims to reduce a powerful and potentially dangerous being into something biddable and useful. This poem can be read in light of the fact that the Abortion Act of 1967, which legalized abortion under a large number of circumstances in the rest of the United Kingdom, did not apply to Northern Ireland. This meant that, until October 2019, the Offences against the Person Act of 1861, under which carrying out an abortion was a criminal offense with a potential sentence of life imprisonment, was left in force.[38] Gamble grew up while this law was in operation; she also grew up in Belfast during the Troubles. There were few places on earth where the eye of the law was more watchful.[39] At the time this poem was written, the law, which had so assiduously watched the movements of Northern Ireland's disaffected citizenry while Gamble was growing up, now watched and policed women's choices.

A further layer is added to the poem in the next lines, which at first glance seem to signify a shift in preoccupations. The poem takes a turn for the strange, as it morphs into a reflection on the song "Bodies" by the Sex Pistols, several lyrics from which Gamble quotes. The Sex Pistols song from which the poem takes its name contains the words "She was a girl from Birmingham / She just had an abortion," before the roared chorus "Body! I'm not an animal!"[40] In the poem, in which the speaker remembers herself singing along to this song, her sense of liberation in singing along with the record is iconoclastic, drawing its disruptive energy from punk music. The cry of "I'm not an animal!" reflects the same rejective energies that animated the marchers against the Eighth Amendment in the years around the time this poem was written.

Poet Paula Meehan and critic Patricia Boyle Haberstroh have both warned of the potential hazards in attempting to look at women's poetry as a distinct phenomenon. Haberstroh writes that "women poets in Ireland share many of the themes, strategies and settings with all poets; one need not necessarily use the qualifying adjective 'women' to consider or judge them as poets."[41] These are cautionary words for anyone who seeks to write a chapter that deals only with poets who are women and a reminder that any attempt to critique a set of ideas runs the risk of unconsciously reinforcing these same ideas. Furthermore, looking at poems that respond directly or indirectly to laws relating to women is to select a single strand in a rich and varied tapestry. However, this approach is perhaps justified by the fact that women have, in Ireland, historically been subject to different laws than men.[42]

The legal changes regarding abortion that were ratified in 2018 in Ireland and in Northern Ireland in 2019 occurred as a result of women seeing themselves differently, reimagining their own lives, and assuming new possibilities for themselves. This meant not only rejecting the narratives and ideas than had been created for them in earlier times, but also inventing new ones to take their place. A sense of the necessity of renewal, and also of the excitement and urgency of these new ideas, is strongly depicted in and engendered by Ní Ghríofa's "Birthburst" (*Clasp*, 2015).

"Birthburst" celebrates a moment of liberation, a change of state and of status, whereby a girl is born and, also, just perhaps, a woman is reborn. Certainly, it is hard to tell which person the pronoun "her" belongs to in this work:

> many months, to float in warmth
> womb-wet swell
> stirred with each murmur of her world
> until
> surges
> stir
>
> Now   the caesarean slice
>   Now   mother's girl-cries
>   Now   the hospital light[43]

This poem of birth is a poem of "now," the word repeated eight times, insisting on contemporaneity and immediacy. Each "Now" is also a movement in time, as processes get under way and develop, each "Now" moving further toward the right-hand margin, reflecting both the progress of the baby toward birth and also containing hints of the possibility of other changes as well.

By its end this poem verges on the edge of becoming concrete poetry; the shape it traces is an upward trajectory, tumbling and roiling before tapering to a summit on the singular sliver of the free-floating "I."

> so now I must become
> I,
> I am,
> I.[44]

The culmination on the poem on the personal pronoun is significant. Physically, the column of letter *I*s resembles the row of stitches that seals the incision after a caesarean birth. The word "I" at this point in the poem might be the baby, separated and individuated, its cord cut. However, it also suggests a reclaiming of the subjective point of view, a confident claim on one's own life and story.

The "I am" that comes at the end of the poem is the opposite of the statements of rejection, the "I am not" that was such a prominent feature of the protesters' banners in 2018, yet this positive assertion seems contingent on rejections like these. A pivotal line in this poem is "so now I must become." It is not a poem of enclosure within a category, but one of finding oneself in a new mode of being. The Constitution had sought to limit women; the tone and form of this poem suggest that not just a new life but a new era is in the process of being born. Coming from the years that preceded the repeal of the Eighth Amendment, this poem reads as a premonitory work—a powerfully articulated dream of the possibility, in all senses, of a changed state.

Conclusion

Contending Remembrances

This book began with Seamus Heaney imagining a jail-breaking poet in his poem "The Unacknowledged Legislator's Dream" (*North*, 1975). In picturing his poet protagonist sinking his crowbar into the walls of "the Bastille," there was irony, of course: here was a master of what Yeats called the "sedentary trade" of poetry highlighting the limitations, not to say the ridiculousness, of a poet considering the use of force. But in among the drafts, there were crossings-out and reformulations that indicated that Heaney was aware of the power of invoking, even in an ostensibly lighthearted poem, the state's jealously guarded role of enforcing the law, punishing wrongdoing, and promoting justice.

In imagining himself taking a crowbar to a prison, Heaney was playing with ideas of challenging one of the defining characteristics of the state: its monopoly on the use of force. This doctrine was influentially propounded in Thomas Hobbes's *Leviathan* (1651), which insisted on a state monopoly on force as a bulwark against "the condition of meer Nature, and of warre of every one against his neighbour."[1] To Max Weber, centuries later, the monopoly of force was constitutive of the state's legitimacy. In his 1918 lecture "Politics as a Vocation," Weber stated that "one can define the modern state sociologically only in terms of the specific means peculiar to it [. . .], namely, the use of physical force."[2] When Heaney pictured his protagonist with crowbar in hand, he was actually playing, however whimsically, with ideas of delegitimization.

The modern state rhetorically yokes together the institutions by which it administers law and the idea of justice. Both the Irish and the UK government departments responsible for the administration of courts and prisons are called the "Ministry of Justice," and in both countries senior judiciary are given the title "Justice." These are the linguistic means by which the transcendent quality and the earthly apparatus are attempted to be made equivalent. The state has good reason to attempt this linkage: influential American philosopher John Rawls described the promotion of justice as "the first virtue of social institutions" and a precondition for their continued existence. "Laws and institutions no matter how efficient and well-arranged," Rawls writes, "must be reformed or abolished if they are unjust."[3] The apparatus of the state that manages and administers its courts and prisons must do a great deal if it is to live up to its name.

There are those, including Rawls himself, who would contend that the power of the state obviates its ability to be an agent of justice.[4] In the words of philosopher Simone Weil, justice is "that fugitive from the camp of conquerors," a condition that is easily subject to the downward gravitational pull exerted by earthly power.[5] Seen from a perspective that is suspicious of the motivations of the powerful, poetry, by its ability to record and remember what "conquerors" find uncomfortable or would rather forget, can be an agent of justice in ways that perhaps a state cannot. In Ireland, for reasons that extend from its history of governance and popular memory, the suspicion that justice and the law are fundamentally at odds is never far beneath the surface.

"Writer and Righter" was the title of a speech that Seamus Heaney gave to the Irish Human Rights Commission in 2009. In it, he circumspectly addresses the delicate lines of connection between the shared social world of courts and statutes and the more interior dynamics of reading literature. Several times during this speech Heaney yokes together the words "memory and conscience," including in this closing declaration: "An artist whose work is capable of entering the place of ultimate suffering and decision in his or her own being will bring readers to a realization of that same stratum of humanity in themselves. The work will strike them, as John Keats said poetry should strike its readers, as a remembrance, and as it begins its obscure pilgrimage through memory and conscience, the human condition will be registered at a private personal level, yet the experience will involve a sense of common human belonging."[6] Poetry, to Heaney, does not necessarily promise to endorse the shared societal values that are ostensibly encoded in laws but, rather, can give access down to a shared stratum of humanity. In Heaney's vision, words are arks or time capsules; they are able to create structuring forms that might be resilient enough to endure the erosive qualities of the passage of time. By presenting something as a poem, one of the things a writer is asking is that a reader keep it in mind, make it a part of their memories. Poems are, as Keats said, a "remembrance"; they are small wars with forgetfulness.

The law, like poetry, can be a powerful engine of collective memory. The authors of a 2007 review article titled "Law and Collective Memory," following Émile Durkheim, observe that "law is an especially powerful institution for the creation of collective memory because it involves highly effective rituals."[7] The words that are in laws, court judgments, and constitutions, by their very presence in these things, all partake in the power of ritual; the words that constitute them are intended to be launched into the future where they might linger, haunt, and be drawn on as part of an accretive process of precedent and tradition.[8] Both laws and poetry are forms of remembrance, and it seems natural, even inevitable, that these sources of memory might not easily align with each other.

Poems might hold things of which the state might, through intention or obliviousness, lose sight. In this book I have explored how this dialectical relationship has been a consistent theme in Irish poetry since partition and the foundation of an Irish state. Yeats's protest at the "neglect" of "monuments of unageing intellect" in the first stanza of *The Tower* is akin to his Senate speeches arguing for the preservation and protection of the artifacts in the National Museum, the inheritance of the Irish language, and much else. In the late 1920s Austin Clarke's *Pilgrimage* stood as a vision of what Ireland might be again if it revived its artistic inheritances and sloughed off its state-sponsored moral authoritarianism. The work of Rhoda Coghill, a much more neglected Irish poet, with its "criminal" chestnut tree and its robin whose song contends with the voice of a priest, subtly, subversively, suggests a remade role for women in the jurisdiction. Coghill's spirits of the hilltop and greenwood remind us that, beyond the imaginings of legislators and the drafts of constitutions, there are potent modes of being and forms of expression beyond ones that are officially sanctioned.

More recent poets have inherited these approaches. Thomas Kinsella's voice in the middle of the twentieth century, amid the bright, inflationary language of the state's economic plans, is a monitory one. Do not forget, it seems to say, that in the heart of the independent Ireland is a dark machinery that was forged in a very different time. Seamus Heaney's works can be seen as part of a lifelong attempt to create an alternative space, an imaginative structure that both recognizes and is not bound by inherited limitations. In the 1980s, Paula Meehan and Paul Durcan both drew on the words of the state's foundational documents to deeply ironic effect, as promises of gender equality and cherishing all children of the nation equally went unfulfilled. In the last chapter of this book I discuss how contemporary poetry by Irish women often draws on similarly iconoclastic energies to those of their 1980s predecessors and how, through their works, the occluded elements of women's existences are spoken of, remembered, and passed forward in time to future readers.

Looking back over the century of poetry that I have explored while writing this book, it is hard to avoid the conclusion that the desire to create a counternarrative to the stories and norms instituted by constitutional provisions, court judgments, and official laws has been a consistent impetus behind the publication of poetry on the island of Ireland. The relationship between poetry and law in modern Ireland has been dynamic because it has been so often contestatory. The positive declarations of law create narratives, and these narratives, of necessity, create absences that invite counterspeech. The creation of a pale provokes imaginative people to ask what might lie beyond that pale. This is all to say that poetry can be a place to remember what the state would rather was forgotten.[9]

In 2019 poet Kimberly Campanello published *MOTHERBABYHOME*, a monumental work of 796 transparent vellum pages held in a small oak box. The writing on these pages cannot be read in a conventional manner: overwritings, deletions, and repetitions place these pages partway between literature and visual art. The number of pages in this work, which the author describes as a "'report' comprised of conceptual and visual poetry," is significant: it is the number of children who are recorded to have died at the Saint Mary's Mother and Baby Home in Tuam, County Galway, which was run by the Bon Secours Sisters.[10] This was an institution for unmarried mothers and their children that existed between 1925 and 1961. The infant mortality rate at "homes" of this kind was estimated to be exceptionally high: around 15 percent; at Tuam, the death rate was double this. Many of the children at Tuam were buried without coffins. On each page of *MOTHERBABYHOME* is the name of a child who died at this institution, their date of death, and the age at which they died. The fact that a small, simple wooden box is part of this poetry-object is a reminder of the decent treatment that these children's remains were not afforded.

MOTHERBABYHOME parallels and shadows the report of a government-initiated commission of investigation. In 2014, as a result of the public pressure that was instigated by investigations by the historian Catherine Corless, the Irish government convened a commission of investigation into eighteen of these "homes." As well as the extraordinary death rates at these institutions, the commission considered the mistreatment of their inmates, commercial medical trials that took place without parental consent, and allegations of forced adoptions. The commission's report, published in early 2021, immediately incited controversy. Legal academic Máiréad Enright enumerated the inconsistencies, irregularities, self-contradictions, and methodological shortcomings of the report, while many criticized Taoiseach Micheál Martin's statement that the whole of society, rather than the religious orders who ran the "homes," or the state that empowered them to do so, was to blame for what happened there.[11]

MOTHERBABYHOME may be in some ways restitutive, something that supplies in belated shadow form some of the rites that the children who died at the institution in Tuam were denied. Poet and critic Ailbhe Darcy has speculated on this in an illuminating article that addresses a recording of Campanello's three-hour durational performance of the poem: "I wonder if Campanello is offering us another kind of ritual in the shape of her poem and its performance," she writes.[12] In the wake of the publication of the commission's 2021 report, the issue of recordings themselves took on a central significance. Further outcry was occasioned by news of the erasure of hundreds of recordings of witness testimony and the government's plans for legislation that would the exclude the institutions' mass burial sites from the jurisdiction of a coroner.[13] The government also planned that, once the agency overseeing exhumations and identifications was dissolved, their documents and records would be sealed for thirty years.[14] Though the government justified its actions and plans in part on the grounds of protecting survivor anonymity, there was a grim and widespread suspicion that the Irish state was trying to enforce forgetfulness.

In January 2021, Campanello posted a tweet that read "MOTHERBABYHOME is a report. [. . .] It draws entirely different conclusions from the Commission's report." In thinking of her work in this way, Campanello is writing in a tradition that is influenced by Thomas Kinsella's *Butcher's Dozen*, which itself was a kind of dissenting report on a legal report.[15] In an interview, Kinsella outlined the common areas of concern of poetry and the law in ways that are germane to Campanello's work: "the subject matter is not different," he said;

both poetry and law are concerned with "opposing troubled parties, death, current concerns rooted in the past."[16] The past endures in legal reports, in court transcripts, and in the whole apparatus of the state-sanctioned legal system.[17] Legal documents are exercises in the creation of collective memories: it is no wonder that the quality of remembrance that inheres in poetry and in laws is so often at odds. As Campanello's *MOTHERBABYHOME* reminds us, though poems can never substitute for legal scrutiny, or replace the need for the pursuit of justice by a legal system, we should nevertheless not underestimate what they can do. They are spaces that exist outside the narratives, and therefore the elisions and erasures, of the state. Indeed, as is the case in Campanello's poetry-object, they can enact new forms in which these elisions and erasures become visible. In this way, poems can be, in the words of John Keats that Seamus Heaney quoted in "Writer and Righter," "a remembrance."

Notes

Bibliography

Index

Notes

Introduction

1. A draft manuscript titled "The Unacknowledged Legislator," published in amended form as "The Unacknowledged Legislator's Dream," in Seamus Heaney, *North*, 56.

2. A banner urging the destruction of "the Irish Bastille" was flown by volunteers during a march in Belfast on July 14, 1792, according to Jennifer Orr in *Literary Networks and Dissenting Print Culture in Romantic-Period Ireland.* Marion Green records that "the remand prisoners in Crumlin Road Prison labeled it "the Bastille of Belfast" because of the inhuman and degrading conditions." Green, *The Prison Experience: A Loyalist Perspective*, 16.

3. Internment began on August 9, 1971. See the CAIN database, "Internment: A Chronology of the Main Events," www.cain.ulst.ac.uk/events/intern/chron.htm.

4. I am indebted for the information in this paragraph to Mary Clancy's essay "Aspects of Women's Contribution to the Oireachtas Debate in the Irish Free State, 1922–37"; and Yvonne Scannell's essay "The Constitution and the Role of Women," both in *The Irish Women's History Reader*, ed. Alan Hayes and Diane Urquhart.

5. Kathy D'Arcy and Lucy Collins have done a great deal to bring the poetry of Coghill and other midcentury women out of the library stacks and back toward the light. See in particular Collins's anthology *Poetry by Women in Ireland: A Critical Anthology, 1870–1970.*

6. This phrase is attributed to Oliver St. John Gogarty. Declan Kiberd, "Irish Literature and Irish History," 230–31.

7. The words from the *Freeman's Journal* are quoted in Bernard G. Krimm, *W. B. Yeats and the Emergence of the Irish Free State, 1918–1939: Living in the Explosion*, 60.

8. Yeats quoted in R. F. Foster, *W. B. Yeats: A Life*, 2:209.

9. Danny Morrison, "Seamus Heaney."

10. This occurred in 2010, when Heaney was invited to run by Irish political party Fine Gael. See Justine McCarthy, "No President Heaney," *Sunday Times*,

Mar. 20, 2011. The former deputy first minister of Northern Ireland Martin McGuinness also wrote poetry.

11. Enda Kenny quoted in Roger Pearson, *Unacknowledged Legislators: The Poet as Lawgiver in Post-revolutionary France*, 1.

12. Thomas Bartlett, *Ireland: A History*, 1.

13. This poem was popularized by Robert Graves in *The White Goddess: A Historical Grammar of Poetic Myth*, 9. It is quoted by Paul Muldoon in To Ireland, I, 4. Additional information on Amergin comes from Peter Kavanagh, ed., *Irish Mythology: A Dictionary*, s.v. "Amergin"; and James MacKillop, ed., *Dictionary of Celtic Mythology*, s.v. "Amairgin."

14. Laurie L. Patton, "Space and Time in the 'Immacallam in dá Thuarad,'" 92.

15. Muldoon, *To Ireland*, I, 4.

16. The significance of poets in early Ireland is the reason that much of the recent scholarship on law and literature in Ireland has focused on the medieval period. See, for example, the essays on Ireland in Joseph F. Eska, ed., *Literature, Law and Society.*

17. Fergus Kelly, *A Guide to Early Irish Law*, 47. Laurence Ginnell wrote of how Old Irish laws were in verse as a means of memorization and transmission in his *Handbook of Brehon Law*, 78. See also Noelle Higgins, "The Lost Legal System: Pre–Common Law Ireland and the Brehon Law."

18. Eric Falci notes that the early Irish poets were, among other things, "historians, judges, political operatives." Falci, *Continuity and Change in Irish Poetry, 1966–2010*, 10.

19. Fourteenth-century chronicler Jean Froissart records that, contrary to English custom, Irish kings allowed their "minstrels" to eat at the highest table. Froissart, *The Chronicles of Froissart: Translated by John Bourchier, Lord Berners*, n.p.

20. Michèle Lowrie, Writing, *Performance, and Authority in Augustan Rome*, 327.

21. Thomas C. Grey, *The Wallace Stevens Case: Law and the Practice of Poetry*, 15.

22. Pearson, *Unacknowledged Legislators.*

23. Benjamin N. Cardozo, *The Growth of the Law*, 89. I am grateful to Eugene McNulty for bringing this passage to my attention. Here, as elsewhere, ellipses in square brackets indicate that I have omitted words from the quotation.

24. Books that stress the educative function of law and literature studies include James Boyd White's *The Legal Imagination* and Ian Ward's *Law and Literature: Possibilities and Perspectives.* Richard Posner, who has been so influential in this field, discusses the salutary power of Yeats's vivid, arresting language in

several places, including in *Law and Literature: Being the Fifth John Maurice Kelly Memorial Lecture*. Martha Nussbaum's *Poetic Justice: The Literary Imagination and Public Life* focuses on the necessity of the reintegration of law, founded on rational principles of political economy, with imaginative literature, arguing that the humanities, true to their name, can humanize the social sciences.

25. Northrop Frye, "Literature and the Law (1970)," quoted by C. R. B. Dunlop in "Literature Studies in Law Schools," 77–78. Again, I am grateful to Eugene McNulty for bringing this passage to my attention.

26. The idea that literature and law find their common ground in "the social imagination" is explored in Kieran Dolin's introduction to *Law and Literature*.

27. Jahan Ramazani, *Poetry and Its Others: News, Prayer, Song and the Dialogue of Genres*, 59. Ramazani also states that the links between poetry and law can be taken too far: whereas laws should ideally aim at clarity, the effects of poems are often achieved by other means. The links between poems and laws are also explored in Edward J. Eberle and Bernhard Grossfeld, "Law and Poetry."

28. Richard Posner, too, elaborates on this idea in *Law and Literature: A Misunderstood Relation*, 2.

29. These ideas are explored in Richard H. Weisberg's *The Failure of the Word: The Protagonist as Lawyer in Modern Fiction*, 5; and by Peter Lin in "Wittgenstein, Language and Legal Theorizing: Toward a Non-reductive Account of Law."

30. Lon L. Fuller, *The Morality of Law*, 39–40. I am grateful to Patrick O'Callaghan for bringing Fuller's work to my attention.

31. Michael Brown and Seán Patrick Dolan, eds., *The Laws and Other Legalities of Ireland, 1689–1850*, 20.

32. Heather Laird has written of this historic clash of jurisdictions in *Subversive Law in Ireland: From "Unwritten Law" to the Dáil Courts*, 12ff.

33. This tradition of Irish poems includes Fear Dorcha Ó Mealláin's "Exodus to Connacht," which laments the victims of a 1652 act to dispossess the British Parliament's defeated enemies who lived east of the Shannon. Seán Ó Tuama and Thomas Kinsella, eds., *An Duanaire, 1600–1900: Poems of the Dispossessed*, 103–9.

34. Eibhlín Dhubh Ní Chonaill, "Caoineadh Airt Uí Laoghaire" / "Lament for Art Ó Laoghaire."

35. Ní Chonaill, "Caoineadh Airt Uí Laoghaire" / "Lament for Art Ó Laoghaire," 219.

36. Declan Kiberd, *Irish Classics*, 49–54. Daniel Corkery also writes of courts of poetry in *The Hidden Ireland: A Study of Gaelic Munster in the Eighteenth Century*, 98.

37. Notable explorations of the contentious status of official law in colonial Ireland include Charles Townsend's *Political Violence in Ireland: Government*

and Resistance since 1848, Heather Laird's *Subversive Law*, and Joseph Brooker's "'Estopped by Grand Playsaunce': Flann O'Brien's Post-colonial Lore," 17.

38. Theo Dorgan, "Law, Poetry and the Republic," 184.

39. Anthony Cronin, *The End of the Modern World*, 18.

40. John Hewitt, "The Colony," in *Collected Poems*, 76–79.

41. Donoghue quoted in Richard Rankin Russell, *Poetry and Peace: Michael Longley, Seamus Heaney and Northern Ireland*, 1.

42. The early formation of Yeats's aesthetic by the work of his nationalist predecessors has been anatomized by R. F. Foster in his essay "Oisin Comes Home: Yeats as Inheritor," *Words Alone: Yeats and His Inheritances*, 129–73.

43. W. B. Yeats, "To Ireland in the Coming Times," in *Collected Poems of W. B. Yeats*, 46.

44. Alex Davis and Lee M. Jenkins have drawn attention to the destabilizing effects on poetry of the "linguistic turn" in philosophy at the outset of the twentieth century in their introduction to their edited volume *A History of Modernist Poetry*, 8. See also Margaret Drabble, *The Oxford Companion to English Literature*, s.v. "modernism."

45. Nicholas Allen discusses the simultaneous appearance of the high point of literary modernism in English and of the two Irish states in *Modernism, Ireland and Civil War*, 8. Joe Cleary also discusses this phenomenon in *The Cambridge Companion to Irish Modernism*, 4.

46. This section on postmodernism is indebted to the discussion of the term in Andrew Bennett and Nicholas Royle, *An Introduction to Literature, Criticism and Theory*, 248–57.

47. Muldoon, *To Ireland, I*, 6ff.

48. Patrick Kavanagh, "Epic," in *Collected Poems* (2004), 184.

49. Colin Graham, *Ideologies of Epic: Nation, Empire, and Victorian Epic Poetry*, 13–14.

50. Patrick Kavanagh, "The Hero," *Collected Poems* (2004), 196.

51. Derek Mahon, "The Last of the Fire Kings," in *The Snow Party*, 9; Paul Muldoon, "Lunch with Pancho Villa," in *Mules*, 12. In the early 1970s, Michael Longley pictured his first-person speaker dicing with death, piloting a "rickety biplane" under the Arc de Triomphe in "Ars Poetica" (*Man Lying on a Wall*, 1976), collected in *Collected Poems*, 109.

52. Heaney acknowledged the pressure of these expectations in other ways. Remembering the years during which he wrote "The Unacknowledged Legislator's Dream," he wrote of "pivoting his understanding in an attempt to bear his portion of the weight of the world." Seamus Heaney, "Crediting Poetry," in *Opened Ground: Poems, 1966–1996*, 458.

53. Brice Dickson, *The European Convention on Human Rights and the Conflict in Northern Ireland*, 53.

54. Dickson, *European Convention on Human Rights*, 54. See also Clive Walker, *Terrorism and the Law*, 203ff.

55. Heaney, *North*, 56

56. Laura McAtackney, *Archaeology of the Troubles: The Dark Heritage of Long Kesh / Maze Prison*, 16. Marion Green's *Prison Experience* reproduces loyalist documents referring to Long Kesh's "compounds" (12).

57. Heaney, "Christmas, 1971," in "Belfast," in *Preoccupations: Selected Prose, 1968–1978*, 30.

58. Jean Allain and Siobhán Mullally, eds., *The Irish Yearbook of International Law, 2007*, 28; Dickson, *European Convention on Human Rights*, 146ff. Descriptions of the interrogation techniques can be found in Donald W. Jackson, *The United Kingdom Confronts the European Convention on Human Rights*, 37ff.

59. Heaney remarked in an interview that he "liked the flightiness" of the piece. This intensely revised draft now lodged in the National Library of Ireland shows how hard-won this "flightiness" was. See Heaney to Dennis O'Driscoll in Stepping Stones: Interviews with Seamus Heaney, 181.

60. W. H. Auden, "Writing," in *The Dyer's Hand, and Other Essays*, 27. Auden's comment is in the same spirit in which Geoffrey Hill later warned that "poets are not legislators unless they happen to be so employed." Hill, "Our Word Is Our Bond," in *Collected Critical Writings*, 169. It is interesting to note that Hill later repudiated his own words as "mean and impoverished" in a lecture, "Milton as Muse."

61. Fiona McCann has written about poetry by women republican prisoners in "Writing by and about Republican Women Prisoners: 'Willful Subjects.'"

62. There are enlightening discussions of the semantic complications in describing the jurisdictions of the island of Ireland in both Conor Cruise O'Brien's *States of Ireland*, 103; and the introduction to Ray Ryan, ed., *Writing in the Irish Republic: Literature, Culture, Politics, 1949–99*, 2ff.

63. Bobby Sands, "The Rhythm of Time," in *Prison Poems*, 82.

64. Eugene McNulty, "Law in Contemporary Anglophone Literature," 223.

65. Ian Ward paraphrases Richard Rorty's contention that poets are the heroes of democracy owing to their ability to communicate with the future. Ward, *Law and Literature*, 13.

66. Percy Bysshe Shelley, "A Defence of Poetry (1821)," 850.

67. Alexander Martin Freeman claims Peacock's essay is a misunderstood joke in *Thomas Love Peacock: A Critical Study*, 277. I have drawn on the overview of the dispute between Peacock and Shelley in Pearson, *Unacknowledged Legislators*, 9ff.

68. William Godwin, *Life of Geoffrey Chaucer, the Early English Poet*, 1:370.

69. Rhoda Coghill, *The Bright Hillside*, 9.

70. R. F. Foster outlines these initiatives in *Modern Ireland: 1600–1972*, 578–80.

71. Miriam Gamble, "Bodies," in *Pirate Music*, 60.

1. The New Laws of the 1920s

1. W. B. Yeats, *The Senate Speeches of W. B. Yeats*, 127. Though Yeats's idea was voted down, the Irish government later selected robes for office that Yeats had been instrumental in having designed (132).

2. Yeats quoted by Sir John Keane in *Senate Speeches*, 129.

3. W. B. Yeats, *The Variorum Edition of the Poems of W. B. Yeats*, 408.

4. This information is from the section of the Yeats exhibition at the National Library of Ireland titled "Poetry in Progress: Building *The Tower*."

5. I address Yeats's Senate contributions on divorce and primary education later in this chapter and his Senate agitation against censorship in the chapter on Austin Clarke. Yeats's most forthright statements on censorship were aired not in his Senate speeches but in his article "The Irish Censorship," which he published in the *Spectator* on September 28, 1928, and which is collected in his *Later Articles and Reviews: Uncollected Articles, Reviews and Radio Broadcasts Written after 1900*, vol. 10 of *The Collected Works of W. B. Yeats*, 214–18.

6. W. B. Yeats to Olivia Shakespear, June 28 [1923], uncollected letter, available at CL InteLex 4342.

7. Yeats gave this famous speech on June 11, 1925 (*Senate Speeches*, 99). Yeats versified some of the ideas from this speech in his poem "The Three Monuments," in *Variorum Edition of the Poems*, 460.

8. Yeats's Senate record shows that he spoke on the preservation of ancient monuments on August 3, 1923 (*Senate Speeches*, 56), and June 10, 1925 (88), and on the protection of more modern buildings (including the old parliament building in College Green, the Four Courts, and the Royal Hospital, Kilmainham) on March 15, 1923 (36); July 11, 1923 (53); and May 1, 1924 (66). In addition to these speeches, Yeats made a number of speeches on fire precautions at the National Museum, which I discuss later in this chapter.

9. Yeats, *Senate Speeches*.

10. This debate is set out in Philip O'Leary, *The Prose Literature of the Gaelic Revival, 1881–1921: Ideology and Innovation*.

11. The preservation of monuments from heedless encroachments or neglect was also a matter of personal interest to Yeats during his years in the Senate, engaged as he was in restoring a medieval tower near Coole Park in County Galway.

12. Yeats, *Variorum Edition of the Poems*, 407.

13. Yeats, *Senate Speeches*, 88.

14. Yeats, *Variorum Edition of the Poems*, 415.

15. Yeats, "Lapis Lazuli," in *Variorum Edition of the Poems*, 565.

16. These were, to use Yeats's terms, primary and antithetical gyres. See *A Vision: The Original 1925 Version*, 13ff.

17. Yeats, *Senate Speeches*, 125.

18. These are recorded in the *Senate Speeches*, respectively, on 61, 33, 54, and 60.

19. Yeats, "The Song of the Happy Shepherd," in *Variorum Edition of the Poems*, 65. The idea that lawyers are vain and more concerned with self-advancement than justice has a long pedigree in English poetry. It goes back at least as far as Chaucer's Sergeant of the Lawe, whose "fees and robes" are the most remarkable things about him (*The Canterbury Tales*, 28).

20. W. B. Yeats, *The Variorum Edition of the Plays of W. B. Yeats*, 259.

21. Yeats, *Variorum Edition of the Plays*, 483.

22. W. B. Yeats, "Samhain: 1904: First Principles," in *Explorations*, 141–63. Yeats discusses the legal frustrations that accompanied his theater work in another piece, "Samhain: 1904: The Dramatic Movement," in *Explorations*, 124–40. I am grateful to Hugh Haughton for drawing these essays to my attention.

23. Yeats and Lady Augusta Gregory had to deal with a law that permitted performances in Dublin only in the three existing large theaters; intervention was needed by W. E. H. Lecky to amend the law. W. N. Osborough in *The Irish Stage: A Legal History*, 117. Christopher Morash writes of legal travails that attended the foundation of the Abbey Theatre and, later, the legal "game of bluff and brinksmanship" that surrounded the Abbey's production of G. B. Shaw's *The Shewing-Up of Blanco Posnet* in 1909 (*A History of Irish Theatre*, 116, 144).

24. Yeats read the *Transactions of the Ossianic Society for the Year 1857*, ed. Owen Connellan. The introduction states that Amergin, the first bard, was appointed by the Milesians to a role in "their government of this country" (xvi). It also states that laws were taught "through the medium of poetry" and quotes historian Geoffrey Keating in saying that Old Irish laws "were poetical compositions, and set to music" (xx).

25. Lady Francesca Speranza Wilde, *Ancient Legends, Mystic Charms, and Superstitions of Ireland*, 159–63; Edwin J. Ellis, *Sancan the Bard*.

26. Yeats's marked-up copy of "A Defence of Poetry" is held in the Yeats Library at the National Library of Ireland.

27. Something stronger than a suspicion of lawyers is given notable expression in Yeats's friend William Morris's prose work *A Dream of John Ball*, which appeared in the journal *Commonweal* in late 1886 and early 1887. A character refers to "some accursed lawyer with his false lying sheepskin and forged custom."

Morris, *"A Dream of John Ball" and "The King's Lesson."* Yeats was friendly with Morris at the time this story was first published. Foster, *W. B. Yeats: A Life*, 1:66ff.

28. Alvin Jackson, *Home Rule: An Irish History, 1800–2000*, 183. The prime minister at the time, Lloyd George, denied that there was a link between the introduction of Home Rule and conscription. See *Hansard*, April 9, 1918, http://hansard.millbanksystems.com/commons/1918/apr/09/home-rule-bill.

29. Krimm, *Yeats and the Emergence of the Irish Free State*, 10.

30. Yeats, *Variorum Edition of the Poems*, 328.

31. Heroes of Yeats's who rejected popular approval included J. M. Synge and Charles Stewart Parnell. Others members of Yeats's pantheon acted in deliberate defiance of the law, like John O'Leary, Oscar Wilde, and Roger Casement.

32. In Stephen Maxfield Parrish and James Allan Painter's edited *A Concordance of the Poems of W. B. Yeats*, the section under "law" shows twelve entries, fully three-quarters of which are framed negatively. Three of these negative references are from poems written between the years 1918 and 1921.

33. Townsend, *Political Violence in Ireland*, 350.

34. Yeats, *Variorum Edition of the Poems*, 791.

35. This is shown in the parliamentary records for the days between November 17 and 25, 1920, "Hansard, 1803–2005."

36. Foster, *W. B. Yeats: A Life*, 2:196.

37. Yeats, *Variorum Edition of the Poems*, 428.

38. Quoted in Foster, *W. B. Yeats: A Life*, 2:188.

39. Quoted in Krimm, *Yeats and the Emergence of the Irish Free State*, 55. Yeats was not the only unlikely person to endorse the justice of the Dáil Courts at around this time. In July 1920 Lord Dunraven paid tribute to their ability to administer "justice promptly and equably." Laird, *Subversive Law*, 124.

40. Mary Kotsonouris has written a history of these courts, *Retreat from Revolution: The Dáil Courts, 1920–24*. Heather Laird writes about the establishment and structure of the Dáil Court system in *Subversive Law*, 124–28.

41. Michael Wood, *Yeats and Violence*, 161.

42. Cited in Foster, *W. B. Yeats: A Life*, 2:206.

43. This is set out in Gemma Clark, *Everyday Violence in the Irish Civil War.*

44. Yeats's close encounters with violence and the destruction of the other senators' houses are described in Foster, *W. B. Yeats: A Life*, 2:230.

45. Yeats, *Variorum Edition of the Poems*, 430.

46. Yeats, *Variorum Edition of the Poems*, 425, 438.

47. Yeats's *Senate Speeches* record speeches on the risk of fire on four occasions: June 4, 1924 (67); June 19, 1924 (77); and twice on July 16, 1924 (82, 85). These include an extraordinary passage from a speech in which he repeats the words "fireproof door" five times in the space of a single paragraph (84).

48. Yeats, *Variorum Edition of the Plays*, 775.

49. Yeats, *Variorum Edition of the Plays*, 1044.

50. Osborough explores this comparison in *Irish Stage.*

51. Yeats, *Variorum Edition of the Plays*, 426.

52. Elizabeth Cullingford, "How Jacques Molay Got Up the Tower: Yeats and the Irish Civil War."

53. Yeats, *Variorum Edition of the Poems*, 475, 476.

54. Yeats, *Variorum Edition of the Poems*, 634.

55. Reiner Stach, *Kafka: The Decisive Years.*

56. The poem "The New Faces" (*Variorum Edition of the Poems*, 435) is given this date. Chronologically, this poem is very much an outlier: the next oldest poems in the collection are from 1917. From the display "Poetry in Progress: Building *The Tower*," in the Yeats exhibition, National Library of Ireland.

57. Niall Whelehan, "The Irish Revolution, 1912–23," 621.

58. Yeats, *Variorum Edition of the Poems*, 431.

59. At the time Yeats was coming to maturity in the late 1880s, there was a very real impetus to revive the ancient memories of Old Irish law as well as literature. As well as reading about it in the *Proceedings of the Ossianic Society for 1857*, Yeats also would have come across these ideas in Sophie Bryant's *Celtic Ireland*, which he reviewed. In this book, Bryant presented law and literature as central to life in Celtic Ireland (x, 144). At the center of this law-and-literature-loving society was the bard: "The bard is in the place of honour higher than the warrior, and he has a definite duty to the society that supports and honours him" (xi). Ronald Schuchard reiterated these points in 2008, writing that Yeats had an "intuitive awareness of the bardic poet's responsibility to the imaginative and aesthetic life of his culture and of his essential role in creating the images, shaping the values and restoring the dignity of a beleaguered nation." Schuchard, *The Last Minstrels: Yeats and the Revival of the Bardic Arts*, xxi.

60. Krimm, *Yeats and the Emergence of the Irish Free State*, 60.

61. Yeats, *Variorum Edition of the Plays*, 259.

62. Yeats, *Variorum Edition of the Poems*, 427.

63. Yeats, "Compulsory Gaelic," in *Collected Works of Yeats*, 10:176.

64. Yeats, *Collected Works of Yeats*, 10:231.

65. The distinction of being the first person to quote a poem in the Senate did not, therefore, belong to Senator Sir John Keane when arguing with Yeats over judges' costumes but, rather, belonged to Yeats himself.

66. Yeats, *Senate Speeches*, 89.

67. Yeats, *Senate Speeches*, 89.

68. Senate Proceedings for June 10, 1925, available at http://debates.oireachtas.ie/Senate/1925/06/10/printall.asp.

69. Philip L. Marcus takes this view in *Yeats and Artistic Power*, 134, as does Geraldine Higgins in *Heroic Revivals from Carlyle to Yeats*, 146. Marcus's view that he quoted these lines to disparage them is, however, unlikely. He earlier described them as "the Gaelic lyric come close to perfection" (*Collected Works of Yeats*, 9:282). In the early 1920s Yeats recorded that "after five and twenty years I continually murmur to myself [Rolleston's] lyric, 'In the quiet watered land, a land of roses.'" W. B. Yeats, *Memoirs: Autobiography, First Draft Journal*, 51.

70. Yeats to Edmund Dulac, January 28, 1924, uncollected letter, available at CL InteLex 4462.

71. Yeats, *Senate Speeches*, 63–64. Yeats made similar points on a speech on the stained-glass industry (80–81).

72. W. B. Yeats, *Collected Works of Yeats*, 5:46.

73. Yeats recollected in his essay "If I Were Four-and-Twenty" that "one day when I was twenty-three or twenty-four this sentence seemed to form in my head, without my willing it, much as sentences form when we are half-asleep: 'Hammer your thoughts into unity.' For days I could think of nothing else, and for years I tested all I did by that sentence." Yeats, *Collected Works of Yeats*, 5:34.

74. Yeats, *Autobiographies*, 167–68.

75. Yeats, *A Vision* (1925), 159.

76. In "Four Years: 1887–1891," an autobiographical work first published in 1922, Yeats recalled how "I wished for a world where I could discover the tradition" of "an almost infallible Church of poetic tradition" all around him, "not in pictures and in poems only, but in tiles round the chimney-piece and in the hangings that kept out the draught." Yeats, *Autobiographies*, 115.

77. This idea was prompted by a comment by Alex Davis, whose generous help with this chapter I gratefully acknowledge.

78. Yeats, *Variorum Edition of the Poems*, 443.

79. Yeats, *Variorum Edition of the Poems*, 443.

80. Maura O'Connor writes of the educational debates in the early Free State in "The Theories on Infant Pedagogy of Dr. Timothy Corcoran, Professor of Education, University College, Dublin."

81. Yeats, *Senate Speeches*, 96ff.

82. Yeats, *Senate Speeches*, 34.

83. Yeats, *Variorum Edition of the Poems*, 424.

2. Jurisdictions of the Past

1. Austin Clarke, *Pilgrimage, and Other Poems*, 45. "Parliament passes laws against temptations" was an uncanny turn of phrase: just three years later, his

novel *The Bright Temptation* (1932) would be banned by the board that was appointed under the 1929 censorship legislation.

2. Quoted in Terence Brown, *Ireland: A Social and Cultural History, 1922–2002*, 30.

3. The Censorship of Publications Act of 1929 was described in its headnote as "an Act to make provision for the prohibition of the sale and distribution of unwholesome literature." www.irishstatutebook.ie/eli/1929/act/21/enacted/en/print. Francis Hutton-Williams makes a convincing case for the idea that censorship was imposed with a high degree of popular support. Hutton-Williams "Against Irish Modernism: Towards an Analysis of Experimental Irish Poetry."

4. John Goodby makes this point in *Irish Poetry since 1950: From Stillness into History*, 19. Lucy Collins also makes this observation in the introduction to *Poetry by Women in Ireland*, 39.

5. Clarke, "The Young Woman of Beare," in *Pilgrimage, and Other Poems*, 33.

6. Warwick Gould, "'Satan, Satan Smut & Co': Yeats and the Suppression of Evil Literature in the Early Years of the Free State," 200.

7. Clarke, "The Young Woman of Beare," in *Pilgrimage, and Other Poems*, 33.

8. The reference to the "President of Munster" places the poem in sixteenth- or seventeenth-century Ireland.

9. Eiléan Ní Chuilleanáin, in her article "The Ages of a Woman and the Middle Ages," describes the speaker of the original Old Irish poem as "a human creature who accepts time and age, who asserts the splendour of the past and refuses to be sorry for the pleasures she knew then" (199). Robert Welch uses the Cailleach as the organizing principle of his study of Irish literature since the earliest times. Welch, *The Cold of May Day Monday: An Approach to Irish Literary History.*

10. Augustine Martin, "The Rediscovery of Austin Clarke," in *Bearing Witness: Essays on Anglo-Irish Literature*, 172. This theme has also been pursued by W. J. McCormack in "The Poet as Scapegoat of Modernism," 77.

11. Heather Laird, "Law, Colonialism and Anti-colonial Resistance." Text kindly provided by the author.

12. James C. Meredith, "Desirable Ameliorations of the Law." I am grateful to Heather Laird for bringing this article to my attention.

13. Clarke, "Pilgrimage," in *Pilgrimage, and Other Poems*, 9.

14. W. B. Yeats, *A Critical Edition of Yeats's "A Vision" (1925)*, 190.

15. Frank Leslie Cross and Elizabeth A. Livingstone, eds., *The Oxford Dictionary of the Christian Church*, s.v. "Celtic Churches."

16. This term is what Austin Clarke uses in the notes to *Later Poems* (1961), reprinted in *Collected Poems* (1974), 545. Though he characterized it as his "Celtic

Romanesque" volume, in fact, as Maurice Harmon points out in *Austin Clarke, 1896–1974: A Critical Introduction*, just five of the poems are set recognizably in this world: "Pilgrimage," "Celibacy," "The Confession of Queen Gormlai," "The Scholar," and "The Cardplayer" (60). However, because the poems set in this world include the title poem, and because it is such a short volume, these five do much to give the whole work its tone.

17. Tessa Garton, "Masks and Monsters: Some Recurring Themes in Irish Romanesque Sculpture."

18. John McAuliffe is an exception to a critical tendency to associate Clarke with insularity; he illuminatingly internationalizes Clarke's technical innovations in *Pilgrimage* by comparing them to Pound's Provençal metrical experiments in "Against Irish Studies: Reading Austin Clarke and His Critics," 256.

19. Austin Clarke, *The Bright Temptation: A Romance*, 2.

20. *Saorstát Eireann Irish Free State Official Handbook* (Dublin: Talbot Press, 1932).

21. Clarke, "Love in Irish Poetry and Drama" (1932), quoted by John Goodby in "From Irish Mode to Modernisation," 28.

22. Clarke, "Pilgrimage," in *Pilgrimage, and Other Poems*, 9.

23. W. B. Yeats, *Oxford Book of Modern Verse, 1892–1935*, xxxvi. Edna Longley points out that the earliest of his own poems that he includes are from 1913. Longley, *Yeats and Modern Poetry*, 35.

24. Yeats referred to Clarke in a 1932 letter as "as it were part of my propaganda." Quoted in Kit Fryatt, *Austin Clarke*, 13.

25. Samuel Beckett, "Recent Irish Poetry," 72–73. Beckett later satirized Clarke through the characters of "Austin Ticklepenny" and the catatonic "Clarke" in his novel *Murphy* (1938).

26. Patrick Kavanagh, "The Paddiad," in *Collected Poems* (1984), 90.

27. Clarke wrote about his "interest in the Celtic-Romanesque period" in relation to his schooling in "The Black Church," 226. He writes of his discussions with F. R. Higgins in *A Penny in the Clouds: More Memories of Ireland and England*, 17.

28. Clarke, *Collected Poems* (1974), 545.

29. The designs of the 1908–15 editions of Clarke's school magazine the *Belvederian* are heavily influenced by Celtic religious art. The summer 1908 edition contains, among other things, a vividly imagined article called "A North Dublin School in the Ninth Century" (26–32).

30. Clarke wrote in a letter to Augustine Martin that he wished "we had a small church here as in Brittany, but we seem to have taken over, since the establishment of the Republic, the imperial and evangelical spirit of the British race." Augustine Martin, "The Rediscovery of Austin Clarke," in *Bearing Witness*, 176.

31. J. J. Lee has written of how William Cosgrave's first minister for education, Eoin MacNeill, "believed that the early Christian period, when 'the Irish were the schoolmasters of Europe,' was the greatest in Irish history." Lee, *Ireland, 1912–1985: Politics and Society*, 129.

32. Austin Clarke, "Pilgrimage," in *Pilgrimage, and Other Poems*, 10.

33. Clarke, "Pilgrimage," in *Pilgrimage, and Other Poems*, 11.

34. Fryatt, *Austin Clarke*, 9.

35. Chrystel Hug, *The Politics of Sexual Morality in Ireland*, 12–15.

36. R. F. Foster records the debates that surrounded the banning of divorce in *W. B. Yeats: A Life*, 2:296.

37. Clarke, "The Confession of Queen Gormlai," in *Pilgrimage, and Other Poems*, 16.

38. Clarke, "The Confession of Queen Gormlai," in *Pilgrimage, and Other Poems,* 16. The same queen is the subject of Clarke's novel *The Singing Men at Cashel* (1936), which was banned. Maurice Harmon writes of the life of Queen Gormlai in *Austin Clarke*, 67.

39. This aspect of Gaelic society was understood at the time Clarke was writing. Laurence Ginnell had commented on the ease of divorce in ancient Ireland in his *Handbook of Brehon Law*, 212.

40. In her paper "Law, Colonialism and Anti-colonial Resistance in Ireland," Heather Laird points out that "under the Brehon laws, a wife could divorce a husband who was, for example, infertile, impotent or obese. Moreover, she could divorce a husband who committed certain acts against her, such as slandering her, ridiculing her, beating her so as to leave a mark, or abandoning her for another woman." Peter Kuch shows in *Joyce's Ulysses / Irish Divorce* that divorce was a realistic option for Irish people from many backgrounds into the early twentieth century.

41. Lucy Collins writes of the Committee of Enquiry in *Poetry by Women in Ireland*, 39.

42. The page on which this provision appears in Yeats's copy of this act, held in the National Library of Ireland, has its corner folded down. Yeats quoted from the same page in the Senate on March 11, 1927. Yeats, *Senate Speeches*, 136.

43. Yeats, *Senate Speeches*, 132, 136, 144, 145.

44. Adrian Hardiman discusses common-law notions of decency in *Joyce in Court*, 248.

45. Seán O'Faoláin, "The Dangers of Censorship" (1936), 91.

46. Yeats, "The Irish Censorship," in *Collected Works of Yeats*, 10:215.

47. E. Longley, *Yeats and Modern Poetry*, 23.

48. Austin Clarke, "Banned Books" (1953), 123.

49. Mary Colum, *Life and the Dream*, 122.

50. Seán O'Faoláin, *Vive Moi! An Autobiography*, 270.

51. T. Brown, *Ireland, 1922–2002*, 155.

52. Clarke, *Collected Poems* (1936), 56.

53. Colm Campbell, *Emergency Law in Ireland, 1918–1925*, 167.

54. Among these collections set in pagan Irish prehistory, *The Fires of Baal* (1921) stands out for being set outside Ireland. Even in this Old Testament setting, however, the links to Ireland are obvious: the poem centers on a chosen people finally coming to their promised land.

55. Clarke, "The Pedlar," *The Cattledrive in Connaught, and Other Poems*, 18.

56. Alan Gillis suggests that the way in which Tara is blown away in "The Pedlar" in *The Cattledrive in Connaught* shows Clarke's ambivalence toward the new Irish state. Gillis, *Irish Poetry of the 1930s*, 83.

57. Thomas MacDonagh, *Literature in Ireland: Studies in Irish and Anglo-Irish*.

58. As Robert Welch recently and memorably asked of this time, "What other reaction can there be when you are lost and lonely other than to cling for safety to strict laws, enforced sanctities, desperate pieties?" Welch, *Cold of May Day Monday*, 178. Michael G. Cronin explores similar ideas in *Impure Thoughts: Sexuality, Catholicism and Literature in Twentieth-Century Ireland*.

59. Austin Clarke wrote of being briefly detained by Black and Tans in Dublin in "The Room Upstairs," collected in *Reviews and Essays of Austin Clarke*, 238.

60. Harmon, *Austin Clarke*, 10.

61. Hugh Maxton records this in his introduction to Clarke's *Selected Poems*, 7.

62. Vivien Mercier notes that the word "pride" appears in the volume a half-dozen times in "Mortal Anguish, Mortal Pride: Austin Clarke's Religious Lyrics," 98.

63. Clarke, "Martha Blake," in *Collected Poems* (1974), 184.

64. The idea of unthinking submission before religious authority appears in lines like "the simple prayer / That gave obedience to the knee," or "The sanctuary lamp is lowered / In witness of our ignorance." Clarke, *Collected Poems* (1974), 181, 192.

65. Clarke, "The Straying Student," in *Collected Poems* (1974), 189. This line was taken by John Goodby as a starting point for a feminist reappraisal of Clarke's work, "'The Prouder Counsel of Her Throat': Towards a Feminist Reading of Austin Clarke."

66. Mercier, "Mortal Anguish, Mortal Pride," 98.

67. Yeats, *Senate Speeches*, 99.

68. W. B. Yeats, "The Three Monuments," in *Collected Poems of Yeats*, 234.

69. Clarke, "Penal Law," in *Collected Poems* (1974), 189.

70. Senia Paseta writes of how "the Archbishop of Tuam warned Irish Catholics that they must 'shun . . . as you would a pestilence' all imported literature." Paseta, "Censorship and Its Critics in the Irish Free State," 196.

71. Clarke, "Penal Law," in *Collected Poems* (1974), 192.

72. See, for example, Welch, *Cold of May Day Monday*, 182; and Gillis, *Irish Poetry of the 1930s*, 92.

73. Clarke, *Collected Poems* (2008), 202, 232. My understanding of these and other poems by Clarke has been greatly enhanced by Kit Fryatt's monograph *Austin Clarke.*

74. Clarke, "Celebrations," in *Collected Poems* (1974), 195.

75. Treasonable Offences Act of 1925, www.irishstatutebook.ie.

3. Sounding Justice

1. Lucy Collins has perhaps done more than anyone to keep Coghill's work in the living stream of Irish literature. She inaugurated a revival of critical interest in Coghill's work by publishing a selection of her poetry in *Poetry by Women in Ireland.*

2. This Donne-like note of religious darkness has been noted by Anne Fogarty in her article "'The Influence of Absences': Eavan Boland and the Silenced History of Irish Women's Poetry." In this article she writes that the "fascination with absence and death is evident in Coghill's work, although often these themes are given a religious cast."

3. Rhoda Coghill, "Summer in Sheephaven," in *The Bright Hillside*, 2.

4. John Redmond, *Poetry and Privacy: Questioning Public Interpretations of Contemporary British and Irish Poetry.*

5. Lucy Collins has written about Coghill's response to the subordinate position of women in midcentury Ireland in "'I knew what it meant / Not to be at all': Death and the (Modernist) Afterlife in the Work of Irish Women Poets of the 1940s."

6. Coghill, "In Wicklow," in *The Bright Hillside*, 1

7. Coghill, *The Bright Hillside*, 4.

8. Coghill, "In the City," in *The Bright Hillside*, 6.

9. Richard Pine cited by Laura Watson, "Epitaph for a Musician: Rhoda Coghill as Pianist, Composer and Poet," 7.

10. "'I have my own notion of how things should be'" (obituary for Rhoda Coghill), *Irish Times*, Feb. 19, 2000, www.irishtimes.com/news/i-have-my-own-notion-of-how-things-should-be-1.246947.

11. Kathy D'Arcy, "Why Uncomplicated Recovery Isn't Enough: Rhoda Coghill, Her Letters, and the Fired! Movement."

12. Heather Ingman, *Twentieth-Century Fiction by Irish Women: Nation and Gender*, 10.

13. Coghill's second collection, *Time Is a Squirrel*, was published in 1956. D'Arcy makes a powerful case for the recovery of both Coghill's and other neglected work in "Why Uncomplicated Recovery Isn't Enough."

14. D'Arcy, "Why Uncomplicated Recovery Isn't Enough."

15. Mary Clancy has written of the "significant desire to extend control over aspects of women's lives in general" in the legislative moves of the Free State in "Aspects of Women's Contribution," 66.

16. Coghill, *The Bright Hillside*, 8.

17. D'Arcy, "Why Uncomplicated Recovery Isn't Enough."

18. D'Arcy, "Why Uncomplicated Recovery Isn't Enough."

19. Watson, "Epitaph for a Musician," 8.

20. See Johannah Duffy's article "Jazz, Identity and Sexuality in Ireland during the Interwar Years"; Jim Smyth's article "Dancing, Depravity and All That Jazz: The Public Dance Halls Act of 1935"; and Gearóid Ó hAllmhuráin's "Dancing on the Hobs of Hell: Rural Communities in Clare and the Dance Halls Act of 1935."

21. Duffy, "Jazz, Identity and Sexuality," 68.

22. Coghill, "In the Morning," in *The Bright Hillside*, 16.

23. Coghill, "Spring Doggerel," in *The Bright Hillside*, 14.

24. Coghill, "The Bright Hillside," in *The Bright Hillside*, 19.

25. Coghill, "The Chestnut Tree," in *The Bright Hillside*, 12.

26. Kathy D'Arcy, "Almost Forgotten Names: Irish Women Poets of the 1930s, 1940s and 1950s," 118.

27. Coghill, "Afternoon by the Lake at Clogherrevagh," in *The Bright Hillside*, 4.

28. Coghill, *The Bright Hillside*, 15.

29. Coghill, *The Bright Hillside*, 24.

30. David Wheatley, "Aspermatic Nights and Days: Samuel Beckett and an Anti-genealogy of Contemporary Irish Poetry (I)," 48.

31. Siobhán Mullally outlined the controversy that this constitutional provision caused in the *Second Report of the Convention on the Constitution* (2013), available online at https://cdn.thejournal.ie/media/2013/05/convention-on-the-constitution-role-of-women-report.pdf.

32. Julie Morrissy makes this point in a striking manner in her visual piece "Positions Gendered Male in Bunreacht na hÉireann / 1937 Constitution of Ireland" (vinyl installation, "TULCA Festival of Visual Arts: The Law Is a White Dog," Galway 2020). There are, according to Morrissy, 110 references to men in the Irish Constitution; there are 7 references to women.

33. Caitríona Beaumont, "Women, Citizenship and Catholicism in the Irish Free State, 1922–1948," 567.

34. Both the review and the telegram are from two envelopes of Coghill's correspondence, drafts, and other papers that are held by the estate of Rhoda Coghill. I am very grateful to Kathy D'Arcy for sharing scans of these papers with me.

4. The Civil Servant as Poet

1. Michael Mays notes that the *Irish Times* gave Whitaker this title in *Nation States: The Cultures of Irish Nationalism*, 178.

2. Thomas Kinsella in interview with Adam Hanna, "A Dual Arrangement: Thomas Kinsella."

3. Historian Diarmaid Ferriter contextualizes these new ideas in postwar economic changes, writing in his essay "De Valera's Ireland: 1932–58" that "the arrival of Marshall Aid funds was significant in forcing Irish economists to think internationally" (682).

4. T. Brown, *Ireland, 1922 to the Present*, 241.

5. Gary Murphy writes of midcentury civil service recruitment in *In Search of the Promised Land: The Politics of Post-war Ireland*. He notes that civil servant Todd Andrews complained that want of opportunities in industry in the new state meant that too many talented people were going into the civil service (128).

6. Bryan Fanning has written, in *The Quest for Modern Ireland: The Battle of Ideas, 1912–1986*, of the restricted latitude granted to prose writers in the civil service, at least in the mid-twentieth century (193). It is intriguing to compare these restrictions to the freedom granted to Kinsella. When he found his work on *The Táin* was not progressing, Whitaker enabled him to take a year's leave of absence, and Kinsella, perhaps by way of thanks, later dedicated his and Seán Ó Tuama's 1981 anthology, *An Duanaire*, to him.

7. John Goodby writes that poetry was "rarely a target" of the censors in *Irish Poetry since 1950*, 19.

8. Justin Quinn, *The Cambridge Introduction to Modern Irish Poetry*, 100.

9. Michael Hartnett, "A Farewell to English," in *A Farewell to English, and Other Poems*, 33.

10. Dorgan, "Law, Poetry and the Republic," 201.

11. Kinsella, interview with the author, Aug. 17, 2017.

12. Kinsella quoted by Andrew Fitzsimons in "The Sea of Disappointment: Thomas Kinsella's 'Nightwalker' and the New Ireland," 347.

13. Terence Brown writes of the economic ideas that gave rise to "the new Ireland" of the early 1960s in *Ireland: A Social and Cultural History, 1922 to the Present*, 185–204.

14. Something of the buoyancy of this period is communicated in Fergal Tobin's *The Best of Decades: Ireland in the Nineteen Sixties*. Conor McCarthy has written about the cultural consequences of changes in economic ideas, and their weakening of traditional narratives of Irish nationality, in *Modernisation, Crisis and Culture in Ireland, 1969–1992*.

15. Thomas Kinsella, "Nightwalker," in *Collected Poems*, 82.

16. Margaret Scanlan, *Culture and Customs of Ireland*, 85. Tom Inglis, too, has written of the bourgeois Victorian British origins of much of independent Ireland's sexual morality in "Origins and Legacies of Irish Prudery: Sexuality and Social Control in Modern Ireland."

17. J. J. Lee quoted in Brooker, "'Estopped by Grand Playsaunce,'" 19.

18. Brooker, "'Estopped by Grand Playsaunce,'" 22.

19. Kinsella quoted in Fitzsimons, "Sea of Disappointment," 347.

20. This era was imagined in this way by William Cosgrave and Eamon De Valera, for example, at different times in the Free State's history. Michael Kennedy, *Ireland and the League of Nations, 1919–1946: International Relations, Diplomacy and Politics*, 47; Tim Pat Coogan, *Ireland in the Twentieth Century*, 427.

21. Yvonne Whelan, "The Construction and Destruction of a Colonial Landscape: Monuments to British Monarchs in Dublin before and after Independence," 519ff.

22. Kinsella, "Another September," in *Collected Poems*, 20.

23. Hanna, "Dual Arrangement," 71. I mention the ideas of Carl Jung as they have been so influential on Kinsella himself, as Brian John records in *Reading the Ground: The Poetry of Thomas Kinsella*.

24. Martin Kayman has written extensively about the semiotics of representations of Justice in statuary, including in "The Law and the Statuesque."

25. Heather Laird has written about the inverted relationship between official law and justice that colonialism in Ireland fostered in *Subversive Law*.

26. Kinsella lived on Baggot Street when he started at the civil service; it is around the corner from Government Buildings, where the Department of Finance was based (interview with the author, Aug. 17, 2017).

27. Karen E. Brown, *The Yeats Circle, Verbal and Visual Relations in Ireland, 1880–1939*, 96. Curlews appear in poems by Yeats, including "He Reproves the Curlew" (*The Wind among the Reeds*, 1899) and "Paudeen" (*Responsibilities*, 1913).

28. Kinsella, "Baggot Street Deserta," in *Collected Poems*, 12.

29. This impression was augmented by large-scale emigration, which kept the population of the Republic beneath three million throughout the 1940s and 1950s.

30. The phrase is John V. Kelleher's, quoted in T. Brown, *Ireland, 1922 to the Present*, 241.

31. R. F. Foster outlines these initiatives in *Modern Ireland: 1600–1972*, 578–80.

32. Though most accounts focus on the changes this program envisaged, Conor McCabe has sought to highlight continuities, noting that the document did not so much imagine a diminished role for agriculture in the future Irish economy as envision an increase in the use of credit. McCabe, *Sins of the Father: Tracing the Decisions That Shaped the Irish Economy*, 85.

33. *Programme for Economic Expansion* (Dublin: Stationery Office, 1958).

34. *Programme for Economic Expansion*, 34. The visual corollary of the ethos of the *Programme for Economic Expansion* was in the film that accompanied the RTÉ shutdown and anthem in the early 1960s. It showcased, among other props of technocratic modernity, an electricity substation, a new school made of plate glass and concrete, and a passenger jet taking off from Shannon Airport.

35. Kinsella, "A Country Walk," in *Collected Poems*, 44–47.

36. Goodby, *Irish Poetry*, 78.

37. Alex Davis has pointed out how Kinsella's work, though it later turns against the economic imperatives of the Department of Finance, is nevertheless implicated in the same ideas. Davis, *A Broken Line: Denis Devlin and Irish Poetic Modernism*, 128; Davis, "Irish Poetry to 1966," 354.

38. Thomas Kinsella, "The Irish Writer," 629.

39. Alex Davis points out that American poetry was a significant influence in Kinsella's work from the time of *Downstream* (1962) onward in his article "Thomas Kinsella and the Pound Legacy: His Jacket on the 'Cantos.'" Kinsella underscored the importance of American poets to his work in a radio talk in the 1970s, in which he stated that "the great innovators, discoverers and refreshers of poetry in the twentieth century have been without exception I think American" (BBC script titled "The Arts in Ireland."

40. Kinsella, "Nightwalker," in *Collected Poems*, 77.

41. Gerald Dawe has noted that Kinsella's innovation was to take Irish poetry into "governmental offices and the political chambers" (quoted in Fitzsimons, "Sea of Disappointment," 335).

42. John Montague, *The Rough Field*, 70, 71.

43. Kinsella, "Nightwalker," in *Collected Poems*, 78.

44. T. K. Whitaker states this central aim in *The New Ireland: Its Progress, Problems and Aspirations.* This text is from a speech Whitaker delivered in Brussels on May 3.

45. George W. Potter, *To the Golden Door: The Story of the Irish in Ireland and America.*

46. Kinsella, "Nightwalker," in *Collected Poems*, 82.

47. *Programme for Economic Expansion*, 8.

48. By arguing for the necessity for lower wages and the end of rent controls, the *Programme* contains the strong suggestion that the burden of the economic shift it proposes should be borne by those individuals at the lower end of the income scale. This regressive thinking was in keeping with other economic developments at the time. As Diarmaid Ferriter has written, "In the 1950s, borrowed American dollars were of crucial importance to the post-war Irish economy, but they came at a price, and those who paid the biggest penalty were the poorest" ("De Valera's Ireland," 684). For an analysis of the more positive outcomes of the scheme, see T. Brown, *Ireland, 1922 to the Present*, 241.

5. Unwritten Laws

1. Seamus Heaney, *The Burial at Thebes*, 21. I am indebted to Eugene McNulty's illuminating discussion of this play in "Words into Action: Re-hearing Antigone's Claim in *The Burial at Thebes*."

2. See, for example, Sergio Cotta, "Positive Law and Natural Law."

3. Oliver Wendell Holmes associated natural law with an uncompromising sense of the ideal in "Natural Law."

4. Heaney, *The Burial at Thebes*, 20.

5. Heaney quotes Hegel in "Title Deeds."

6. This summary of Gurvitch's ideas comes from Alan Hunt, "On Georges Gurvitch, *Sociology of Law*," 148.

7. In the centuries that have followed the first performance of *Antigone*, writers have used Sophocles's play to air this dangerous idea in several contested jurisdictions, including Nazi-occupied France, apartheid-era South Africa, and modern Northern Ireland. McNulty writes about the performance history of *Antigone* in "Words into Action," 115–16.

8. Heaney, "Title Deeds."

9. Conor Cruise O'Brien republished this piece in revised form in *States of Ireland* (New York: Pantheon, 1972). Tom Paulin wrote a critique of O'Brien's revised version in "The Making of a Loyalist."

10. The background to the civil rights movement is set out in J. R. Hill, ed., *A New History of Ireland*, iii, lxiv.

11. Conor Cruise O'Brien in *The Listener*, Oct. 1968, quoted in Marilynn J. Richtarik, *Acting between the Lines: The Field Day Theatre Company and Irish Cultural Politics, 1980–1984*, 217.

12. Politicians swear to uphold "unwritten law" in Seamus Heaney, "From the Republic of Conscience," in *The Haw Lantern*, 12–13.

13. Heaney, "From the Republic of Conscience," in *The Haw Lantern*, 13.

14. Nathan Wallace, *Hellenism and Reconciliation in Ireland from Yeats to Field Day*, 101.

15. Laird, *Subversive Law*.

16. The idea of "unwritten law" is explored in D. Jordan, "The Irish National League and the 'Unwritten Law': Rural Protest and Nation-Building in Ireland, 1882–1890"; and Laird, *Subversive Law*.

17. Heaney, "Punishment," in *North*, 38. Notably critical responses include ones by Ciaran Carson and Edna Longley. Carson, "Escaped from the Massacre? Seamus Heaney's *North*"; Longley, "'Inner Émigré' or 'Artful Voyeur'? Seamus Heaney's *North*," in *Poetry in the Wars*, 140–69. Yxta Maya Murray has written a perceptive law-and-literature account of this poem in "Punishment and the Costs of Knowledge."

18. The poems from which these lines come are, respectively, "The Strand at Lough Beg"; "Casualty" (both in Seamus Heaney, *Field Work*, 17, 23); and "Clearances," in *The Haw Lantern*, 25.

19. Heaney, "Craig's Dragoons," quoted in Neil Corcoran, *The Poetry of Seamus Heaney: A Critical Study*, 249.

20. Historians Graham Ellison and Jim Smyth termed the period 1922–68 one of "imposed normality" in *The Crowned Harp: Policing Northern Ireland*, 42. The existence, from 1920, of an entirely Protestant body of special constables called "B-Specials" led to, Heaney wrote, a "shared understanding that the police were a paramilitary force" in pre-Troubles Northern Ireland. Seamus Heaney, "The Interesting Case of Nero, Chekhov's Cognac and a Knocker," xxi.

21. See "Key Events: The Deployment of British Troops, 14 August 1969," www.cain.ulster.ac.uk.

22. Heaney told O'Driscoll that Miller published the poem first (*Stepping Stones*, 111). Details of the edition of the *Review* in which it is published are from Alain Thomas Yvon Sinner, "'Protective Colouring': The Political Commitment in the Poetry of Seamus Heaney."

23. The events of the day are summarized on the CAIN website, http://cain.ulst.ac.uk/events/bsunday/sum.htm.

24. Seamus Heaney, "The Road to Derry."

25. Seamus Heaney discusses his reasons for this with Dennis O'Driscoll in *Stepping Stones*, 118–19.

26. See, in particular, Seamus Heaney, "A Northern Hoard," in *Wintering Out*, 29–35.

27. John, *Reading the Ground*, 143. The poem took Kinsella eight days to write from the date of the publication of the report; an "octave" is the eighth day after a feast day in the liturgical calendar.

28. Thomas Kinsella, *Butcher's Dozen: A Lesson for the Octave of Widgery.*

29. *Kinsella's Oversight: A Reply to "The* [sic] *Butcher's Dozen," a Poem on Bloody Sunday.*

30. Heaney, "A Constable Calls," prose version published in *The Wearing of the Black: An Anthology of Contemporary Ulster Poetry*, ed. Padraic Fiacc, 47.

31. Heaney, *Field Work*, 45.

32. Heaney quotes these passages in his lecture "Title Deeds."

33. Notable examples of poems featuring members of the constabulary are "A Constable Calls," in *North*, 72; "The Nod," in *District and Circle*, 33; and "The Wood Road," *Human Chain*, 22 (which I discuss at the end of this chapter).

34. Heaney, "The Haw Lantern," in *The Haw Lantern*, 7.

35. Heaney, "The Ministry of Fear," in *North*, 64.

36. Corcoran, *Poetry of Seamus Heaney*, 238; Seamus Heaney, "Belfast," in *Finders Keepers: Selected Prose, 1971–2001*, 41.

37. Heaney, "The Strand at Lough Beg," in *Field Work*, 17. Michael Longley also wrote of his memories of traveling by car with Heaney amid the threat of fake roadblocks in "Room to Rhyme: Some Memories of Seamus Heaney."

38. This period is discussed in J. Hill, *A New History of Ireland*, vii, 347.

39. Mitchel P. Roth, *Prisons and Prison Systems: A Global Encyclopaedia*, 163.

40. Committee on the Administration of Justice, "Prisons and Prisoners in Northern Ireland: Putting Human Rights at the Heart of Prison Reform."

41. Heaney, "Whatever You Say, Say Nothing," in *North*, 60.

42. A handwritten draft contents page among Heaney's papers relating to his Faber-published volume *North* suggests that at one point he intended most of the poems in *Stations* to be published in it. File l.vi., *North*.

43. Seamus Heaney, "Visitant," in *Stations*, 17.

44. Roth, *Prisons and Prison Systems*, 163.

45. Margaret Thatcher, speech delivered at Parliament Buildings, Stormont Belfast, Mar. 5, 1981.

46. The specifics of the "criminalization" process are set out in Smyth and Ellison, *Crowned Harp*, 82ff.

47. This period is discussed by F. Stuart Ross in *Smashing H-Block: The Rise and Fall of the Popular Campaign against Criminalization, 1976–1982*.

48. Seamus Heaney, "Chekhov on Sakhalin," in *Station Island*, 18.

49. Heaney interview in O'Driscoll, *Stepping Stones*, 259.

50. Heaney, "Away from It All," in *Station Island*, 17.

51. BBC, "Demonstration against Internment on Magilligan Strand," www.bbc.co.uk/bitesize/clips/z6v2n39.

52. Heaney, "Exposure," in *North*, 73.

53. Yeats, "Easter 1916," in *Variorum Edition of the Poems*, 393.

54. Seamus Heaney, "Station Island," in *Opened Ground*, 261.

55. Nathan Wallace discusses Heaney's association with Amnesty International in "Seamus Heaney's Poetics of Human Rights," in *Hellenism and Reconciliation*, 90ff.

56. Terence Brown discusses the importance of "Paudeen" to Heaney in "Seamus Heaney's Tender Yeats."

57. Yeats, "Paudeen," in *Variorum Edition of the Poems*, 291.

58. Some of them can be found in the manuscripts archive that was opened at the National Library of Ireland in 2012 and others in the letters archive at Emory University that was reopened after several years of partial closure in early 2016.

59. Bernard O'Donoghue, "Remembering Seamus Heaney," 278.

60. I am grateful to John McAuliffe for sending me information about Jack Mitchell.

61. Box 45, MSS 960, FF4, in the Stuart A. Rose Library, Emory University, Atlanta. The poem typescript of *GiB: A Modest Exposure*, attributed to "Paul Macdonnell," was published under the name "Jack Mitchell" in 1990 by Fulcrum Press in Dublin.

62. Heaney to O'Driscoll in *Stepping Stones*, 260.

63. "Death on the Rock," Thames Television documentary episode, Apr. 1988.

64. These killings are explored in Kader Asmal, *Shoot to Kill? International Lawyers' Inquiry into the Lethal Use of Firearms by the Security Forces in Northern Ireland*.

65. Quoted in "John Stalker Obituary," *Times*, Feb. 8, 2019.

66. Stephanie Palmer, "'Death on the Rock' and the European Convention on Human Rights," 1.

67. Heaney, note on a draft letter to Niall Farrell (brother of Mairéad Farrell), Jan. 17, 1989.

68. Seamus Heaney, "Settings, xiii," in *Seeing Things*, 69.

69. These poems include "Summer Home," in *Wintering Out*, 59–61; "Summer 1969," in *North*, 69–70; and "High Summer," in *Field Work*, 45–46. It is worth noting that the latter two of these poems reflect on the use of disproportionate force by the authorities against nationalists.

70. Richard Rankin Russell, not unreasonably considering its associations with sunlight and whitewash, has recently situated this poem at Heaney's childhood farmhouse, Mossbawn, in *Seamus Heaney: An Introduction*, 157. This follows Helen Vendler's approach to the poem, which she quotes in a discussion of "return-poems" in which Heaney "returns as a conscious adult to some scene from youth" (*Seamus Heaney*, 138). John Goodby labeled *Seeing Things* "unsettled" immediately after quoting this poem in "Review: *Seeing Things* by Seamus Heaney

and *Gorse Fires* by Michael Longley," 451. Irene Gilsenan Nordin, perhaps not taking account of the whole range of ideas associated with the bird, writes that the image of a cormorant creates a "sense of suspense" in *Crediting Marvels in Seamus Heaney's "Seeing Things,"* 132.

71. I am grateful to Colin Graham, who brought this version of the poem to my attention.

72. Richard J. King, *The Devil's Cormorant: A Natural History*, 256.

73. In the year *Seeing Things* was published, Desmond Fennell published an antipathetic piece that claimed that Heaney's "poetry says nothing, plainly or figuratively, about the war" (quoted in Eugene O'Brien, *Seamus Heaney and the Place of Poetry*. Less antagonistically, Neil Corcoran has called "Squarings" "the most purely pleasurable and unexacerbated of Heaney's poems" (*Poetry of Seamus Heaney: A Critical Study*, 185). Helen Vendler, too, emphasizes the aerial qualities of this volume in her chapter "Airiness: *Seeing Things*," in *Seamus Heaney*, 136–54. The deracinated turn in Heaney's work has been labeled Heaney's "'walking on air' turn in the mid-1980s" by Catriona Clutterbuck in "'Pilot and Stray in One': Sustaining Nothingness in the Travel Poems of Early Heaney."

74. Typescript of *GiB: A Modest Exposure*.

75. Séamus Deane, introduction to *GiB: A Modest Exposure*, by Jack Mitchell, iii.

76. Heaney, draft letter to Farrell, Jan. 17, 1989.

77. Sands's poems, in spite of Heaney's advice, were posthumously published by Sinn Féin's publicity department.

78. This post is reported by Henry McDonald, "Strangers on a Train: Heaney and Sinn Féin," *Guardian*, Feb. 15, 2009, www.theguardian.com/politics/2009/feb/15/seamus-heaney-sinn-fein-hunger-strikes.

79. Morrison, "Seamus Heaney Disputed."

80. Seamus Heaney, "The Flight Path," in *The Spirit Level*, 25; Heaney to O'Driscoll in *Stepping Stones*, 257–58.

81. Seamus Heaney, *The Redress of Poetry*, 187.

82. Seamus Heaney, "New Worlds."

83. In "The Defense of Poesy (Written c. 1579)," Sir Philip Sidney writes of nature that "her world is brazen, the poets only deliver a golden" (937). William Shakespeare affirms through Theseus in *A Midsummer Night's Dream* that "as imagination bodies forth the forms of things unknown, the poet's pen turns them to shape" (866).

84. Late in his life, Heaney wrote a piece called "Writer and Righter," a lecture he gave in front of a gathering of human rights lawyers in 2009. In it he quoted Camus on a theme that Heaney explored in "New Worlds": the existence of "an unknown prisoner, abandoned to humiliations at the other end of the world, is

enough to draw the writer out of his exile [. . .] in the midst of the privileges of freedom."

85. Heaney, "Crediting Poetry," in *Opened Ground*, 455.

86. Heaney, "The Flight Path," in *The Spirit Level*, 25.

87. Heaney, "The Wood Road," in *Human Chain*, 22.

88. Heaney, "The Wood Road," *Magma* 36 (2006): 28.

89. In his lecture, Heaney drew a parallel on the outcry in the village of Toome, where the body of hunger striker Francis Hughes was handed over to his family by the RUC in 1981, and the events at Thebes. As Luz Mar González-Arias observes, Heaney's "putting 'burial' in the title signals to a new audience what the central concern of the play is going to be." From "'A Pedigree Bitch, Like Myself': (Non) Human Illness and Death in Dorothy Molloy's Poetry," 126.

90. Helen Meany, review of *The Burial at Thebes*, by Heaney, *Irish Times*, Apr. 7, 2004; Neil Corcoran, review of *The Burial at Thebes*, by Heaney, *Guardian*, Apr. 30, 2004. Later, another critic exhibited uncertainty, writing that "it seems the playwright deemed the political environment of 2004 one for stark, unrelenting verse." Katie Fabel, "Streamlined *The Burial at Thebes* Is Clean Take on Greek Classic," nj.com, Jan. 29, 2016, nj.com/entertainment/2016/01/streamlined_the_burial_at_thebes_is_clean_take_on.html.

91. Heaney, "Title Deeds."

92. Heaney quoted Simone Weil's observation in a piece called "Human Rights, Poetic Redress," *Irish Times*, Mar. 15, 2008.

6. Legislators of the Unacknowledged

1. Paula Meehan, "The Statue of the Virgin at Granard Speaks," in *The Man Who Was Marked by Winter*, 40.

2. "After Ann Lovett," 36. The author goes on to say that "the whole ethos of Ireland, (and it's not confined to the South) is such that everybody wants rid of the responsibility for taking about sex. Indeed for using the word. So everyone kicks to touch."

3. Christy Moore, "Middle of the Island," in *Voyage* (1989).

4. Andrew Auge, "The Apparitions of 'Our Lady of the Facts of Life': Paula Meehan and the Visionary Quotidian," 50.

5. "A Poem for Ireland" short list available at https://apoemforireland.rte.ie/shortlist/.

6. Karen Steele, "Refusing the Poisoned Chalice: The Sexual Politics of Rita Ann Higgins and Paula Meehan," 323. Colm Tóibín's edited collection *Seeing Is Believing: Moving Statues in Ireland* contains several perspectives on the phenomenon.

7. Andrew Auge, *A Chastened Communion: Modern Irish Poetry and Catholicism*, 194.

8. This point was made by Jill Franks, who reflected that "there was no one to indict for this tragedy, only a generalized attitude of Irish people that says avoiding shame is better than letting a fellow human being suffer" (*British and Irish Women Writers and the Women's Movement: Six Literary Voices of Their Times*, 49).

9. Steele writes about the linkage of Lovett's death and the changes to law in the popular imagination in "Refusing the Poisoned Chalice" (323). This is illustrated in the above-mentioned *Hot Press* piece, whose author argued that if similar tragedies were not to occur in the future, there had to be a public conversation about contraception, the sale of which was restricted by law. (The law then in force regarding contraception was the Health [Family Planning] Act of 1979, which meant that contraceptives were available at a restricted number of places and could be obtained only with a prescription.)

10. Eavan Boland, "The Communal Art of Paula Meehan," 19.

11. All these things are named in Heaney's "The Mud Vision," in *The Haw Lantern*, 42.

12. Heaney quoted in O'Driscoll, "Heaney in Public," 58.

13. Brendan Kennelly quoted in Michael Murphy, "Brendan's Voyage." The story of this scandal is told by Nell McCafferty in *The Kerry Babies Case: A Woman to Blame.*

14. Nor were they the only ones: Meehan's "The Statue of the Virgin at Granard Speaks" is not the only poem to address Lovett's death. There are also Nuala Ní Dhomhnaill's "Thar Mo Chionn / Mea Culpa" and Biddy Jenkinson's "I gCuimhne Shíle." I am indebted to a talk by Caitlín Nic Íomhair about these poems, given at Trinity College Dublin on February 5, 2016.

15. Paul Durcan's collections written wholly or partly in the 1980s include *Jesus, Break His Fall*; *Ark of the North*; *Jumping the Train Tracks with Angela*; *The Berlin Wall Café*; *Going Home to Russia*; and *Daddy, Daddy.*

16. Bernard McKenna, "Paul Durcan."

17. Bunreacht na hÉireann—Constitution of Ireland.

18. Paul Durcan, "Wife Who Smashed Television Gets Jail," in *Teresa's Bar*, 23.

19. Article 41.2, Bunreacht na hÉireann—Constitution of Ireland.

20. Scannell, "Constitution and the Role of Women," 72.

21. In one poem, a woman at a job interview is complimented for her looks before being told, "You have no right to a job here or anywhere." Durcan, "Interview for a Job," in *Jumping the Train Tracks with Angela*, 35.

22. Durcan, "Catholic Father Prays for His Daughter's Abortion," in *The Berlin Wall Café*, 32. Sociologist Linda Connolly, in *The Irish Women's Movement: From Revolution to Devolution*, has identified a period of abeyance in Irish

feminism that lasted from the Civil War until the end of the 1960s. This forty-year period was then followed, according to Connolly, by a period of rapid change in the 1970s, which saw (among other developments) the principle of equal pay for equal work enshrined in law and the limited legalization of contraception.

23. Catriona Clutterbuck, "Irish Women's Poetry and the Republic of Ireland: Formalism as Form," 18. She records that the decade saw an increase in the very low numbers of poetry books by women, with more than thirty-five women achieving their first publication of a volume in that decade.

24. These collections are *Return and No Blame*, *Reading the Sky*, and *The Man Who Was Marked by Winter.*

25. Meehan's childhood experience of the dispersal of her city-center tenement community was one of the formative events of her life, and, in the first poem of her first volume, the speaker opines that "They will tear down my city, / [. . .] My little streets" ("A Decision to Stalk," in *Return and No Blame*, 7). Many of the streets that Meehan writes of were demolished in the late 1960s; many of their occupants—including Meehan herself—relocated to newly built estates on the edges of Dublin. This internal migration, too, was linked to legal moves: while the government was planning new houses at the edge of the city, it facilitated the destruction of buildings in the city center through the Local Government (Sanitary Services) Act of 1964.

26. Meehan quoted in Luz Mar González-Arias, "'Playing with the Ghosts of Words': Interview with Paula Meehan," 198.

27. *Oxford English Dictionary*, s.v. "citizen."

28. Article 40, Bunreacht na hÉireann—Constitution of Ireland.

29. These sessions are described in Franks, *British and Irish Women Writers.*

30. Meehan, "Ard Fheis," in *Man Who Was Marked by Winter*, 21.

31. Meehan quoted in González-Arias, "'Playing with the Ghosts of Words,'" 203 (emphasis in the original).

32. The constitutional and legal measures that limited the freedom of women in twentieth-century Ireland are starkly set out by Scannell in "Constitution and the Role of Women."

33. Durcan also treats it irreverently in "Study of a Figure in Landscape" (*Daddy, Daddy*), a poem in which its opening invocation of "the name of God and of the dead generations" becomes a father's cross demand to his small son: "What in the name of the Mother of God / And the dead generations is the matter with you?" (104).

34. Durcan, "'Windfall,' 8 Parnell Hill, Cork," in *Jumping the Train Tracks with Angela*, 45.

35. Durcan, "Bewley's Oriental Café, Westmoreland Street," in *The Berlin Wall Café*, 13.

36. Durcan, "This Week the Court Is Sleeping in Loughrea," in *Jesus, Break His Fall*, 50.

37. Durcan, "The Boy Who Was Conceived in the *Leithreas*," in *Jesus, Break His Fall*, 56.

38. Derek Mahon, "Orpheus Ascending: The Poetry of Paul Durcan," 163–64.

39. In another poem, "On Seeing Two Bus Conductors Kissing Each Other in the Middle of the Street," the speaker wonders "when I will see / Two policemen at a street corner caressing each other?" (*Jesus, Break His Fall*, 50).

40. Durcan, *Ark of the North*, 22.

41. Lucy Collins acutely identifies the cultivation of oppositional stances and marginal perspectives as one of the chief characteristics of Irish poetry in the public sphere in her article "Irish Poets in the Public Sphere," 209.

42. Fintan O'Toole quoted in Jonathan Allison, "Acts of Memory: Poetry and the Republic of Ireland since 1949," 52.

43. Durcan, *Jesus, Break His Fall*, 43, 58.

44. Durcan, "The Hole, Spring, 1980," in *Jesus, Break His Fall*, 61.

45. *Oxford English Dictionary*, s.v. "anarchy."

46. In 1986 an amendment to remove the constitutional prohibition on divorce was defeated by two-thirds of voters in a referendum.

47. Handwritten and typescript drafts of poems for *Jesus, Break His Fall* and notes relating to publication, Paul Durcan Papers. Other themes include "Mixture of Satire and Love" and "The HORRORS of University Life." Divorce is also the subject of "An Anatomy of Divorce by Joe Commonwealth" (*Jesus, Break His Fall*, 40) and features prominently in "The Haulier's Wife Meets Jesus on the Road Near Moone" (*The Berlin Wall Café*, 4)

48. Durcan, "The Divorce Referendum, Ireland, 1986," in *Going Home to Russia*, 27.

49. Diarmaid Ferriter, *Occasions of Sin: Sex and Society in Modern Ireland*, 495ff.

50. T. Brown, *Ireland, 1922 to the Present*, 266.

51. Durcan, *Daddy, Daddy*, 115.

52. R. F. Foster, *Luck & the Irish: A Brief History of Change, c. 1970–2000*, 49.

53. Julia Carlson, ed., *Banned in Ireland*, 2, 5.

54. Meehan, "The Dark Twin," in *Man Who Was Marked by Winter*, 37.

55. Meehan, "No Go Area," in *Reading the Sky*, 7.

56. Meehan continues to translate images from Northern Ireland into conditions closer to home in the second poem in *Reading the Sky*, "Circle Charm." It centres on an unhappy romantic relationship, but is written in terms that recall the Maze prison. Ostensibly a poem to a special person, the space the speaker

keeps for the beloved is reimagined as a prison cell: "I come back when your hair is long and matted // And you've smeared the walls with your own fear," Meehan writes.

57. Meehan, "Borders," in *Return and No Blame*, 21.

58. Durcan, "Poem Not Beginning with a Line from Pindar," in *Daddy, Daddy*, 140.

59. Lucy Collins points out that, here, "the private and public roles of the man—at once judge and father—also reflect the interaction between exterior and interior worlds" ("Irish Poets in the Public Sphere," 217).

60. Though her interest in how Irish society defined its transgressors, and how it indicted itself by its treatment of them, would later find its most stark expression in her play *Cell* (2000), this interest is already visible in her poetry from the 1980s.

61. Paula Meehan, "Hunger Strike," in *Reading the Sky*, 9.

62. T. Brown, *Ireland, 1922 to the Present*, 261. The legal systems of both the Republic and Northern Ireland were highly preoccupied with this conflict, and a 1983 report stated that Northern Ireland had "the highest number of prisoners per head of population in Western Europe."

63. Durcan, "Ulysses," in *Daddy, Daddy*.

64. Conor Farnan writes how "Durcan has repeatedly invoked *Ulysses* as a touchstone of humanistic tolerance in the face of the fanatical violence of Republican terrorism" in "The Most Subversive Unit in Society: Depicting the Family in *Daddy, Daddy* and *The Laughter of Mothers*."

65. Meehan, "The Pattern," in *Man Who Was Marked by Winter*, 18.

66. Paula Meehan quoted in Jody Allen Randolph, "The Body Politic: A Conversation with Paula Meehan," 257.

67. George Oppen, "Disasters," quoted in Lyn Graham Barzilai, *George Oppen: A Critical Study*, 156.

68. Meehan, "The Statue of the Virgin," in *Man Who Was Marked by Winter*, 41.

7. The Body of the Law in New Poetry

1. The text of the Irish Constitution is available online at www.irishstatutebook.ie/eli/cons/en/html.

2. The ways in which the Constitution seeks to direct the lives of women is set out in Scannell, "Constitution and the Role of Women," 71. This chapter starkly sets out the bleak legislative landscape with regard to women and shows how laws that sought to limit the opportunities available to women were underwritten by the 1937 constitution.

3. Beaumont, "Women, Citizenship and Catholicism," 576.

4. Scannell, "Constitution and the Role of Women," 71ff.

5. Beaumont, "Women, Citizenship and Catholicism," 566, 576, 571, 573.

6. L. Connolly, *Irish Women's Movement*, 120–26.

7. Fintan O'Toole, foreword to *The Child Sex Scandal and Modern Irish Literature: Writing the Unspeakable*, by Joseph Valente and Margot Gayle Backus. A significant exploration of this part of the story of modern Ireland is Caelainn Hogan's *Republic of Shame: Stories from Ireland's Institutions for "Fallen Women."*

8. Margaret Fine-Davis, *Gender Roles in Ireland: Three Decades of Attitude Change*, 189.

9. Lia Mills, "'I Won't Go Back to It: Irish Women Poets and the Iconic Feminine.'"

10. Eavan Boland, "Mise Eire," in *The Journey, and Other Poems*, 10–11. Catriona Clutterbuck has written an article on the contested place of this poem in the canon of Irish works on gender, "'Mise Eire,' Eavan Boland." Boland also recounts a tense, regretful encounter with the Shan Van Vocht in "In Coming Days," in *Domestic Violence*, 56.

11. Eavan Boland, "Anna Liffey," in *In a Time of Violence*, 41–46. I am indebted to Patricia Boyle Haberstroh's illuminating discussion of the work of Boland, O'Donnell, and others in "Poetry, 1970–Present," 299ff.

12. Paula Meehan, "Not Your Muse," in *Pillow Talk*, 24.

13. Bernard O'Donoghue, "The Aisling."

14. Mary O'Donnell, "The Rib," in *Spiderwoman's Third Avenue Rhapsody*, 21.

15. Mary O'Donnell, "Eve's Maternity," in *Spiderwoman's Third Avenue Rhapsody*, 26–27.

16. Dorothy Macardle, "The Portrait of Roisin Dhu," in *Earth-Bound: Nine Stories of Ireland*, 90–101.

17. Macardle, "The Portrait of Roisin Dhu," in *Earth-Bound*, 100.

18. Claire Connolly, "Introduction: Ireland in Theory," 3.

19. This phenomenon is discussed by Irene Gilsenan Nordin in the introduction to her edited collection *The Body and Desire in Contemporary Irish Poetry*, 6.

20. Julie Morrissy, "Civil Regulations Amendment Act 1956: Retirement of Women Civil Servants on Marriage."

21. Niamh O'Mahony, "'Releasing the Chaos of Energies': Communicating the Concurrences in Trevor Joyce's Appropriative Poems."

22. M. NourbeSe Philip, *Zong!*

23. I am indebted to Ellen Howley's excellent discussion of this poem in "The Sea and Memory: Poetic Reconsiderations of the *Zong* Massacre."

24. M. NourbeSe Philip quoted in Wendy W. Walters, "'Still in the Difficulty': The Afterlives of Archives," 184.

25. Paula Meehan spoke of patriarchal motivations behind the prescription of sedatives to unhappy women to Luz Mar González-Arias in "'Playing with the Ghosts of Words,'" 198. Betty Friedan discussed the same phenomenon in *The Feminine Mystique.*

26. Linda Connolly, "Symphysiotomy Report Begets More Questions," *Irish Examiner*, Nov. 29, 2016, www.irishexaminer.com. The practice continued until the 1980s, and 399 women were awarded up to €150,000 each by the High Court in 2016.

27. Morrissy, "Civil Regulations Amendment Act 1956."

28. Elaine Feeney, "History Lesson," in *Rise*, 47.

29. Heike Felzmann, "Bringing Abortion to Ireland? The Protection of Life during Pregnancy Act 2013," 197.

30. Doireann Ní Ghríofa, Moving Poems, http://movingpoems.com/poet/doireann-ni-ghriofa/.

31. Fiona de Londras, "Protection of Life during Pregnancy Act, 2013," n.p.

32. A quotation by Ní Ghríofa to this effect can be found at Moving Poems, http://movingpoems.com/poet/doireann-ni-ghriofa/.

33. Ní Ghríofa, "Waking," in *Clasp*, 27. An earlier version of this poem was published as "Recovery Room, Maternity Ward (for Savita Halappanavar)," *Irish Examiner*, Sept. 10, 2013, www.irishexaminer.com.

34. Ní Ghríofa quoted at Moving Poems.

35. Gamble, "Misrecognition," in *Pirate Music*, 32.

36. Gamble, "Childhood," in *Pirate Music*, 49.

37. Gamble, "Bodies," in *Pirate Music*, 60.

38. The history of abortion law in Northern Ireland is summarized in Marie Fox and Sheelagh McGuinness, "In the Matter of an Application for Judicial Review by the Northern Ireland Human Rights Commission, 2015," n.p.

39. This lasting effect of the Troubles can also be witnessed in Paul Muldoon's surveillance-oriented collection *One Thousand Things Worth Knowing: Poems*, with its military watchtower on the cover.

40. I am grateful to a pseudonymous commenter on the *Guardian* website who made the link between the Sex Pistols song and Gamble's poem. The lyrics "she's a bloody disgrace" have led some, including Gamble herself, to voice misgivings about this song. Singer John Lydon (also known as Johnny Rotten) has stated in an interview he was reflecting the views of others, not condemning abortion himself.

41. Haberstroh, "Poetry, 1970–Present," 295. Tracy Brain's review of *Pillow Talk* reports Meehan's remarks on the phrase "woman writer": "It's often used to ghettoise women. I don't find the label . . . an insult, but I'm wary that it can be used to try and marginalise women." Brain, "Nobody's Muse: *Pillow Talk* with Paula Meehan," 11–12.

42. Haberstroh has raised the idea of a distinct female Irish poetic tradition that is inflected by law, writing that "challenging gender stereotypes propagated by the church and state, Irish women writers have sought to interrogate the limited 'wife and mother in the home' model embedded in the 1937 Irish Constitution, and to question the sexual taboos imposed upon the culture by both church and state." Haberstroh, "Poetry, 1970–Present," 295.

43. Ní Ghríofa, "Birthburst," Body website, https://bodyliterature.com/2014/10/28/doireann-ni-ghriofa/. A slightly amended version of this poem was published in *Clasp*, 44.

44. Ní Ghríofa, *Clasp*, 44.

Conclusion

1. Thomas Hobbes, *Leviathan; or, The Matter, Forme and Power of a Commonwealth Ecclesiasticall and Civil*, 242. André Munro makes the link between Hobbes and Weber in *Encyclopaedia Britannica*, s.v. "state monopoly on violence," www.britannica.com/topic/state-monopoly-on-violence.

2. Max Weber, "Politics as Vocation."

3. John Rawls, *A Theory of Justice*, 3.

4. John Rawls writes that the state is too self-interested to be an agent of justice in *The Law of Peoples: With the Idea of Public Reason Revisited*, 28. His ideas have been questioned by Onora O'Neill in "Agents of Justice."

5. Quoted in Seamus Heaney, *The Redress of Poetry*, 3.

6. Heaney, "Writer and Righter," 17.

7. Joachim J. Savelsberg and Ryan D. King, "Law and Collective Memory," 190.

8. The sometimes terrible power of legal rituals is the subject of Colin Dayan's seminal study *The Law Is a White Dog: How Legal Rituals Make and Unmake Persons*.

9. Though I do not write of the Irish state's notorious "Direct Provision" system for refugees in this book, I discuss its spectral presence in the work of Doireann Ní Ghríofa in a forthcoming chapter, "Connection and Citizenship in Doireann Ní Ghríofa's *Clasp*," in *Law and Literature: The Irish Case*, ed. Adam Hanna and Eugene McNulty (Liverpool: Liverpool Univ. Press, forthcoming). This system is the subject of the edited collection compiled by Stephen Rea and Jessica Traynor, *Correspondences: An Anthology to Call for an End to Direct Provision*.

10. The information in this paragraph comes from Kimberly Campanello's *MOTHERBABYHOME* website, www.kimberlycampanello.com/motherbabyhome; Emer O'Toole, "The Report into Abuses at Ireland's Mother and Baby Homes Does Not Go Far Enough—There Must Be Criminal Justice Proceedings," *Independent*,

Jan. 14, 2021, www.independent.co.uk/voices/ireland-mother-baby-homes-abuse-report-b1787252.html.

11. Máiréad Enright, "Responding to Ireland's Mother and Baby Homes Commission Report." See also Máiréad Enright, "The Mother and Baby Homes Commission Report Misses the Point on Redress," *Thejournal.ie*, Jan. 23, 2021, www.thejournal.ie/readme/mother-and-baby-homes-2-5324302-Jan2021/.

12. Ailbhe Darcy, "Recent Documentary Poetry in Performance," 61.

13. Shane Phelan, "IHREC Concern over Bill Allowing Graves at Mother and Baby Homes to Be Exhumed," *Independent.ie*, Feb. 22, 2021, www.independent.ie/irish-news/ihrec-concern-over-bill-allowing-graves-at-mother-and-baby-homes-to-be-exhumed-40116312.html.

14. Ailbhe Conneely, "Deadline Nears for Mother-and-Baby Home Burial Submissions," Rte.ie, Feb. 21, 2021, www.rte.ie/news/ireland/2021/0221/1198370-mother-and-baby-home-burial-submissions-deadline-nears/.

15. Darcy comments on the consonances between Kinsella's and Campanello's work in "Recent Documentary Poetry in Performance," 64.

16. Kinsella to Adam Hanna, quoted in "Dual Arrangement," 71.

17. Barbara A. Misztal, in an essay on Durkheim and collective memory, writes of his position that that "memory is codified in law. [. . .] The past endures in the present in legislation." Misztal, "Durkheim on Collective Memory," 132.

Bibliography

Archival and Manuscript Materials

Coghill, Rhoda. Correspondence, drafts, and other papers. 2 envelopes. Held by the estate of Rhoda Coghill.

Durcan, Paul. Handwritten and typescript drafts of poems for *Jesus, Break His Fall* and notes relating to publication. MS 45,761/1, 1978–80. Paul Durcan Papers. National Library of Ireland, Dublin.

Heaney, Seamus. Draft letter to Niall Farrell (brother of Mairéad Farrell) with annotated typescript of *GiB: A Modest Exposure*, by Paul Macdonnell, and letter from Niall Farrell. MSS 960, box 45, FF4, Jan. 17, 1989. Seamus Heaney Papers. Stuart A. Rose Library, Emory Univ., Atlanta.

———. Draft manuscript of "The Unacknowledged Legislator." File I.vi.4. Seamus Heaney Literary Papers, 1963–2010. National Library of Ireland, Dublin.

———. File l.vi. *North*. Seamus Heaney Literary Papers, 1963–2010. National Library of Ireland, Dublin.

———. "New Worlds." A contribution to *The Prison of His Days: A Miscellany for Nelson Mandela on His Seventieth Birthday* [1988]. MSS, box 74, 960, FF22. Seamus Heaney Papers. Stuart A. Rose Library, Emory Univ., Atlanta.

———. "Title Deeds." Typescript lecture with manuscript additions, delivered to the American Philosophical Society on Apr. 23, 2004. MSS 960, box 98, FF57. Seamus Heaney Papers. Stuart A. Rose Library, Emory Univ., Atlanta.

Kinsella, Thomas. BBC script titled "The Arts in Ireland." Photocopied typescript dated Jan. 23, 1973. Box 99, MSS 960, FF1. Seamus Heaney Archive. Stuart A. Rose Library, Emory Univ., Atlanta.

Yeats, W. B. Marked-up copy of "A Defence of Poetry." In *Essays and Letters by Percy Bysshe Shelley*, edited by Ernest Rhys (London: Walter Scott, 1886). MS 40, 568/215. Yeats Library, National Library of Ireland, Dublin.

Other Sources

"After Ann Lovett." *Hot Press* 8, no. 4 (1984): 36.

Allain, Jean, and Siobhán Mullally, eds. *The Irish Yearbook of International Law, 2007.* Oxford: Hart, 2009.

Allen, Nicholas. *Modernism, Ireland and Civil War.* Oxford: Oxford Univ. Press, 2009.

Allison, Jonathan. "Acts of Memory: Poetry and the Republic of Ireland since 1949." In *Writing in the Irish Republic: Literature, Culture, Politics, 1949–1999*, edited by Ray Ryan, 44–63. Basingstoke: Macmillan Press, 2000.

———, ed. *Yeats's Political Identities.* Ann Arbor: Univ. of Michigan Press, 1996.

Asmal, Kader. *Shoot to Kill? International Lawyers' Inquiry into the Lethal Use of Firearms by the Security Forces of Northern Ireland.* Cork: Mercier Press, 1985.

Auden, W. H. *The Dyer's Hand, and Other Essays.* New York: Vintage Books, 1968.

Auge, Andrew. "The Apparitions of 'Our Lady of the Facts of Life': Paula Meehan and the Visionary Quotidian." *An Sionnach: A Journal of Literature, Culture and the Arts* 5, nos. 1–2 (2009): 50–64.

———. *A Chastened Communion: Modern Irish Poetry and Catholicism.* Syracuse, NY: Syracuse Univ. Press, 2013.

Bartlett, Thomas. *Ireland: A History.* Cambridge: Cambridge Univ. Press, 2010.

Barzilai, Lyn Graham. *George Oppen: A Critical Study.* Jefferson, NC: McFarland, 2006.

Beaumont, Caitríona. "Women, Citizenship and Catholicism in the Irish Free State, 1922–1948." *Women's History Review* 6, no. 4 (1997): 563–85.

Beckett, Samuel. "Recent Irish Poetry." In *Disjecta: Miscellaneous Writing*, edited by Ruby Cohn, 70–76. London: John Calder, 1983.

Bennett, Andrew, and Nicholas Royle. *An Introduction to Literature, Criticism and Theory*. 3rd ed. Harlow: Pearson, 2004.

Boland, Eavan. "The Communal Art of Paula Meehan." *An Sionnach: A Journal of Literature, Culture and the Arts* 5, nos. 1–2 (2009): 17–24.

———. *Domestic Violence*. Manchester: Carcanet, 2007.

———. *In a Time of Violence*. Manchester: Carcanet, 1994.

———. *The Journey, and Other Poems*. Manchester: Carcanet, 1987.

Brain, Tracey. "Nobody's Muse: *Pillow Talk* with Paula Meehan." *Irish Studies Review* 3, no. 10 (1995): 11–15.

Brooker, Joseph. "'Estopped by Grand Playsaunce': Flann O'Brien's Postcolonial Lore." In *Law and Literature*, edited by Patrick Hanafin, Adam Gearey, and Joseph Brooker, 15–37. Oxford: Blackwell, 2004.

Brown, Karen E. *The Yeats Circle, Verbal and Visual Relations in Ireland, 1880–1939*. Farnham: Ashgate, 2011.

Brown, Michael, and Seán Patrick Dolan, eds. *The Laws and Other Legalities of Ireland, 1689–1850*. Abingdon: Routledge, 2011.

Brown, Terence. *Ireland: A Social and Cultural History, 1922 to the Present*. Ithaca, NY: Cornell Univ. Press, 1985.

———. *Ireland: A Social and Cultural History, 1922–2002*. London: Harper Perennial, 2004.

———. "Seamus Heaney's Tender Yeats." Éire-Ireland 49, nos. 3–4 (2014): 301–19.

Bryant, Sophie. *Celtic Ireland*. London: Kegan Paul, Trench, 1889.

Bunreacht na hÉireann—Constitution of Ireland. Dublin: Stationery Office, 2015. www.taoiseach.gov.ie.

Campanello, Kimberly. *MOTHERBABYHOME*. Manchester: zimZalla, 2019.

Campbell, Colm. *Emergency Law in Ireland, 1918–1925*. Oxford: Clarendon Press, 1994.

Campbell, Matthew, ed. *The Cambridge Companion to Contemporary Irish Poetry*. Cambridge: Cambridge Univ. Press, 2003.

Cardozo, Benjamin N. *The Growth of the Law*. 1924. Reprint, Westport, CT: Greenwood Press, 1966.

Carlson, Julia, ed. *Banned in Ireland*. London: Routledge, 1990.

Carson, Ciaran. "Escaped from the Massacre? Seamus Heaney's *North*." In *A Twentieth Century Literature Reader*, edited by Suman Gupta and David Johnson, 267–71. London: Routledge, 2005.

Cavanagh, Clare. *Lyric Poetry and Modern Politics: Russia, Poland and the West.* New Haven, CT: Yale Univ. Press, 2009.

Chaucer, Geoffrey. *The Canterbury Tales.* In *The Riverside Chaucer*, edited by Larry D. Benson. 3rd ed. Oxford: Oxford Univ. Press, 1988.

Chubb, Basil. *The Politics of the Irish Constitution.* Dublin: Institute of Public Administration, 1991.

Clancy, Mary. "Aspects of Women's Contribution to the Oireachtas Debate in the Irish Free State, 1922–37." In *The Irish Women's History Reader*, edited by Alan Hayes and Diane Urquhart, 64–70. London: Routledge, 2001.

Clark, Gemma. *Everyday Violence in the Irish Civil War.* Cambridge: Cambridge Univ. Press, 2014.

Clarke, Austin. "Banned Books" [1953]. In *Reviews and Essays of Austin Clarke*, edited Gregory A. Schirmer, 123–25. Gerards Cross: Colin Smythe, 1995.

———. "The Black Church." In *Reviews and Essays of Austin Clarke*, edited Gregory A. Schirmer, 224–28. Gerards Cross: Colin Smythe, 1995.

———. *The Bright Temptation: A Romance.* Dublin: Dolmen Press, 1932.

———. *The Cattledrive in Connaught, and Other Poems.* London: Allen & Unwin, 1925.

———. *Collected Poems.* London: Allen & Unwin, 1936.

———. *Collected Poems.* Edited by Liam Miller. Dublin: Dolmen Press, 1974.

———. *Collected Poems.* Edited by R. Dardis Clarke. Manchester: Carcanet, 2008.

———. *A Penny in the Clouds: More Memories of Ireland and England.* London: Routledge, 1968.

———. *Pilgrimage, and Other Poems.* London: George Allen and Unwin, 1929.

———. "The Room Upstairs." In *Reviews and Essays of Austin Clarke*, edited by Gregory A. Schirmer, 234–39. Gerards Cross: Colin Smythe, 1995.

———. *Selected Poems.* Dublin: Liliput Press, 1991.

Cleary, Joe. *The Cambridge Companion to Irish Modernism.* Cambridge: Cambridge Univ. Press, 2014.

Clutterbuck, Catriona. "Irish Women's Poetry and the Republic of Ireland: Formalism as Form." In *Writing in the Irish Republic: Literature, Culture, Politics, 1949–1999*, edited by Ray Ryan, 17–43. Basingstoke: Macmillan Press, 2000.

———. "'Mise Eire,' Eavan Boland." *Irish University Review* 39, no. 2 (2009): 289–300.

———. "'Pilot and Stray in One': Sustaining Nothingness in the Travel Poems of Early Heaney." *Irish Review* 49–50 (2014–15): 106–21.

Coghill, Rhoda. *The Bright Hillside*. Dublin: Hodges, Figgis, 1948.

———. *Time Is a Squirrel*. Dublin: the author, 1956.

Collins, Lucy. "'I knew what it meant / Not to be at all': Death and the (Modernist) Afterlife in the Work of Irish Women Poets of the 1940s." In *Modernist Afterlives in Irish Literature and Culture*, edited by Paige Reynolds, 23–34. Atlanta: Anthem, 2016.

———. "Irish Poets in the Public Sphere." In *The Cambridge Companion to Contemporary Irish Poetry*, edited by Matthew Campbell, 209–38. Cambridge: Cambridge Univ. Press, 2003.

———, ed. *Poetry by Women in Ireland: A Critical Anthology, 1870–1970*. Liverpool: Liverpool Univ. Press, 2012.

Colum, Mary. *Life and the Dream*. New York: Doubleday, 1947.

Committee on the Administration of Justice. "Prisons and Prisoners in Northern Ireland: Putting Human Rights at the Heart of Prison Reform." Dec. 2010. www.caj.org.uk/files/2011/01/17/prisons_report_web2.pdf.

Connellan, Owen, ed. *Transactions of the Ossianic Society for the Year 1857*. Vol. 5. Dublin: Ossianic Society, 1860.

Connolly, Claire. "Introduction: Ireland in Theory." In *Theorizing Ireland*, edited by Claire Connolly, 1–13. New York: Palgrave, 2004.

Connolly, Linda. *The Irish Women's Movement: From Revolution to Devolution*. Basingstoke: Palgrave, 2002.

Coogan, Tim Pat. *Ireland in the Twentieth Century*. London: Arrow Books, 2004.

Corcoran, Neil. *The Poetry of Seamus Heaney: A Critical Study*. London: Faber and Faber, 1998.

Corkery, Daniel. *The Hidden Ireland: A Study of Gaelic Munster in the Eighteenth Century*. Dublin: Gill & Macmillan, 1924.

Cotta, Sergio. "Positive Law and Natural Law." *Review of Metaphysics* 37, no. 2 (1983): 265–85.

Coughlan, Patricia, and Alex Davis, eds. *Modernism and Ireland: The Poetry of the 1930s.* Cork: Cork Univ. Press, 1995.

Cronin, Anthony. *The End of the Modern World.* Dublin: New Island, 2016.

Cronin, Michael G. *Impure Thoughts: Sexuality, Catholicism and Literature in Twentieth-Century Ireland.* Manchester: Manchester Univ. Press, 2012.

Cross, Frank Leslie, and Elizabeth A. Livingstone, eds. *The Oxford Dictionary of the Christian Church.* Oxford: Oxford Univ. Press, 2005.

Crotty, Patrick. *The Penguin Book of Irish Poetry.* London: Penguin, 2010.

Cullingford, Elizabeth. "How Jacques Molay Got Up the Tower: Yeats and the Irish Civil War." *ELH* 50, no. 4 (1983): 763–89.

Darcy, Ailbhe. "Recent Documentary Poetry in Performance." *Poetry Ireland Review* 132 (2020): 59–68.

D'Arcy, Kathy. "Almost Forgotten Names: Irish Women Poets of the 1930s, 1940s and 1950s." In *Irish Literature: Feminist Perspectives*, edited by Patricia Coughlan and Tina O'Toole, 99–123. Dublin: Carysfort Press, 2008.

———. "Why Uncomplicated Recovery Isn't Enough: Rhoda Coghill, Her Letters, and the Fired! Movement." *Honest Ulsterman*, June 2020. humag.co/features/why-uncomplicated-recovery-isn-t-enough.

Davis, Alex. *A Broken Line: Denis Devlin and Irish Poetic Modernism.* Dublin: Univ. College Dublin Press, 2000.

———. "Irish Poetry to 1966." In *A Companion to Twentieth Century Irish Poetry*, edited by Neil Roberts, 343–56. Oxford: Blackwell, 2001.

———. "Thomas Kinsella and the Pound Legacy: His Jacket on the 'Cantos.'" *Irish University Review* 31, no. 1 (2001): 38–53.

Davis, Alex, and Lee M. Jenkins, eds. *A History of Modernist Poetry.* Cambridge: Cambridge Univ. Press, 2015.

Dayan, Colin. *The Law Is a White Dog: How Legal Rituals Make and Unmake Persons.* Princeton, NJ: Princeton Univ. Press, 2011.

de Londras, Fiona. "Protection of Life during Pregnancy Act, 2013." In *Women's Legal Landmarks: Celebrating the History of Women and Law in the UK and Ireland*, edited by Erika Rackley and Rosemary Auchmuty. Oxford: Hart, 2018.

Dickson, Brice. *The European Convention on Human Rights and the Conflict in Northern Ireland.* Oxford: Oxford Univ. Press, 2010.

Dolin, Kieran, ed. *Law and Literature.* Cambridge: Cambridge Univ. Press, 2018.

Dorgan, Theo. "Law, Poetry and the Republic." In *Up the Republic! Towards a New Ireland*, edited by Fintan O'Toole, 182–207. London: Faber and Faber, 2012.

Drabble, Margaret. *The Oxford Companion to English Literature.* Oxford: Oxford Univ. Press, 1995.

Duffy, Johannah. "Jazz, Identity and Sexuality in Ireland during the Interwar Years." *IJAS Online*, no. 1 (2009): 62–71.

Dunlop, C. R. B. "Literature Studies in Law Schools." *Cardozo Studies in Law and Literature* 3, no. 1 (1991): 63–110.

Durcan, Paul. *Ark of the North.* Dublin: Raven Arts, 1982.

———. *The Berlin Wall Café.* Belfast: Blackstaff, 1985.

———. *Daddy, Daddy.* Belfast: Blackstaff, 1990.

———. *Going Home to Russia.* Belfast: Blackstaff, 1987.

———. *Jesus, Break His Fall.* Dublin: Raven Arts, 1980.

———. *Jumping the Train Tracks with Angela.* Dublin: Raven Arts, 1983.

———. *Teresa's Bar.* Oldcastle, Co. Meath: Gallery Press, 1976.

Eberle, Edward J., and Bernhard Grossfeld. "Law and Poetry." *Roger Williams University Law Review* 11, no. 2 (2006) 353–401.

Ellis, Edwin J. *Sancan the Bard.* London: Ward and Downey, 1895.

Ellison, Graham, and Jim Smyth. *The Crowned Harp: Policing Northern Ireland.* London: Pluto Press, 2000.

Enright, Máiréad. "Responding to Ireland's Mother and Baby Homes Commission Report." OxHRH blog, Jan. 20, 2021. http://ohrh.law.ox.ac.uk/responding-to-irelands-mother-and-baby-homes-commission-report/.

Eska, Joseph F., ed. *Literature, Law and Society.* Dublin: Four Courts Press, 2008.

Falci, Eric. *Continuity and Change in Irish Poetry, 1966–2010.* Cambridge: Cambridge Univ. Press, 2012.

Fanning, Bryan. *The Quest for Modern Ireland: The Battle of Ideas, 1912–1986.* Dublin: Irish Academic Press, 2008.

Farnan, Conor. "The Most Subversive Unit in Society: Depicting the Family in *Daddy, Daddy* and *The Laughter of Mothers.*" www.academia.edu.

Feeney, Elaine. *Rise*. Co. Clare: Salmon, 2017.

Felzmann, Heike. "Bringing Abortion to Ireland? The Protection of Life during Pregnancy Act 2013." *International Journal of Feminist Approaches to Bioethics* 7, no. 1 (2014): 192–98.

Ferriter, Diarmaid. "De Valera's Ireland: 1932–58." In *The Oxford Handbook of Modern Irish History*, edited by Alvin Jackson, 670–92. Oxford: Oxford Univ. Press, 2014.

———. *Occasions of Sin: Sex and Society in Modern Ireland*. London: Profile Books, 2009.

Fiacc, Padraic, ed. *The Wearing of the Black: An Anthology of Contemporary Ulster Poetry*. Belfast: Blackstaff, 1974.

Fine-Davis, Margaret. *Gender Roles in Ireland: Three Decades of Attitude Change*. New York: Routledge, 2015.

Fitzpatrick, David. "Yeats in the Senate." *Studia Hibernica* 12 (1972): 7–26.

Fitzsimons, Andrew. "The Sea of Disappointment: Thomas Kinsella's 'Nightwalker' and the New Ireland." *Irish University Review* 36, no. 2 (2006): 335–52.

Fogarty, Anne. "'The Influence of Absences': Eavan Boland and the Silenced History of Irish Women's Poetry." *Colby Quarterly* 35, no. 4 (1999): 256–74.

Foster, R. F. *Luck & the Irish: A Brief History of Change, c. 1970–2000*. London: Penguin, 2007.

———. *Modern Ireland: 1600–1972*. London: Penguin, 1988.

———, ed. *The Oxford Illustrated History of Ireland*. Oxford: Oxford Univ. Press, 1989.

———. *W. B. Yeats: A Life*. Vol. 1, *The Apprentice Mage, 1865–1914*. Oxford: Oxford Univ. Press, 1997.

———. *W. B. Yeats: A Life*. Vol. 2, *The Arch-Poet, 1915–1939*. Oxford: Oxford Univ. Press, 2003.

———. *Words Alone: Yeats and His Inheritances*. Oxford: Oxford Univ. Press, 2011.

Fox, Marie, and Sheelagh McGuinness. "In the Matter of an Application for Judicial Review by the Northern Ireland Human Rights Commission, 2015." In *Women's Legal Landmarks: Celebrating the History of Women and Law in the UK and Ireland*, edited by Erika Rackley and Rosemary Auchmuty. London: Hart, 2018.

Franks, Jill. *British and Irish Women Writers and the Women's Movement: Six Literary Voices of Their Times*. Jefferson, NC: McFarland, 2013.

Freeman, Alexander Martin. *Thomas Love Peacock: A Critical Study*. London: M. Secker, 1911.

Friedan, Betty. *The Feminine Mystique*. New York: W. W. Norton, 1963.

Froissart, Jean. *The Chronicles of Froissart: Translated by John Bourchier, Lord Berners*. Edited by G. C. Macaulay. London: Macmillan, 1899.

Fryatt, Kit. *Austin Clarke*. Aberdeen: Aberdeen Univ. Press, 2020.

Fuller, Lon L. *The Morality of Law*. New Haven, CT: Yale Univ. Press, 1969.

Gamble, Miriam. *Pirate Music*. Hexham: Bloodaxe, 2014.

Garton, Tessa. "Masks and Monsters: Some Recurring Themes in Irish Romanesque Sculpture." In *From Ireland Coming*, ed. Colum Hourihane, 121–40. Princeton, NJ: Princeton Univ. Press, 2001.

Gillis, Alan. *Irish Poetry of the 1930s*. Oxford: Oxford Univ. Press.

Ginnell, Laurence. *Handbook of Brehon Law*. London: T. Fisher Unwin, 1894.

Godwin, William. *Life of Geoffrey Chaucer, the Early English Poet*. London: Richard Phillips, 1804.

González-Arias, Luz Mar. "'A Pedigree Bitch, Like Myself': (Non)Human Illness and Death in Dorothy Molloy's Poetry." In *Animals in Irish Literature and Culture*, edited by Kathryn Kirkpatrick and Borbála Faragó, 119–34. Basingstoke: Palgrave Macmillan, 2015.

———. "'Playing with the Ghosts of Words': Interview with Paula Meehan." *Atlantis* 22, no. 1 (2000): 187–204.

Goodby, John. "From Irish Mode to Modernisation." In *The Cambridge Companion to Contemporary Irish Poetry*, edited by Matthew Campbell, 21–41. Cambridge: Cambridge Univ. Press, 2003.

———. *Irish Poetry since 1950: From Stillness into History*. Manchester: Manchester Univ. Press, 2000.

———. "'The Prouder Counsel of Her Throat': Towards a Feminist Reading of Austin Clarke." *Irish University Review* 29, no. 2 (1999): 321–40.

———. "Review: *Seeing Things* by Seamus Heaney and *Gorse Fires* by Michael Longley." *Studies: An Irish Quarterly Review* 81, no. 324 (1992): 448–52.

Gould, Warwick. "'Satan, Satan Smut & Co': Yeats and the Suppression of Evil Literature in the Early Years of the Free State." *Yeats Annual* 21 (2018): 123–212.

Graham, Colin. *Ideologies of Epic: Nation, Empire, and Victorian Epic Poetry*. Manchester: Manchester Univ. Press, 1998.

Graves, Robert. *The White Goddess: A Historical Grammar of Poetic Myth*. New York: Noonday Press, 1966.

Green, Marion. *A Prison Experience: A Loyalist Perspective*. Belfast: Ex-Prisoners' Interpretative Centre, 1998. https://cedarlounge.files.wordpress.com/2012/01/loyalprisondoc.pdf.

Grey, Thomas C. *The Wallace Stevens Case: Law and the Practice of Poetry*. Cambridge, MA: Harvard Univ. Press: 1991.

Grimes, Richard H., and Patrick T. Horgan. *Introduction to Law in the Republic of Ireland: Its History, Principles, Administration and Substance*. Dublin: Wolfhound Press, 1981.

Haberstroh, Patricia Boyle. "Poetry, 1970–Present." In *A History of Modern Irish Women's Literature*, edited by Heather Ingman and Clíona Ó Gallchoir, 294–311. Cambridge: Cambridge Univ. Press, 2018.

Hanna, Adam. "A Dual Arrangement: Thomas Kinsella." *Poetry Ireland Review* 124 (2018): 69–71.

Hansard, 1803–2005. http://hansard.millbanksystems.com/commons.

Hardiman, Adrian. *Joyce in Court*. Dublin: Head of Zeus, 2016.

Harmon, Maurice. *Austin Clarke, 1896–1974: A Critical Introduction*. Dublin: Wolfhound Press, 1989.

Hartnett, Michael. *A Farewell to English, and Other Poems*. Dublin: Gallery Press, 1975.

Hayes, Alan, and Diane Urquhart, eds. *The Irish Women's History Reader*. London: Routledge, 2001.

Heaney, Seamus. *The Burial at Thebes*. London: Faber and Faber, 2004.

———. *District and Circle*. London: Faber and Faber, 2006.

———. *Field Work*. London: Faber and Faber, 1979.

———. *Finders Keepers: Selected Prose, 1971–2001*. London: Faber and Faber, 2002.

———. *The Government of the Tongue: The 1986 T. S. Eliot Memorial Lectures, and Other Critical Writings*. London: Faber and Faber, 1988.

———. *The Haw Lantern*. London: Faber and Faber, 1987.

———. *Human Chain*. London: Faber and Faber, 2010.

———. "The Interesting Case of Nero, Chekhov's Cognac and a Knocker." In *The Government of the Tongue: The 1986 T. S. Eliot Memorial*

Lectures, and Other Critical Writings, xi–xxiii. London: Faber and Faber, 1988.

———. *North*. London: Faber and Faber, 1975.

———. *Opened Ground: Poems, 1966–1996*. London: Faber and Faber, 1998.

———. *Preoccupations: Selected Prose, 1968–1978*. London: Faber and Faber, 1980.

———. *The Redress of Poetry*. London: Faber and Faber, 1995.

———. "The Road to Derry." *Derry Journal*, Jan. 31, 1997. www.derry journal.com.

———. *Seeing Things*. London: Faber and Faber, 1991.

———. *The Spirit Level*. London: Faber and Faber, 1995.

———. *Station Island*. London: Faber and Faber, 1984.

———. *Stations*. Belfast: Ulsterman, 1975.

———. *Wintering Out*. London: Faber and Faber, 1972.

———. "The Wood Road." *Magma* 36 (2006): 28.

———. "Writer and Righter." Fourth Irish Human Rights Commission Annual Human Rights Lecture, Dec. 9, 2009. Dublin: Irish Human Rights Commission, 2010. www.ihrec.ie/documents/writer-righter-by-seamus-heaney/.

Hewitt, John. *Collected Poems*. Edited by Frank Ormsby. Belfast: Blackstaff, 1991.

Higgins, Geraldine. *Heroic Revivals from Carlyle to Yeats*. Basingstoke: Palgrave Macmillan, 2012.

———. "The Quotable Yeats: Modified in the Guts of the Living." *South Carolina Review* 32, no. 1 (1999): 184–92.

Higgins, Noelle. "The Lost Legal System: Pre–Common Law Ireland and the Brehon Law." In *Legal Theory Practice and Education*, edited by Carsten Gerner-Beuerle and David A. Frenkel, 193–205. Athens: ATINER, 2011.

Hill, Geoffrey. *Collected Critical Writings*. Edited by Kenneth Haynes. Oxford: Oxford Univ. Press, 2008.

———. "Milton as Muse." Lecture delivered at Lady Margaret Lecture, Cambridge, Oct. 28, 2008. www.christs.cam.ac.uk/files/hill.mp3.

Hill, J. R., ed. *A New History of Ireland*. 9 vols. Oxford: Oxford Univ. Press, 2003.

Hobbes, Thomas. *Leviathan; or, The Matter, Forme and Power of a Commonwealth Ecclesiasticall and Civil.* 1651. Reprint, Oxford: James Thornton, 1881.

Hogan, Caelainn. *Republic of Shame: Stories from Ireland's Institutions for "Fallen Women."* London: Penguin Books, 2019.

Holmes, Oliver Wendell. "Natural Law." *Harvard Law Review* 32, no. 1 (1918): 40–44.

Howes, Marjorie, and John Kelly, eds. *The Cambridge Companion to W. B. Yeats*. Cambridge: Cambridge Univ. Press, 2006.

Howley, Ellen. "The Sea and Memory: Poetic Reconsiderations of the *Zong* Massacre." *Journal of Commonwealth Literature* 45, no. 3 (2019): 371–88.

Hug, Chrystel. *The Politics of Sexual Morality in Ireland.* Basingstoke: Macmillan, 1999.

Hunt, Alan. "On Georges Gurvitch, *Sociology of Law.*" In *Classic Writings in Law and Society*, edited by A. Javier Treviño, 141–63. London: Transaction, 2009.

Hutton-Williams, Francis. "Against Irish Modernism: Towards an Analysis of Experimental Irish Poetry." *Irish University Review* 46, no. 1 (2016): 20–37.

Inglis, Tom. "Origins and Legacies of Irish Prudery: Sexuality and Social Control in Modern Ireland." Éire-Ireland 40, nos. 3–4 (2005): 9–37.

Ingman, Heather. *Twentieth-Century Fiction by Irish Women: Nation and Gender.* London: Routledge, 2007.

Jackson, Alvin. *Home Rule: An Irish History, 1800–2000.* Oxford: Oxford Univ. Press, 2003.

———, ed. *The Oxford Handbook of Modern Irish History.* Oxford: Oxford Univ. Press, 2014.

Jackson, Donald W. *The United Kingdom Confronts the European Convention on Human Rights.* Gainesville: Univ. Press of Florida, 1997.

John, Brian. *Reading the Ground: The Poetry of Thomas Kinsella.* Washington, DC: Catholic Univ. of America Press, 1996.

Jordan, D. "The Irish National League and the 'Unwritten Law': Rural Protest and Nation-Building in Ireland, 1882–1890." *Past & Present* 158 (1998): 146–71.

Kavanagh, Patrick. *Collected Poems.* London: Martin Brian and O'Keeffe, 1984.

———. *Collected Poems*. Edited by Antoinette Quinn. London: Allen Lane, 2004.

Kavanagh, Peter, ed. *Irish Mythology: A Dictionary*. Newbridge, Co. Kildare: Goldsmith Press, 1988.

Kayman, Martin. "The Law and the Statuesque." *Law and Critique* 24, no. 1 (2013): 1–22.

Kelly, Fergus. *A Guide to Early Irish Law*. Dublin: Dublin Institute for Advanced Studies, 1988.

Kennedy, Michael. *Ireland and the League of Nations, 1919–1946: International Relations, Diplomacy and Politics*. Dublin: Irish Academic Press, 1996.

Kiberd, Declan. *Irish Classics*. London: Granta Books, 2000.

———. "Irish Literature and Irish History." In *The Oxford History of Ireland*, edited by R. F. Foster, 230–81. Oxford: Oxford Univ. Press, 1989.

King, Richard J. *The Devil's Cormorant: A Natural History*. Oxford: Oxford Univ. Press, 2015.

Kinsella, Thomas. *Butcher's Dozen: A Lesson for the Octave of Widgery*. Dublin: Peppercanister, 1972.

———. *Collected Poems*. Manchester: Carcanet Press, 2001.

———. "The Irish Writer" [1966]. In vol. 3 of *The Field Day Anthology of Irish Writing*, edited by Seamus Deane, 625–29. Derry: Field Day, 1991.

Kinsella's Oversight: A Reply to "The [sic] *Butcher's Dozen," a Poem on Bloody Sunday*. Belfast: British and Irish Communist Organisation, 1973.

Kotsonouris, Mary. *Retreat from Revolution: The Dáil Courts, 1920–24*. Dublin: Irish Academic Press, 1994.

Krimm, Bernard G. *W. B. Yeats and the Emergence of the Irish Free State, 1918–1939: Living in the Explosion*. New York: Whitston, 1981.

Kuch, Peter. *Joyce's Ulysses / Irish Divorce*. New York: Palgrave, 2017.

Laird, Heather. "Law, Colonialism and Anti-colonial Resistance." Unpublished presentation at the Northern/Irish Feminist Judgments Project, Univ. College Cork, Feb. 2015.

———. *Subversive Law in Ireland, 1879–1920: From "Unwritten Law" to the Dáil Courts*. Dublin: Four Courts Press, 2005.

Larrissy, Edward. *Yeats the Poet: The Measures of Difference*. London: Harvester Wheatsheaf, 1994.

Lee, J. J. *Ireland: Politics and Society, 1912–1985.* Cambridge: Cambridge Univ. Press, 1989.

Lin, Peter. "Wittgenstein, Language and Legal Theorizing: Toward a Non-reductive Account of Law." *University of Toronto Faculty of Law Review* 47 (1989): 939–47.

Longley, Edna. *Poetry in the Wars.* Newcastle: Bloodaxe, 1986.

———. *Yeats and Modern Poetry.* Cambridge: Cambridge Univ. Press, 2013.

Longley, Michael. *Collected Poems.* London: Jonathan Cape, 2006.

———. "Room to Rhyme: Some Memories of Seamus Heaney." *Irish Review* 49–50 (2014–15): 33–37.

Lowrie, Michèle. *Writing, Performance, and Authority in Augustan Rome.* Oxford: Oxford Univ. Press, 2009.

Macardle, Dorothy. *Earth-Bound: Nine Stories of Ireland.* Dublin: self-published at Frankfort House, 1924.

MacDonagh, Thomas. *Literature in Ireland: Studies in Irish and Anglo-Irish.* Dublin: Talbot Press, 1916.

MacKillop, James, ed. *Dictionary of Celtic Mythology.* Oxford: Oxford Univ. Press, 1998.

Mahon, Derek. "Orpheus Ascending: The Poetry of Paul Durcan." In *The Kilfenora Teaboy: A Study of Paul Durcan*, edited by Colm Tóibín, 163–70. Dublin: New Island Books, 1996.

———. *The Snow Party.* London: Oxford Univ. Press, 1975.

Marcus, Philip L. *Yeats and Artistic Power.* Syracuse, NY: Syracuse Univ. Press, 2001.

Martin, Augustine. *Bearing Witness: Essays on Anglo-Irish Literature.* Dublin: UCD Press, 1996.

Mays, Michael. *Nation States: The Culture of Irish Nationalism.* Lanham, MD: Lexington Books, 2007.

McAtackney, Laura. *Archaeology of the Troubles: The Dark Heritage of Long Kesh / Maze Prison.* Oxford: Oxford Univ. Press, 2008.

McAuliffe, John. "Against Irish Studies: Reading Austin Clarke and His Critics." In *New Voices in Irish Criticism*, edited by P. J. Mathews, 255–59. Dublin: Four Courts Press, 2000.

McCabe, Conor. *Sins of the Father: Tracing the Decisions That Shaped the Irish Economy.* Dublin: History Press, 2011.

McCafferty, Nell. *The Kerry Babies Case: A Woman to Blame*. Cork: Cork Univ. Press, 2010.

McCann, Fiona. "Writing by and about Republican Women Prisoners: 'Willful Subjects.'" *Irish University Review* 47 (2017): 502–14.

McCarthy, Conor. *Modernisation, Crisis and Culture in Ireland, 1969–1992*. Dublin: Four Courts Press, 2000.

McCormack, W. J. "The Poet as Scapegoat of Modernism." In *Modernism and Ireland: The Poetry of the 1930s*, edited by Alex Davies and Patricia Coughlan, 75–102. Cork: Cork Univ. Press, 1995.

McGowan Smyth, John. *The Theory and Practice of the Irish Senate*. Dublin: Institute of Public Administration, 1972.

McKenna, Bernard. "Paul Durcan." In *Modern Irish Writers: A Bio-critical Sourcebook*, edited by Alexander G. Gonzalez, 69–72. London: Greenword Press, 1997.

McNulty, Eugene. "Law in Contemporary Anglophone Literature." In *Law and Literature*, edited by Kieran Dolin, 220–35. Cambridge: Cambridge Univ. Press, 2018.

———. "Words into Action: Re-hearing Antigone's Claim in *The Burial at Thebes*." In *Hearing Heaney: The Sixth Seamus Heaney Lectures*, edited by Eugene McNulty and Ciarán Mac Murchaidh, 111–23. Dublin: Four Courts Press, 2015.

McNulty, Eugene, and Ciarán Mac Murchaidh, eds. *Hearing Heaney: The Sixth Seamus Heaney Lectures*. Dublin: Four Courts Press, 2015.

Meehan, Paula. *Cell: A Play in Two Parts for Four Actors and a Voice*. Dublin: New Island, 2000.

———. *The Man Who Was Marked by Winter*. Oldcastle, Co. Meath: Gallery Press, 1991.

———. *Pillow Talk*. Oldcastle, Co. Meath: Gallery Press, 1994.

———. *Reading the Sky*. Dublin: Beaver Row Press, 1986.

———. *Return and No Blame*. Dublin: Beaver Row Press, 1984.

Mercier, Vivien. "Mortal Anguish, Mortal Pride: Austin Clarke's Religious Lyrics." *Irish University Review* 4, no. 1 (1974): 91–99.

Meredith, James C. "Desirable Ameliorations of the Law." *Journal of the Statistical and Social Inquiry Society of Ireland* 16 (1939–40): 63–74.

Mills, Lia. "'I Won't Go Back to It': Irish Women Poets and the Iconic Feminine." *Feminist Review* 50 (Summer 1995): 69–88.

Misztal, Barbara A. "Durkheim on Collective Memory." *Journal of Classical Sociology* 3, no. 2 (2003): 123–43.

Mitchell, Jack. *GiB: A Modest Exposure.* Dublin: Fulcrum Press, 1990.

Montague, John. *The Rough Field.* 2nd ed. Dublin: Dolmen Press, 1974.

Morash, Christopher. *A History of Irish Theatre.* Cambridge: Cambridge Univ. Press, 2002.

Morris, William. *"A Dream of John Ball" and "The King's Lesson."* London: Reeves & Turner, 1888.

Morrison, Danny. "Seamus Heaney Disputed." Jan. 31, 2009. www.dannymorrison.com.

Morrissy, Julie. "Civil Regulations Amendment Act 1956: Retirement of Women Civil Servants on Marriage." *Poetry Ireland Review* 122 (Aug. 2017): 12.

Muldoon, Paul. *Mules.* London: Faber and Faber, 1977.

———. *One Thousand Things Worth Knowing: Poems.* New York: Farrar, Straus & Giroux, 2015.

———. *To Ireland, I.* Oxford: Oxford Univ. Press, 2000.

Murphy, Gary. *In Search of the Promised Land: The Politics of Post-war Ireland.* Cork: Mercier Press, 2009.

Murphy, Michael. "Brendan's Voyage." *Hot Press* 9, no. 1 (1985): 9–10.

Murray, Yxta Maya. "Punishment and the Costs of Knowledge." In *Hearing Heaney: The Sixth Seamus Heaney Lectures*, edited by Eugene McNulty and Ciarán Mac Murchaidh, 136–54. Dublin: Four Courts Press, 2015.

National Library of Ireland. "Poetry in Progress: Building *The Tower.*" www.nli.ie/yeats/main.html.

Ní Chonaill, Eibhlín Dhubh. "Caoineadh Airt Uí Laoghaire" / "Lament for Art Ó Laoghaire." In *An Duanaire, 1600–1900: Poems of the Dispossessed*, edited by Seán Ó Tuama and Thomas Kinsella, 200–219. Dublin: Dolmen Press, 1981.

Ní Chuilleanáin, Eiléan. "The Ages of a Woman and the Middle Ages." *Irish University Review* 45, no. 2 (2015): 199–214.

Ní Ghríofa, Doireann. *Clasp.* Dublin: Dedalus Press, 2015.

Nordin, Irene Gilsenan, ed. *The Body and Desire in Contemporary Irish Poetry.* Dublin: Irish Academic Press, 2006.

———. *Crediting Marvels in Seamus Heaney's "Seeing Things."* Uppsala: Uppsala Univ., 1999.

Nussbaum, Martha. *Poetic Justice: The Literary Imagination and Public Life*. Boston: Beacon Press, 1995.

O'Brien, Conor Cruise. *Passion and Cunning*. London: Paladin, Grafton Books, 1990.

———. *States of Ireland*. London: Hutchinson, 1972.

O'Brien, Eugene. *Seamus Heaney and the Place of Poetry*. Gainesville: Univ. Press of Florida, 2002.

O'Connor, Laura. "W. B. Yeats and Modernist Poetry." In *The Cambridge Companion to Irish Modernism*, edited by Joe Cleary, 77–94. Cambridge: Cambridge Univ. Press, 2014.

O'Connor, Maura. "The Theories on Infant Pedagogy of Dr. Timothy Corcoran, Professor of Education, University College, Dublin." *Irish Educational Studies* 23, no. 1 (2004): 35–47.

O'Donnell, Mary. *Spiderwoman's Third Avenue Rhapsody*. Dublin: Salmon, 1993.

O'Donoghue, Bernard. "The Aisling." In *A Companion to Poetic Genre*, edited by Eric Martiny, 420–34. Oxford: Wiley-Blackwell, 2011.

———. "Poetry in Ireland." In *The Cambridge Guide to Modern Irish Culture*, edited by Joe Cleary and Claire Connolly, 173–89. Cambridge: Cambridge Univ. Press, 2005.

———. "Remembering Seamus Heaney." *Hungarian Journal of English and American Studies* 21, no. 2 (2015): 277–80.

O'Driscoll, Dennis. "Heaney in Public." In *The Cambridge Companion to Seamus Heaney*, edited by Bernard O'Donoghue, 56–72. Cambridge: Cambridge Univ. Press, 2009.

———. *Stepping Stones: Interviews with Seamus Heaney*. London: Faber and Faber, 2008.

O'Faoláin, Seán. "The Dangers of Censorship." In *The Selected Essays of Seán Ó Faoláin*, ed. Brad Kent, 90–96. Montreal-Kingston: McGill–Queen's Univ. Press, 2016.

———. *Vive Moi! An Autobiography*. London: Rupert Hart-Davis, 1965.

Ó hAllmhuráin, Gearóid. "Dancing on the Hobs of Hell: Rural Communities in Clare and the Dance Halls Act of 1935." *New Hibernia Review / Iris Éireannach Nua* 9, no. 4 (2005): 9–18.

O'Leary, Philip. *The Prose Literature of the Gaelic Revival, 1881–1921: Ideology and Innovation*. University Park: Pennsylvania State Univ. Press, 1994.

O'Mahony, Niamh. "'Releasing the Chaos of Energies': Communicating the Concurrences in Trevor Joyce's Appropriative Poems." *Irish University Review* 45, no. 1 (2016): 119–31.

O'Neill, Onora. "Agents of Justice." *Metaphilosophy* 32, nos. 1–2 (2001): 180–95.

Orr, Jennifer. *Literary Networks and Dissenting Print Culture in Romantic-Period Ireland*. Basingstoke: Palgrave, 2015.

Osborough, W. N. *The Irish Stage: A Legal History*. Dublin: Four Courts Press, 2015.

———. *Literature, Judges and the Law*. Dublin: Four Courts Press, 2008.

O'Toole, Fintan. *A Mass for Jesse James: A Journey through 1980s Ireland*. Dublin: Raven Arts, 1990.

Ó Tuama, Seán, and Thomas Kinsella, eds. *An Duanaire, 1600–1900: Poems of the Dispossessed*. Dublin: Dolmen Press, 1981.

Palmer, Stephanie. "'Death on the Rock' and the European Convention on Human Rights." *Cambridge Law Journal* 55, no. 1 (1996): 1–3.

Parrish, Stephen Maxfield, and James Allan Painter, eds. *A Concordance of the Poems of W. B. Yeats*. Ithaca, NY: Cornell Univ. Press, 1983.

Paseta, Senia. "Censorship and Its Critics in the Irish Free State." *Past & Present* 181 (Nov. 2003): 193–218.

Patton, Laurie L. "Space and Time in the 'Immacallam in dá Thuarad.'" *Folklore* 103, no. 1 (1992): 92–102.

Paulin, Tom. "The Making of a Loyalist." In *Writing to the Moment: Selected Critical Essays, 1980–1996*. London: Faber and Faber, 1996.

———. *The Riot Act: A Version of "Antigone" by Sophocles*. London: Faber and Faber, 1985.

Peacock, Thomas Love. *The Works of Thomas Love Peacock*. London: Richard Bentley and Son, 1875.

Pearson, Roger. *Unacknowledged Legislators: The Poet as Lawgiver in Post-revolutionary France*. Oxford: Oxford Univ. Press, 2016.

Philip, M. NourbeSe. *Zong!* Middletown, CT: Wesleyan Univ. Press, 2008.

Posner, Richard A. *Law and Literature: Being the Fifth John Maurice Kelly Memorial Lecture*. Dublin: Univ. College Dublin Faculty of Law, 1999.

———. *Law and Literature: A Misunderstood Relation*. Cambridge, MA: Harvard Univ. Press, 1988.

Potter, George W. *To the Golden Door: The Story of the Irish in Ireland and America*. Boston: Little, Brown, 1960.

Quinn, Justin. *The Cambridge Introduction to Modern Irish Poetry*. Cambridge: Cambridge Univ. Press, 2008.

Ramazani, Jahan. *Poetry and Its Others: News, Prayer, Song and the Dialogue of Genres*. Chicago: Univ. of Chicago Press, 2013.

Randolph, Jody Allen. "The Body Politic: A Conversation with Paula Meehan." *An Sionnach: A Journal of Literature, Culture and the Arts* 5, nos. 1–2 (2009): 239–71.

Rawls, John. *The Law of Peoples: With the Idea of Public Reason Revisited*. 1999. Reprint, Cambridge, MA: Harvard Univ. Press, 2002.

———. *A Theory of Justice*. 1971. Reprint, Cambridge, MA: Harvard Univ. Press, 2009.

Rea, Stephen, and Jessica Traynor, comps. *Correspondences: An Anthology to Call for an End to Direct Provision*. Dublin: Correspondences Press, 2019.

Redmond, John. "Engagements with the Public Sphere in the Poetry of Paul Durcan and Brendan Kennelly." In *The Oxford Handbook of Modern Irish Poetry*, edited by Fran Brearton and Alan Gillis, 403–18. Oxford: Oxford Univ. Press, 2012.

———. *Poetry and Privacy: Questioning Public Interpretations of Contemporary British and Irish Poetry*. Bridgend: Seren Books, 2013.

Richtarik, Marilynn J. *Acting between the Lines: The Field Day Theatre Company and Irish Cultural Politics, 1980–1984*. Washington, DC: Catholic Univ. of America Press, 2001.

Ross, David A. *Critical Companion to William Butler Yeats: A Literary Reference to His Life and Work*. New York: Facts on File, 2009.

Ross, F. Stuart. *Smashing H-Block: The Rise and Fall of the Popular Campaign against Criminalization, 1976–1982*. Liverpool: Liverpool Univ. Press, 2011.

Roth, Mitchel P. *Prisons and Prison Systems: A Global Encyclopaedia*. Westport, CT: Greenwood Press, 2006.

Russell, Richard Rankin. *Poetry and Peace: Michael Longley, Seamus Heaney and Northern Ireland*. Notre Dame, IN: Notre Dame Univ. Press, 2010.

———. *Seamus Heaney: An Introduction*. Edinburgh: Edinburgh Univ. Press, 2016.

Ryan, Ray, ed. *Writing in the Irish Republic: Literature, Culture, Politics, 1949–99*. Basingstoke: Macmillan, 2000.

Sands, Bobby. *Prison Poems*. Dublin: Sinn Féin Publicity Department, 1981.

Savelsberg, Joachim J., and Ryan D. King. "Law and Collective Memory." *Annual Review of Law and Social Science* 3 (2007): 189–211.

Scanlan, Margaret. *Culture and Customs of Ireland*. Westport, CT: Greenwood Press, 2006.

Scannell, Yvonne. "The Constitution and the Role of Women." In *The Irish Women's History Reader*, edited by Alan Hayes and Diane Urquhart, 71–78. London: Routledge, 2001.

Schirmer, Gregory A. Introduction to *Reviews and Essays of Austin Clarke*, edited by Gregory A. Schirmer, ix–xix. Gerards Cross: Colin Smythe, 1995.

Schreibman, Susan. "Irish Women Poets, 1929–1959: Some Foremothers." *Colby Quarterly* 37, no. 4 (2001): 309–26.

Schuchard, Ronald. *The Last Minstrels: Yeats and the Revival of the Bardic Arts*. Oxford: Oxford Univ. Press, 2008.

Shakespeare, William. *A Midsummer Night's Dream*. In *The Norton Shakespeare*, edited by Stephen Greenblatt et al. London: W. W. Norton, 2008.

Shelley, Percy Bysshe. "A Defence of Poetry (1821)." In *The Norton Anthology of English Literature*, edited by Stephen Greenblatt, 2:837–50. London: W. W. Norton, 2006.

Sidney, Sir Philip. "The Defense of Poesy (Written c. 1579)." In *The Norton Anthology of English Literature*, edited by M. H. Abrams, 1:933–54. New York: W. W. Norton, 2000.

Sinner, Alain Thomas Yvon. "'Protective Colouring': The Political Commitment in the Poetry of Seamus Heaney." PhD diss., Univ. of Hull, 1988.

Smyth, Jim. "Dancing, Depravity and All That Jazz: The Public Dance Halls Act of 1935." *History Ireland* 1, no. 2 (1993): 51–54.

Stach, Reiner. *Kafka: The Decisive Years*. Translated by Shelley Frisch. Princeton, NJ: Princeton Univ. Press.

Steele, Karen. "Refusing the Poisoned Chalice: The Sexual Politics of Rita Ann Higgins and Paula Meehan." In *Homemaking: Women Writers and the Politics and Poetics of Home*, edited by Catherine Wiley and Fiona R. Barnes, 313–34. London: Garland, 1996.

Thatcher, Margaret. Speech delivered at Parliament Buildings, Stormont Belfast, Mar. 5, 1981. Margaret Thatcher Foundation. www.margaret thatcher.org.

Tobin, Fergal. *The Best of Decades: Ireland in the Nineteen Sixties*. Dublin: Gill & Macmillan, 1984.

Tóibín, Colm, ed. *The Kilfenora Teaboy: A Study of Paul Durcan*. Dublin: New Island Books, 1996.

———, ed. *Seeing Is Believing: Moving Statues in Ireland*. Mountrath, Co. Laois: Pilgrim Press, 1985.

Townsend, Charles. *Political Violence in Ireland: Government and Resistance since 1848*. Oxford: Oxford Univ. Press, 2003.

Valente, Joseph, and Margot Gayle Backus. *The Child Sex Scandal and Modern Irish Literature: Writing the Unspeakable*. Bloomington: Indiana Univ. Press, 2020.

Vendler, Helen. *Seamus Heaney*. London: HarperCollins, 1998.

Walker, Clive. *Terrorism and the Law*. Oxford: Oxford Univ. Press, 2011.

Wallace, Nathan. *Hellenism and Reconciliation in Ireland from Yeats to Field Day*. Cork: Cork Univ. Press, 2015.

Walters, Wendy W. "'Still in the Difficulty': The Afterlives of Archives." In *Memory as Colonial Capital: Cross-Cultural Encounters in French and English*, edited by Erica L. Johnson and Éloïse Brezault, 179–98. New York: Palgrave, 2017.

Ward, Ian. *Law and Literature: Possibilities and Perspectives*. Cambridge: Cambridge Univ. Press, 1995.

Watson, Laura. "Epitaph for a Musician: Rhoda Coghill as Pianist, Composer and Poet." *Journal of the Society for Musicology in Ireland* 11 (2015–16): 3–23.

Weber, Max. "Politics as Vocation" [1918]. https://socialpolicy.ucc.ie/Weber_Politics_as_Vocation.htm.

Weisberg, Richard H. *The Failure of the Word: The Protagonist as Lawyer in Modern Fiction*. New Haven, CT: Yale Univ. Press, 1984.

Welch, Robert. *The Cold of May Day Monday: An Approach to Irish Literary History*. Oxford: Oxford Univ. Press, 2014.

Wheatley, David. "Aspermatic Nights and Days: Samuel Beckett and an Anti-genealogy of Contemporary Irish Poetry (I)." *PN Review* 42, no. 3 (2016): 48–53.

Whelan, Yvonne. "The Construction and Destruction of a Colonial Landscape: Monuments to British Monarchs in Dublin before and after Independence." *Journal of Historical Geography* 28, no. 4 (2002): 508–33.

Whelehan, Niall. "The Irish Revolution, 1912–23." In *The Oxford Handbook of Modern Irish History*, edited by Alvin Jackson, 621–46. Oxford: Oxford Univ. Press, 2014.

Whitaker, T. K. *The New Ireland: Its Progress, Problems and Aspirations.* Brussels: Institut Royal des Relations Internationales, 1966.

White, James Boyd. *The Legal Imagination.* Cambridge: Cambridge Univ. Press, 1985.

Wilde, Lady Francesca Speranza. *Ancient Legends, Mystic Charms, and Superstitions of Ireland.* London: Ward and Downey, 1887.

Wood, Michael. *Yeats and Violence.* Oxford: Oxford Univ. Press, 2010.

Yeats, W. B. *Autobiographies.* Edited by William H. O'Donnell and Douglas N. Archibald. New York: Scribner, 1999.

———. *The Collected Letters of W. B. Yeats: Electronic Edition: Unpublished Letters (1905–1939).* http://pm.nlx.com.

———. *Collected Poems of W. B. Yeats.* Edited by Augustine Martin. London: Vintage, 1992.

———. *The Collected Works of W. B. Yeats.* Vol. 2, *The Plays.* Edited by David R. Clark and Rosalind E. Clark. Basingstoke: Macmillan, 2001.

———. *The Collected Works of W. B. Yeats.* Vol. 5, *Later Essays.* Edited by William H. O'Donnell. New York: Scribner, 1994.

———. *The Collected Works of W. B. Yeats.* Vol. 9, *Early Articles and Reviews: Uncollected Articles and Reviews Written between 1886 and 1900.* Edited by John P. Frayne and Madeleine Marchaterre. New York: Scribner, 2004.

———. *The Collected Works of W. B. Yeats.* Vol. 10, *Later Articles and Reviews: Uncollected Articles, Reviews and Radio Broadcasts Written after 1900.* Edited by Colton Johnson. New York: Scribner, 2000.

———. *A Critical Edition of Yeats's "A Vision" (1925).* Edited by George Mills Harper and Walter Kelly Hood. London: Macmillan, 1978.

———. *Explorations.* London: Macmillan, 1962.

———. *The Major Works.* Edited by Edward Larrissy. Oxford: Oxford Univ. Press, 2008.

———. *Memoirs: Autobiography, First Draft Journal.* Edited by Denis Donoghue. London: Macmillan, 1973.

———. *The Oxford Book of Modern Verse, 1892–1935.* Oxford: Oxford Univ. Press, 1936.

———. *The Senate Speeches of W. B. Yeats.* Edited by Donald R. Pearce. Bloomington: Indiana Univ. Press, 1960.

———. *The Variorum Edition of the Plays of W. B. Yeats.* Edited by Russell K. Alspach, assisted by Catherine C. Alspach. London: Macmillan, 1966.

———. *The Variorum Edition of the Poems of W. B. Yeats.* Edited by Peter Allt and Russell K. Alspach. New York: Macmillan, 1966.

———. *A Vision: The Original 1925 Version.* Edited by Catherine E. Paul and Margaret Mills Harper. New York: Scribner, 2008.

———. *A Vision: The Revised 1937 Edition.* Vol. 14 of *The Collected Works of W. B. Yeats*, edited by Catherine E. Paul and Margaret Mills Harper. New York: Scribner, 2015.

———. Yeats exhibition. National Library of Ireland, Dublin. www.nli.ie/yeats/main.html.

Index

Adam Hanna is a lecturer in Irish literature in the English Department of University College Cork, Ireland. He joined UCC as an Irish Research Council Government of Ireland Postdoctoral Fellow in 2015. He was raised and educated in Ireland, the United States, and the United Kingdom; trained and practiced as a lawyer in London and Frankfurt; and has taught in the English Departments of Trinity College Dublin, the University of Bristol, and the University of Aberdeen. He is a cofounder of the Irish Network for the Legal Humanities, the author of *Northern Irish Poetry and Domestic Space* (2015), and the coeditor (with Jane Griffiths) of *Architectural Space and the Imagination: Houses in Art and Literature from Classical to Contemporary* (2020). A second edited collection, *Law and Literature: The Irish Case* (coedited with Eugene McNulty), is forthcoming from Liverpool University Press.

Printed in the USA
CPSIA information can be obtained
at www.ICGtesting.com
CBHW032200080324
5159CB00002B/43

9 780815 637660